365
DAYS
of Insights

365
DAYS
of Insights

Peter Legge
with
Tashon Ziara

EAGLET PUBLISHING

Eaglet Publishing
Peter Legge Management Co. Ltd.
4th Floor, 4180 Lougheed Highway
Burnaby, British Columbia, V5C 6A7, Canada
Tel. (604) 299-7311 Fax (604) 299-9188

Library and Archives Canada Cataloguing in Publication

Legge, Peter, 1942-
    365 days of insights / Peter Legge with Tashon Ziara.

Includes bibliographical references.
ISBN 978-0-9781459-9-6

1. Inspiration—Quotations, maxims, etc. 2. Motivation (Psychology)—Quotations, maxims, etc. I. Ziara, Tashon II. Title. III. Title: Three hundred sixty-five days of insights.

PN6081.L45 2011   082   C2011-906872-9

First Printing
Jacket design by Catherine Mullaly; cover illustration by iStock; illustration manipulation by Bernhard Holzmann; electronic imaging by Debbie Craig; typeset by Ina Bowerbank; edited by Kim Mah
Printed and bound in Canada by Friesens

Dedicated to my wife Kay.
A joy and inspiration to
my life every day.

Other Books by the Author

How to Soar With the Eagles
You Can If You Believe You Can
It Begins With a Dream
If Only I'd Said That
If Only I'd Said That: Volume II
If Only I'd Said That: Volume III
If Only I'd Said That: Volume IV
If Only I'd Said That: Volume V
Who Dares Wins
The Runway of Life
Make Your Life a Masterpiece
The Power of Tact
The Power to Soar Higher
The Power of a Dream

Booklets

97 Tips on How to Do Business in Tough Times
97 Tips on Customer Service
97 Tips on How to Jumpstart Your Career

CD

The Runway of Life

Video

How to Do Business in Tough Times
Interview With Jimmy Pattison

Introduction

WHOSE LIFE IS IT, ANYWAY?

Yours, of course! Though you may just need a bit of help to claim back a sense of empowerment.

Some of your power has been given away to the people and situations in your life . . . while in other areas you just haven't been sure what to do, so important decisions have been left in the hands of "fate." But what is fate really? In my opinion, fate isn't simply something that is inevitable and out of your control (as some people believe); rather it is what you run into when you run out of willpower.

Look around you, consider all the important components that make up the life that you're living — where you live, who you live with, how you earn your living, the people you spend the majority of your time with, what you do with your leisure time, whether or not you have the guidance and support you need to make decisions that are good for you — consider the choices you have made in the past five, 10, maybe even 20 years and how they have shaped the life you have today. Are you happy with those choices, is this the life you imagined?

If it isn't, you have the power to change.

If you're thinking change is scary, you're right. But it's also the most effective way of getting what you want.

One of the most useful — and ultimately, effective — things you can do when setting about changing your life is to put the emphasis on taking each day as it comes (it's worked for AA for how many years?) and that is what this daily reader is all about. Instead of becoming overwhelmed and discouraged by looking at this as one big life-altering transformation, we're going to cut it up into little manageable chunks and take small, significant steps, day by day.

This book will focus on seven core elements — you could also call them fundamentals or principles — of a great life. They are:

Strength
Courage
Commitment
Gratitude
Compassion
Integrity
Mindfulness

As we discuss these core elements, we will highlight some important lessons that will help you:

1. Learn to appreciate who you are.

One of the biggest mistakes any of us can make is to try to act like someone else. As any self-actualized person will tell you, each one of us is a unique and original individual and therefore we have something to share with the world that no one else can offer. So, as important as it is to have good role models and to learn from the example of people like Martin Luther King, Winston Churchill or Mother Teresa, it is equally important for us to appreciate and develop our own unique talents and abilities and to appreciate our quirks and foibles.

2. Cultivate a positive attitude.

Attitude can be defined as the way you habitually think and react to life's situations or circumstances. Attitude is everything. It is what helps one person succeed where another fails. The difference between successful people and those who struggle through life is their ability to be optimistic despite difficult circumstances. Smart people are not shaken by circumstances or mishaps and they do not dwell on negatives. They always look for the opportunity in life and the lessons they can learn from disappointments or misfortune.

3. Realize the importance of believing in yourself.

If you are a leader (and all of us are leaders in some capacity, whether we like it or not) but don't believe in yourself, how can you possibly convince others to believe in you? Learning to believe in yourself is the first step in the journey to realize your true potential.

4. Embrace change as a way of life.
In order to grow and develop, smart people put themselves in situations that challenge them to change, mature and keep on growing. They are not scared or intimidated by change and in many circumstances, they initiate change. They act rather than react.

5. Give fate a nudge.
When you don't make plans, you give away your power to the people and situations that end up taking your time and attention away from the things that you want in your life. Fate is always open to negotiation and the best way to tilt the odds in your favour is to make a plan to create the life you want.

6. Understand why it's important to build relationships with quality people.
A leader influences people and is influenced by others. It is in our best interests then to network with people who are going to nurture and motivate us. These are people who will tell us what we need to hear, not just what we want to hear. These are the kind of people who will put us in the hot seat when it is needed and we will learn from their counsel.

7. How true happiness grows from the seeds of compassion.
Genuine compassion is based not on our own projections and expectations, but rather on the rights of the other: irrespective of whether another person is a close friend or an enemy, as long as that person wishes for peace and happiness and wishes to overcome suffering, then on that basis we develop a genuine concern for his or her problems. This is genuine compassion. When we are able to care about the welfare of others, feelings such as anger, frustration, jealousy and insecurity begin to fade and we are able to be truly happy with our place in the world.

8. Never take issues personally.

Smart people focus on situations, not on personalities. Don't take anything personally. What others say and do is a projection of their own reality; it's not about you. When people make insulting or vicious remarks to you, it's a reflection of what's going on inside of them. When you are immune to the opinions and actions of others, you won't be the victim of needless suffering.

9. Realize that negotiation and compromise are the cornerstones of true strength.

The central struggle for every relationship we have is how to handle differences. We cultivate the arts of negotiation and compromise as a means of resolving differences and achieving mutual understanding. Learning how to negotiate can be very challenging; especially when there is an assumption of only one right way to do things. How we compromise with one another and the steps we take to resolve conflict can help build our relationships and create trust.

10. Nurture the people you wish to influence.

The greatness of any leader is not determined by the power he possesses but his ability to empower others. Many leaders want to be feared and revered, but a leader who will win people's hearts is one who is keen on empowering them. Without the admiration and respect of those he is leading, any attempt to influence or control followers will most likely be in vain. What you give is what you get.

11. Make as many mistakes as you can.

"Would you like me to give you a formula for success?" asks IBM founder Thomas J. Watson Sr. "It's quite simple, really. Double your rate of failure. You are thinking of failure as the enemy of success. But it isn't at all. You can be discouraged by failure — or you can learn from it. So go ahead and make mistakes. Make all you can. Because, remember that's where you will find success."

12. Remember to breathe.

How much of the time do you actually spend living in the moment, mindfully aware of what is going on here and now? Too often, we are like robots, automatically living out habitual patterns of self-pity, anger, wish fulfillment, fear, etc. These habitual tendencies can take us over and end up running our lives for us — without our being able to stand back and decide whether this is what we actually want to be doing. When we remember to breathe and allow ourselves to be fully aware of what is happening at the moment, we have the opportunity to choose what happens next.

JANUARY

THREE-WORD RESOLUTIONS

Traditional New Year's resolutions are tricky things — you know the ones, quit smoking, lose 30 pounds, get in shape — we make them with the best of intentions, but more often than not, those good intentions aren't enough to keep us focused and motivated. Nearly 90 per cent of all resolutions fail. So why set yourself up for failure?

Chris Brogan, a social media expert and *New York Times* bestselling co-author of *Trust Agents*, takes a different approach. Instead of making specific resolutions at the beginning of each year, Chris comes up with three words to be the "guiding pillars" that he will focus on in the 12 months ahead.

"These words are not goals," he is quick to point out. Instead, they are guidelines within which we can frame our goals. Think of them as "three-word inspirations" that can be applied to all areas of your life to keep you on track and give you something to reflect upon throughout the year.

On his blog, Chris shared the three words he chose for 2011: reinvest, package and flow. In his life, "reinvest" referred to refocusing on existing commitments and goals and realizing that taking on new projects would take time and energy away from those that he had already committed to.

Here are some more examples of actual three-word resolutions that people have shared:
Creativity, Growth, Simplicity
Focus, Connect, Momentum
Passion, Confidence, Balance
Action, Collaboration, Freedom
Ask, Do, Share
Integrate, Connect, Finish
Integrity, Wisdom, Patience
Produce, Plan, Ask
Honour, Stretch, Organize

— Insight 2011

WHAT ARE YOUR THREE WORDS FOR THIS YEAR?

THE IMPORTANCE OF MENTORS

If you've ever heard me speak or have read one of my books, you know I am very keen on mentors. This is primarily due to the fact that I have been blessed with much support and encouragement throughout my career. In fact, I credit three men with having a great influence on my life. I call them my mentors. They have given freely to me of their wisdom, experience and understanding of life. They have also given me the most precious thing they own — their time.

Sadly, my first mentor Raymond J. Addington, O.B.E., former president of Kelly Douglas Co. Ltd., passed away a few years ago. Ray taught me the significance of character and follow-through.

My second mentor is Dr. Mel Cooper, C.M., O.B.C., LL.D. (Hon), former owner of CFAX Radio in Victoria. I first met Mel when I worked at CKNW early in my career. Mel taught me the importance of a good attitude. He once told me, "Your attitude determines your altitude. How high you go in life is almost entirely due to a positive attitude."

My third mentor is Dr. Joseph Segal, C.M., O.B.C. LL.D (Hon), the legendary businessman and philanthropist who taught me the importance of communication, sharing ideas and never giving up.

Mentors are people who choose you as much as you choose them, and no one is really successful in life unless other people want them to be. The need to associate with successful leaders is imperative if you want to reach your full potential.

— *The Runway of Life*

DO YOU HAVE ONE OR MORE MENTORS TO HELP GUIDE YOU
ON THE ROAD TO SUCCESS? IF NOT, LOOK AROUND YOU, IS THERE
SOMEONE YOU RESPECT AND ADMIRE? WHY NOT
ASK THEM TO BE YOUR MENTOR?

A HEALTHY MINDSET — PART I

When it comes to maintaining a healthy weight, nothing should stand in the way of doing what is best for your body (after all, it's the only one you've got), but all too often bad choices, spurred on by a negative "I just can't do it" mindset, create an environment where not only is it difficult to make positive choices, but you may not even know what options are best.

Here are some straightforward tips to help:

Simply choose to eat less. One of the simplest and most effective changes we can make to improve our diet is to eat smaller portions. However, exercising portion control is a challenge for most of us because we take an all-or-nothing approach when it comes to putting food on our plate — we either indulge to excess or starve ourselves until our cravings get the better of us. Wouldn't it be far more practical to have a little bit of the foods we like, along with the foods we know our bodies need? Nourish your body with quality foods that you can eat more of, such as foods that are high in volume, but low in calories (think fresh fruits and vegetables, as well as whole grains and legumes). This will help to fill your plate and your stomach without overdoing the calories.

Eat more often. It may sound crazy to anyone who is cutting back on their calorie intake in order to lose weight, but when we don't eat, our bodies go into starvation mode and our metabolism slows down to conserve energy. Scientific studies confirm that eating smaller meals every three to four hours is more effective at sustaining metabolism and aiding long-term weight loss than skipping meals or restricting ourselves to a strict low-calorie diet.

A HEALTHY MINDSET – PART II

Walk the dog. This is great for people who have difficulty sticking to an exercise program. A study at the University of Missouri-Columbia showed that simply taking a dog for a walk on a regular basis was more effective over a one-year period than other major weight-loss programs. Researchers had participants begin by walking a dog for 10 minutes a day three days a week, building up to 20 minutes a day five days a week. In one year, they found the dog walkers lost an average of 14 pounds and because they were actually interacting with the dog (as opposed to running on a treadmill or walking alone), they were more motivated to stick with the exercise program long term. So even if you don't have a dog, borrow a neighbour's dog and get walking.

Get enough sleep. Research shows that people who don't get enough sleep (seven to eight hours a night) are more prone to weight gain because sleep deprivation puts more stress on our nervous system. Sleep provides an opportunity for the body to repair and rejuvenate itself and, according to the Division of Sleep Medicine at Harvard Medical School, many of the major restorative functions in the body like muscle growth, tissue repair, protein synthesis and growth hormone release occur mostly, or in some cases only, during sleep. So if you don't get the zzz's you need, you're actually weakening your body.

Manage stress. Last, and most importantly, get your stress under control. Both physical and emotional stress causes our bodies to release cortisol, a steroid that slows down the metabolism. When your metabolism slows, your body automatically begins to store more fat, causing you to gain weight, particularly around the tummy.

— *Make Your Life a Masterpiece*

A HEALTHY LIFESTYLE STARTS WITH YOUR ATTITUDE.

DREAM BIG DREAMS

E very millionaire or billionaire I've ever talked to tells me that the biggest secret to his or her success has been to dream big dreams, plan for the long term and keep moving forward. These people didn't get where they are by taking a leisurely bus ride up the hill, they decided early on that they were going to the very top of the mountain and they began to chart a course that would get them there.

Microsoft founder Bill Gates says that his success in business has largely been the result of his ability to focus on long-term goals and ignore short-term distractions. Despite all of his success, he continues to dream big dreams about developments within his own industry and he creates the opportunities — bringing together the right people and the right technologies — that can make them happen.

Of course, it can be intimidating to compare our own lives to someone like Bill Gates and you might say that he was the right person in the right place at the right time, that he got the breaks, or that no one will ever again succeed quite like he has. When comparing bank accounts, that may well be. But while Mr. Gates may have a special niche in the world, there is also a special niche in the world for you — you just have to find it.

When I talk of dreaming, I'm not talking about daydreaming. Dreaming also involves taking action. We may have to struggle to find what we're looking for, but if we stay focused on what we want to achieve, it will come to fruition.

— *The Power to Soar Higher*

WE HUMANS THRIVE ON ACHIEVEMENT AND THE BIGGER
WE DREAM, THE MORE WE CAN ACHIEVE.

SUCCESS DEFINED

I've heard two great definitions of success. Earl Nightingale said that success is nothing more than the pursuit of a worthy ideal. Nido Qubein defined success as balance.

Unless you have balance in your life and something worthwhile to work towards, you can't be truly successful. If you have all the money in the world but have managed to alienate others to the point that no one wants to spend time with you, you aren't successful. Similarly, if you have a happy marriage and a comfortable home, but don't sleep at night because you can't afford the mortgage payments, you are also out of balance and not successful.

Pursuing a worthy ideal (i.e., making a contribution to the world) and taking the time to build strong relationships with others, that's a recipe for success.

— *Who Dares Wins*

WHILE THERE ARE GUIDELINES,
THERE IS NO UNIVERSAL MEASURE OF SUCCESS.
EACH OF US MUST DEFINE IT FOR OURSELVES.

THE FATHER OF INSPIRATIONAL LITERATURE – PART I

Have you ever thought about who started the ball rolling on all this talk about self-help, inspiration, motivation and leadership? Where did the literary greats of this genre come from, and who exactly influenced the likes of Dale Carnegie, Orison Swett Marden, W. Clement Stone, Norman Vincent Peale, Earl Nightingale and Napoleon Hill?

At the Speakers Roundtable 2009 conference in West Lake Village, California, member Danny Cox put on a seminar titled, "Links to the Past, Strength for the Future." Turns out, the answer is Samuel Smiles (1812-1904), who wrote the first book of its kind, *Self Help*, which was published in 1859, more than 150 years ago.

The eldest of 11 children, Samuel Smile was born to parents who ran a small general store in Haddington, Scotland, where he attended the local school until age 14, when he joined Dr. Robert Lewins as an apprentice.

After making good progress with Dr. Lewins, Smiles went to Edinburgh University in 1829 to study medicine. While in Edinburgh, Smiles became involved in the campaign for parliamentary reform and had several articles on the subject published by the progressive *Edinburgh Weekly Chronicle*. He graduated in 1832 and found work as a doctor in Haddington.

In 1837, Smiles began contributing articles on parliamentary reform to the *Leeds Times*. The following year he was invited to become the newspaper's editor. At this point, he decided to abandon his career as a doctor and become a full-time worker for the cause of political change.

In the 1850s, however, Smiles also abandoned his interest in parliamentary reform and argued that self-help provided the best route to success. His book *Self Help*, which preached industry, thrift and self-improvement, was published in 1859 and by his death in 1904 had sold more than a quarter-million copies.

THE FATHER OF INSPIRATIONAL LITERATURE — PART II

R ead these Samuel Smiles quotes and I am sure you will see his influence in modern day "self-help" books:

A place for everything and everything in its place.

An intense anticipation itself transforms possibility into reality; our desires being often but precursors of the things which we are capable of performing.

Enthusiasm . . . the sustaining power of all great action.

He who never made a mistake, never made a discovery.

Hope is like the sun, which, as we journey toward it, casts the shadow of our burden behind us.

I'm as happy a man as any in the world, for the whole world seems to smile upon me.

It is a mistake to suppose that men succeed through success; they much oftener succeed through failures. Precept, study, advice and example could never have taught them so well as failure.

Life will always be to a large extent what we ourselves make it.

Lost wealth may be replaced by industry, lost knowledge by study, lost health by temperance or medicine, but lost time is gone forever.

Men must necessarily be the active agents of their own well-being and well-doing . . . they themselves must in the very nature of things be their own best helpers.

Men who are resolved to find a way for themselves will always find opportunities enough; and if they do not find them, they will make them.

Practical wisdom is only to be learned in the school of experience. Precepts and instruction are useful so far as they go, but, without the discipline of real life, they remain of the nature of theory only.

The apprenticeship of difficulty is one which the greatest of men have had to serve.

The reason why so little is done is generally because so little is attempted.

— Insight 2010

THE RUNWAY OF LIFE

S everal years ago, my long-time friend and mentor Joe Segal shared an illustration with me that he had drawn on a napkin while we were having lunch together at his favourite restaurant. Basically, he explained as he scribbled, it's a straight line that starts at whatever age you are right now and ends . . . well, that's the thing of it, we never know exactly where or when it's going to end. The only thing we can be sure of is that it will end!

Joe calls that line the Runway of Life and the point he was making in drawing it on a napkin for me is that eventually we all run out of runway (at 89, Joe still has more life in him than anyone else I know).

How long do you think your own runway of life is? If you think your life will end at 85 years and you're 55 now, you've got 30 years left on your runway.

Take a moment to do the math for your own life.

Approaching 70 years of age, my guess is that my runway has about 15 years or 780 weeks left. (Yikes!) The big question is, what will I do with the time that I have and what will you choose to do with your time? In the weeks, months and years you have left, do you have hopes, dreams, vision and purpose for your life?

— *The Runway of Life*

"ALL WE HAVE TO DECIDE IS WHAT TO DO
WITH THE TIME THAT IS GIVEN US."
— Gandalf the Wizard, *The Lord of the Rings*

WHOSE LIFE IS IT ANYWAY?

It's easy to make excuses for why we aren't pursuing our own dreams. "I'm too busy working and earning a living to think about what I really want; I don't have time to set goals; I'd need to go back to school; it's too complicated; my spouse would never understand; it's too late to start over in a new career; I wouldn't be good enough to make a living doing what I enjoy; there's too much competition."

All of these comments come from a place of fear. Some people are afraid of accomplishment or they worry that if they fulfill their potential, they will alienate others. Some people are afraid of the responsibility of living up to their destiny. They know they have the potential to do great things, but they're afraid of what that means. If you don't take your own dreams seriously, who will?

"Consult not your fears, but your hopes and your dreams," said Pope John XXIII. "Think not about your frustrations, but about your unfulfilled potential. Concern yourself not with what you tried and failed in, but with what it is still possible for you to do."

I have a challenge for you. I want you to sit down right now and answer this all-important question:

"Whose life are you living?"

Give it some serious thought and if you're not happy with the answer, it's time to do something about that.

— *The Power of a Dream*

"THIS IS YOUR LIFE, ARE YOU WHO YOU WANT TO BE?"
— Switchfoot (from the lyrics to "This Is Your Life")

WE ALL HAVE MOUNTAINS TO CONQUER

At the time that I was researching and writing my second book, I was also on the board of Variety Clubs International, which met in Vancouver to choose the humanitarian award winner for that year — the award is the highest honour that Variety can bestow. Previous recipients had included Sir Winston Churchill, Bob Hope and Princess Anne.

The annual convention where the award was to be presented was to be held in New Zealand and the candidate who stood out from all the rest was that country's own Sir Edmund Hillary. From every angle, he was a giant, deserving of the highest praise and admiration.

I was in my mid-teens when Sir Edmund became the first person to climb Mount Everest and as with many young people of that time, he became an instant hero to me.

In an interview, Sir Edmund was asked what the biggest challenge was that he faced in becoming the first man to reach the summit of Everest. The biggest obstacle, he responded, was to overcome the psychological barrier — to keep from talking himself out of trying.

In climbing the mountain, Sir Edmund not only showed the world it could be done; most importantly, he showed himself.

"It was not the mountain that we conquered," he said. "It was ourselves."

— *Who Dares Wins*

PREPARE TODAY TO CONQUER
YOUR OWN MOUNTAINS.

PINK-SLIP ENTREPRENEURS

For many, the thought of being laid off, fired, given the boot or otherwise "let go" is the most frightening thing in the world. While for others, it's just the kick in the pants they need to embark on the adventure of being an entrepreneur. In my book, *The Runway of Life*, I tell the story of how those dreaded words, "You're Fired!" led me to start my own publishing company.

Turns out there are plenty of well-known entrepreneurs who got their start the same way. Home Depot's Bernie Marcus and Arthur Blank are pink-slip entrepreneurs, as was David Neeleman of JetBlue Airways and even *Harry Potter* author J.K. Rowling, who lost her job over writing short stories at work.

The great part about launching a business today is that with modern technology, you can run a business from just about anywhere. In fact, statistics show that 49 per cent of U.S. companies are now operated from a home office (I'm sure Canada has similar stats).

The other great part about becoming an entrepreneur — and the reason many people take the plunge — is that you gain control over your life and the direction of your career. That's not to say it isn't hard work; it is. Chances are, in the beginning at least, you will be working longer and putting more energy into your business than you have put into anything in your life. The plus side is that when you're doing it for yourself and you love what you do, it's not really work.

— *The Power of a Dream*

YOU DON'T HAVE TO WAIT FOR A PINK SLIP TO START LIVING THE LIFE YOU WANT. IF YOU HAVE A GOOD IDEA AND THE DRIVE TO BE SUCCESSFUL, THERE'S NO TIME LIKE THE PRESENT TO SET OFF ON YOUR OWN ADVENTURE.

SELF-DISCIPLINE – PART I

Nothing sets you up for success in life like the habit of self-discipline — the ability to make yourself do what you should do, when you should do it, whether you feel like it or not. Even if you don't think that you possess it now, you can master this habit with practice and if you want to test just how important it is, simply think of some public person you once admired and respected — then you found out that they had succumbed to a weakness, perhaps they covered up some misdeed, or they didn't keep their word on an issue that was critical to those they had power over — and remember how that lack of judgment diminished their character in your view.

These are moments of truth that we all encounter in our lives, moments when others let us down or when we let ourselves down.

It takes determination to learn self-discipline, and the best place to start is with little everyday tasks. Learning to be self-disciplined in the little things in life prepares the way for bigger successes.

Begin by identifying the main areas where you lack discipline. They could include:

• Keeping your workspace tidy (find a spot for each of the items you need; get rid of the rest);

• Getting up when the alarm goes off (reward yourself by playing your favourite music while you go about your morning routine);

• Returning phone calls and emails within 24 hours (set aside a half-hour at the end of each workday to return messages);

• Arriving at work on time (try going in to work 10 minutes early and see how it feels to walk into the office and sit down at your desk without feeling stressed — if it feels good, try doing it every day).

SELF-DISCIPLINE — PART II

C hoose one or two items to start working on and add new items as the older ones become part of your regular routine. You'll be amazed at how much easier your day flows when you aren't constantly scrambling to keep up.

More tips:

Get yourself organized. If you don't control your time, everything — and everyone — else will. Make a schedule and stick to it. Have a to-do list of things you need to accomplish and mark them off as you complete them. If you find yourself spending more than five or 10 minutes on something that isn't on your schedule or your list, redirect yourself and get back on track.

Finish what you start. Many people are good at starting projects, far fewer are as good at finishing them. If you're someone whose life is littered with unfinished projects, take heart. The best way to set yourself up for success is to spend more time planning and assembling the resources you will need before you begin and enlist the help of others to provide encouragement and accountability to keep you motivated.

Tackle the most difficult tasks first. Most people do the opposite, spending their time doing the easier, low-priority tasks. But when they run out of time and energy, the difficult, high-priority tasks still remain undone — and that's where we lose credibility with others. When you do the tough stuff first, you can relax and enjoy the easy tasks knowing that you have already taken care of business.

Keep your word. When you make commitments, see them through. An important part of practicing this habit is developing the ability to properly evaluate whether you have the time and capability to do something before you commit to it.

— Make Your Life a Masterpiece

"TODAY'S MIGHTY OAK IS YESTERDAY'S NUT
THAT HELD ITS GROUND."

30 MINUTES A DAY COULD CHANGE YOUR LIFE

R ead something useful, challenging or educational every day. Thirty minutes spent with a book that motivates, excites and educates you will make a world of difference. Charles Scribner said, "Reading is a means of thinking with another person's mind; it forces you to stretch your own."

But don't stop at reading. Share the wealth and share the wisdom. Send articles to friends and business associates. When you find topical information that you think might help someone else, don't hesitate to pass it along. We could all use a little boost now and then in terms of new ideas. It's also a great way to motivate staff members or give a friend or family member extra encouragement.

You could also join a discussion group (in person or online) to share ideas with others and get different perspectives on what you are learning. Taking it a step further, you could even keep a journal for your thoughts and ideas and try to carry it with you so you can add insights that come your way throughout the day. This will help you to track your progress and make your learning more tangible, in addition to being a place where you can record inspiring quotes for future reference and keep a list of books you want to read in the future.

One final idea: Name a library after . . . you! Build your own success library and make sure you include a comfortable chair where you can read every day. It truly is 30 minutes that could change your life.

— *The Runway of Life*

COLLECT BOOKS THAT INSPIRE YOU
AND REVIEW THEM WHENEVER YOU NEED A LITTLE
INSPIRATION OR MOTIVATION IN YOUR LIFE.

BORN EXCITED

Mark Twain was once asked what the reason was for his success. His reply? "I was born excited." That excitement for life and for storytelling attracted people to Twain as if he were a magnet, making him one of the most celebrated writers and enigmatic figures of his time.

"I have always been able to gain my living without doing any work," he explained. "For the writing of books and magazine matter was always play, not work. I enjoyed it; it was merely billiards to me."

Not many things can top the feeling of doing something you love and getting paid for it. But isn't that what we all want from our job or career? To be excited about what lies before us and to know that what we do is valued.

The more excited you are about what you will be doing each day, the more motivated you will be to go above and beyond in performing your job and the more open you will be to identifying new opportunities when they come along — both of which will lead to greater success.

The opposite is also true. If you are trudging through task after task throughout the day and there is nothing for you to look forward to, there are going to be plenty of things that can and will go wrong. When this happens, little frustrations and aggravations can quickly build. "Why is this happening to me?" plays in your mind and quickly turns into "This kind of stuff is always happening to me."

No matter which circumstance you find yourself in, just remember, you always have a choice and the power to change your situation.

So, HOW EXCITED ARE YOU
ABOUT TODAY'S ADVENTURE?

GARBAGE IN, GARBAGE OUT

In life, everything counts. From the moment we are born until the day we check out of Hotel Earth for the last time, we are shaped by our surroundings — our home environment; our education; what we choose to read, listen to and watch; the friends and acquaintances we associate with; our workplace environment; our life partners; the neighbours around us and the communities we belong to — and as a result, the quality of everything we see and do contributes to the evolving beings that we are.

When I think of the implications of this, it reminds me of the computer term, *Garbage In, Garbage Out*, which was coined to keep early programmers mindful of the fact that the applications they produced would only be as good as the planning and data that went into creating them. It's a guiding principle that each one of us can use to determine what we allow in our life.

The philosopher Socrates observed that for every cause there is at least one effect. If we wish, we can go passively through life letting the influences of the world wash over us and allowing ourselves to be shaped by whatever comes our way. We can also, if we choose, be completely unaware that we're part of anything at all. You've met people like this. You can talk to them about all kinds of frivolous things, but try to have a deeper conversation and you hit a dead end. The other option, and the one I choose for myself, is to fill my life with as many challenges, opportunities and positive influences as I can, essentially, to program myself for success.

— *The Power to Soar Higher*

"THE STATE OF YOUR LIFE IS NOTHING MORE
THAN A REFLECTION OF
THE STATE OF YOUR MIND." — Wayne Dyer

WOW, IS IT FRIDAY ALREADY?

I'm always a little saddened when I see people who work in offices give a whoop once a week and shout with relief, "Thank God it's Friday!" Yet it has become the cry of hope for millions who feel trapped in a thankless job.

Don't get me wrong, I like a couple of days off as much as anyone, but I also enjoy what I do in the office — and I do my best as a leader to make sure that the people on our company team enjoy what they're doing too.

Work really shouldn't be something that is dreaded and it's always been quite natural for me to try to create a relaxed office where people share their ideas and feel good about working together. I also think that if you put a happy office next to an unhappy office, the happy office will perform better in almost every way: the people will be more creative, fewer sick days will be taken and generally people will be more open — and you'll see more smiles.

I feel terribly sorry for offices where the CEO comes in every morning with his or her head down, briefcase in hand, heading for another non-communicative day behind a closed door. People like that really haven't progressed much beyond the management style of Ebenezer Scrooge.

Show me a boss who says hello, knows his or her people, does a little management by walking around and takes time to listen to the things people say and I'll show you an office where the end of the week comes and instead of hooting and hollering, what you'll most likely hear is, "Wow, is it Friday already?"

— *How to Soar With the Eagles*

EVERYONE DESERVES TO FEEL APPRECIATED
AND VALUED AT WORK. DO YOU?

DON'T OVERLOOK THE OBVIOUS

In 1936, Dale Carnegie published *How to Win Friends and Influence People*, a book that would become an international bestseller and a classic in its field. Ironically, Carnegie didn't want to publish the book and with its first printing, it was not well received by reviewers, intellectuals and journalists who criticized it as a sign of the decline of public taste. The public viewed it differently and after the sale of 500,000 copies, Carnegie was invited to speak at New York's Dutch Treat Club to editors, publishers, advertising people and others who were amazed by the book's success but skeptical of its literary merit. Carnegie knew they were ready to eat him alive.

"I know there's considerable criticism of my book. People say I'm not profound and there's nothing new to psychology and human relations within my book," he told them in opening. "This is true. Gentlemen, I have never claimed to have a new idea. Of course I deal with the obvious. I present, reiterate and glorify the obvious because the obvious is what people need to be told. The greatest need of people is to know how to deal with other people. This should come naturally to them, but it doesn't."

Like many speakers, I have read Carnegie's classic book many times and refer to it often. Its wisdom may be simple and obvious, but it is as relevant today as it was in 1936.

Here are a few examples:

- Be a good listener. Encourage others to talk about themselves.

- Begin with praise and honest appreciation.

- Try honestly to see things from the other person's point of view.

- Talk about your own mistakes before criticizing someone else.

— *How to Soar With the Eagles*

IF YOU WANT TO WIN FRIENDS AND INFLUENCE PEOPLE,
DON'T OVERLOOK THE OBVIOUS.

GET YOUR PRIORITIES STRAIGHT

Leo Babauta, author of the popular blog *Zen Habits*, reminds us that priorities are not what we say they are — they're what we actually do. It's one thing to set priorities; it's something else again to really live them. He also points out that one of the most common mistakes we make in setting priorities is to overcomplicate things or try to focus on too many things at once. The truth is that we can only focus on a couple of priorities at a time, so we need to be really clear on what they are.

Babauta's advice: Schedule some time each day to do something that supports your most important dream, whatever it might be, so that your life will actually reflect the priorities you set.

Of course, one of the inescapable side effects of setting priorities is that in order to say "yes" to one thing, we have to learn to say "no" to others.

— *The Power of a Dream*

"DON'T WASTE YOUR BREATH PROCLAIMING
WHAT'S REALLY IMPORTANT TO YOU.
HOW YOU SPEND YOUR TIME SAYS IT ALL." — Eric Zorn

LIFE'S TOO SHORT

When my daughters were young, we made a point of introducing them to different foods, including vegetables. While we didn't believe in forcing them to eat foods they really didn't like, our philosophy was that they at least had to try it.

So it was that we attempted to get Samantha to eat Brussels sprouts at Sunday dinner. As usual, when dinner was ready, Kay served up a small portion of vegetables to each child. Unfortunately for Samantha, when the Brussels sprouts landed on her plate it was not love at first sight. As dinner progressed, she managed to eat around the offending vegetables and thinking herself finished, asked to be excused.

"No, you may not," Kay said firmly, "You haven't even tried the Brussels sprouts."

"I don't want to try them," said Samantha. "I already know I don't like them."

Not one to give in, Kay held her ground. "When you've finished what's on your plate you may be excused."

After sitting at the table glaring at the two lonely Brussels sprouts for half an hour, Samantha decided to negotiate (a tactic I would highly recommend to any child in a similar situation).

"If I eat these two Brussels sprouts," she propositioned, "do you promise I'll never have to try them again?"

"Absolutely," Kay agreed. "As long as you try them."

Looking as if a life sentence had been lifted, Samantha quickly ate the vegetables and excused herself.

While I was writing this book, I mentioned to Samantha that I was thinking of including this story in a chapter on priorities.

"Yeah, dad," she said. "That would make a good chapter. After all, life's too short to eat Brussels sprouts."

— *Make Your Life a Masterpiece*

ONCE YOU GET YOUR PRIORITIES STRAIGHT, YOU DON'T
WASTE TIME ON UNIMPORTANT THINGS.

BE THANKFUL FOR YOUR TROUBLES

E very Monday morning for the past 20-plus years, I distribute my weekly *Insight* to everyone in the Canada Wide Media publishing family.

Some people read it and then file it away somewhere where they can refer to it from time to time along with other accumulated wisdom. Others give it a quick read and recycle the message. You never do know how these ideas work or which ones will resonate with specific individuals, but for me, it's a joy to collect the ideas and to know that the thoughts I am sharing have touched at least a few people in a meaningful way.

One of my earliest messages was titled, "Be Thankful for Your Troubles." Maybe not the most inspired headline to start your week, but that was just the headline.

Be thankful for your troubles, I wrote, because they provide about half of your income. Think about it. If it were not for the things that go wrong, the difficult people with whom you deal, the problems and unpleasantries of your working day, someone else could handle your job for half of what it costs to have you doing it.

It's true, isn't it? Think of all the jobs that have been outsourced to Mexico, China, India and elsewhere.

It takes intelligence, resourcefulness, patience, tact and courage to meet the troubles of any job and the more willing you are to deal with the problems that others don't want to, the more sought after you will be in the workforce.

Albert Einstein often said, "In the middle of every difficulty lies opportunity." If you want to get ahead, simply welcome every problem that comes your way as an opportunity for you to shine.

— *How to Soar With the Eagles*

TODAY, FOCUS ON TURNING PROBLEMS
INTO OPPORTUNITIES.

BRAIN FOOD

In addition to feeding our minds with knowledge, we should also remember to eat whole foods that nourish our brains. Research shows that certain foods are high in nutrients that make your brain work better. Including:

B Vitamins — These play an important role in brain function. B6 (pyridoxine) helps to convert tryptophan into serotonin and is found in chicken, pork, liver and kidney, fish, nuts and legumes. Thiamine, or B1, helps build and maintain healthy brain cells. You'll find thiamine in bread, rice, pasta and pork. Folic acid is also an essential brain food and is found in bananas, orange juice, strawberries, melons, lemons, green leafy vegetables, dried pulses and cereals.

Zinc — This mineral helps keep the senses sharp, as well as encouraging a healthy immune system. It is critical for proper growth and development in children. You'll find zinc in sunflower seeds, peanuts, red meats and oysters.

Omega-3 Fatty Acids — Found in fish like salmon and mackerel, Omega-3 can help stave off depression, a common side effect of stress. It is also excellent for improving concentration and energy levels and plays an important role in the reduction of heart disease.

Fruit — As nutritionists will tell you, fresh fruit not only contains many of the vitamins and other nutrients needed for healthy brain function, it also slowly releases natural sugars into the body and gives a sustained effect of mental and physical energy, unlike the "sugar spike" from processed foods and sugary drinks.

Herbs — For many centuries, all kinds of herbs have been used by humans, not only for flavouring foods but also as natural remedies to promote health and wellness. Try ginger to lift the spirits, basil to clear the mind, cinnamon to counteract exhaustion and peppermint to help calm nerves and relieve anger.

— Make Your Life a Masterpiece

FROM PEAK TO PEAK

Here's No. 11 of my success secrets that aren't really secrets at all (there's quite a few of them and I cover them all in my book, *It Begins With a Dream*):

Be prepared to climb from peak to peak.

If you've ever been to the top of a mountain, you know how exhilarating it can be when you finally reach the summit. Mountains have a special way of lifting us above the ordinary and allowing us to survey our world from a new and exciting perspective. It's different up there. All the mediocrity seems to drop away and in the clean air we can breathe deeply a world that's fresher and more spiritually connected, where we can rise above the routine and feel our hearts swell with the thrill of achievement.

For obvious reasons, some people will never have a mountaintop experience because it requires both planning and intention to start climbing. These are perhaps the same people who believe that everything they desire should be handed to them with no effort on their part. They buy a lottery ticket and sit back and wait for the big moment. And despite the famous marketing slogan, "You never know!" the moment rarely ever does come. Meanwhile, time slips by and life goes on.

Those who have been to the mountaintop know that it takes effort to get there, but once you've been, you can't wait to challenge yourself to reach the next peak, even if it means more hard work and more time spent slogging through the valleys to get there.

— *It Begins With a Dream*

IS THERE A MOUNTAIN YOU'VE
BEEN WANTING TO CLIMB?

THE MOMENTUM PRINCIPLE

Remember the momentum principle of success — it is the key to long-term results.

We all know that it takes a lot of energy to get started. However, once you get moving in a particular direction, it takes very little energy to keep going. That's because you have the principle of momentum working in your favour. However, if you stop, it can be even harder to get started again. Don't believe me? Think about the last time you came back from a long vacation when you allowed yourself to become completely relaxed. What happened when you returned to your regular work routine? I bet it took at least a few days before you got back to working at peak efficiency. This is part of the momentum principle.

So how can you use this principle to your advantage?

It's simple actually. Success inspires us and gives us the confidence and momentum to take on ever bigger challenges, which in turn lead to more successes. The opposite is also true; when we don't get the results we want, we can become discouraged and lose momentum, which over time makes us shy of trying to achieve our goals or even believing that we can. When you find yourself in this situation and feel that you are having a problem getting started again, the best thing to do is break that problem up into little pieces that you can tackle one at a time. Then start with the smallest or easiest parts of the problem to begin building your momentum again. As one small success builds on another, you'll regain your momentum and be ready to tackle ever bigger challenges once again.

— *The Runway of Life*

USE THE PRINCIPLE OF MOMENTUM TO
PROPEL YOU FURTHER, FASTER.

IT DOESN'T MATTER WHAT THEY SAY — PART I

E arl Nightingale said, "Difficult things take a long time, impossible things a little longer. Don't let the time it will take to accomplish something stand in the way of your doing it. The time will pass anyway; we might just as well put that passing time to the best possible use."

There was a point in my own life where my dissatisfaction with having "just a job" and answering to someone else's desires overcame any fear or uncertainty I had about becoming an entrepreneur. At once, I realized that I needed to be in control of my own destiny, yet the only way to make it happen was for me to bite the bullet and take a chance.

How did I find the courage?

If you've read the story of how I came to know Joe Segal, you will remember that I used to sell radio advertising for CJOR and at that time, Joe had an office in the back of one of his Fields department stores. You might recall as well that although Joe refused to buy any radio spots from me, I kept returning time after time. Now, you may well wonder why I kept going back to see Joe. The truth is I admired the man — he started out in business with very little money, but a whole lot of determination and ambition — and I wanted to be like him. I wanted to be successful and I figured the best way to learn how to do that was by modelling myself after people like Joe who were living the kind of life I wanted for myself.

IT DOESN'T MATTER WHAT THEY SAY — PART II

J oe also encouraged me and told me that my persistence could more than make up for whatever I lacked in experience or financial resources. So, when the opportunity to buy a little publication called *TV Week* and become a magazine publisher came along, I knew it was now or never and jumped in with both feet.

I soon found out that not everyone was as supportive as Joe. In fact, I was rather surprised at how many people — friends and associates — thought I had taken leave of my senses. "What do you know about publishing?" they asked. "What, are you crazy, there's no money in magazines," they said. I told myself, "It doesn't matter what they say, this is my chance to prove myself."

That skepticism didn't go away for a long time — at our five-, 10- and even 15-year anniversaries, I still encountered people who expected the bottom to fall out at any moment. But I didn't let that stop me, I had a dream. I was determined that my little company, Canada Wide Magazines, would add one new magazine a year to its publication list.

In April 2011, Canada Wide Media Limited celebrated 35 years in business, and guess what? We have consistently managed to stay ahead of my goal of one new magazine per year. We are also the largest independent publisher in Western Canada and have been so for years now. It has been, at once, more exciting, more challenging and more rewarding than I ever imagined. I am thankful that I didn't let the doubt and cynicism of others stop me from pursuing my dream.

— The Runway of Life

NOT EVERYONE WILL BELIEVE IN YOUR DREAM,
BUT THE TRUTH IS, THEY DON'T NEED TO — ONLY YOU DO!

RID YOUR LIFE OF CLUTTER

If you think your workspace is messy, you should see what the late British painter Francis Bacon's studio in London looked like. Bacon, whose *Triptych, 1976* sold for $86 million in 2008, reportedly could not work in a tidy environment. Old photos show every floor and table surface drowning in a sea of debris — papers, paintbrushes, wood, clothing, wine crates and more — leaving little room for the artist to even stand. After his death, the scene was lovingly dismantled and reconstructed in a museum in Dublin — where it took three years to recreate the mess.

Our lives tend to accumulate clutter in every corner: on our desks, in our drawers, on our shelves, in our closets, the garage, the bathroom cabinet, the laundry room, our minds, you name it, clutter finds a way to fill every available space.

If you are determined to sort out the mess once and for all, why not try this innovative approach? Start with nothing and add only what you need. This is a very effective way to remove unnecessary clutter. Rather than look for things to throw away, imagine that the room or space was completely bare and then only add what you really need. This is a great way to decide whether a thing is of practical importance or just there out of habit.

Don't just de-clutter, organize. Most times it is not just a matter of throwing things away; you also need to get organized and find a permanent home for each item you own, so that you don't slowly slip back into your old clutter-bound ways.

— *The Power to Soar Higher*

IF YOU WANT A FRESH PERSPECTIVE ON YOUR LIFE,
GET RID OF THE CLUTTER.

WRITE IT DOWN, MAKE IT HAPPEN — PART I

In one way or another, most of us record the things we have to do. Wherever you go, a business meeting, riding in the elevator or taking the commuter train, you'll see people pulling out their BlackBerries, daytimers or even scraps of paper to record all kinds of things: important information gleaned from a presentation, the date and time of upcoming business and social events, a reminder to get the oil changed on the car.

Technology has made all of this recordkeeping a lot easier for us. With all of our devices synched, we can transfer data at the touch of a button to help keep track of our lives and remind us about what we have to do today, tomorrow and weeks, months or years into the future.

Interestingly, the more we use these devices, the more dependent we become upon them. It's like having an external memory that we can download to so we don't have to carry everything around in our heads. I can tell you, the older you get and the more you have to remember, the more you appreciate these devices, especially when you're wandering around the car park like a fool because you can't remember where you parked the car.

There's nothing wrong or unusual about writing down important things that you want to remember. In fact, it's on my list of secrets that aren't really secrets at all and it works just as well for goals as it does for remembering where the car is.

You wouldn't think that you'd forget what your goals are just because you didn't write them down, but often that's exactly what happens. When you actually have a goal written down and placed in a strategic location, you automatically increase the number of times that you think about your goal.

WRITE IT DOWN, MAKE IT HAPPEN — PART II

S ometimes I think we neglect to write things down because we don't believe we'll really end up doing what we say we'll do. This is a mistake if we truly want to achieve our goals. Writing our goals helps to make them clear, tangible and real. Also, once we've got the "what," it can get our mind working on the "how," even if it's subconsciously. Writing it down can also help identify the smaller steps towards a bigger goal.

So what kinds of things do you need to write down? Realistically, your list should include both short and long-term goals. A good place to start is by thinking about what you *expect* to be doing a year from now and what you would *like* to be doing a year from now. Whatever your goal, write it down and include the steps that will get you there, such as collecting information, doing research and speaking with others who are doing what you want to do.

As you complete the various items on your list, not only will you get a clearer picture of what is needed, you will also be able to determine whether or not you are willing to go the distance and really make it happen. For example, if your present career isn't fulfilling, you can use this process to determine whether you want to make a complete career change or simply move to another job or company in the same industry. However you organize it, the real purpose of writing down your goals is to get moving on them — that's another of my not-so-secret secrets of success.

— *The Power to Soar Higher*

WRITING DOWN YOUR GOALS DOESN'T JUST HELP YOU REMEMBER THEM, IT CAN ALSO BE A USEFUL TOOL IN HELPING YOU DEVELOP A CLEAR SENSE OF DIRECTION.

MINDFULNESS EQUALS HAPPINESS

Despite all of our technology, even in the 21st century, Western science is still playing catch-up with Eastern philosophy. While Buddhists have been practicing mindfulness for centuries, there is now scientific proof that people who are able to stay focused and in the present moment are much happier than those who get distracted and let their mind wander. According to a study published in *Science* magazine, two psychologists at Harvard University found that daydreaming, mind-wandering and spacing out (even when you are thinking about something pleasant) actually lead to unhappiness or dissatisfaction, while staying focused in the moment is linked to higher levels of emotional well-being.

By having people track their level of happiness over a period of time, the researchers found that people spend about 47 per cent of their waking hours thinking about something other than what they're doing and that mind-wandering was linked to feeling unhappy.

Being aware of your behaviour is the first step towards happiness. The next step is practicing mindfulness. Each time you find your mind wandering away from whatever you are doing, consciously guide your thoughts back to the task at hand. Think of it as exercising your mind in the same way that you would run or lift weights to exercise your body. Although it may feel awkward at first, if you do this consistently throughout each day, it will begin to feel more natural and soon you will find that not only do the majority of your thoughts focus on the present moment (which helps you accomplish more in less time), but that the thoughts you are having are much more positive.

— *Insight 2011*

MINDFULNESS MAKES THE PRESENT MORE MEANINGFUL.
DON'T MISS THE OPPORTUNITY TO ENJOY EACH DAY TO ITS FULL
POTENTIAL, BY BEING PRESENT IN THE MOMENT.

FEBRUARY

FIVE GOAL-SETTING STEPS – PART I

I've talked elsewhere about goal setting. It's an important topic and something that most people struggle with. Here are five steps to help you start setting your own goals.

1. Brainstorm

Before you choose a single goal to set and focus on, use a blank sheet of paper to write down as quickly as possible all the things you want in a number of categories, such as: family, career, educational, financial, physical, spiritual, social, etc. Once you have created a list, prioritize each of the items on your list. This will allow you to begin immediately focusing on the potential goals that are most important to you. It is also important to have both long- and short-term goals.

2. Make sure the goals you set are truly your own

The purpose of setting goals is to focus and plan for what you want in your life, not to impress others. Most people don't really know what they want and so they spend countless hours talking about what they don't want, which is something that's not really helpful in the long run. Spend some time each day thinking and talking about what you do want and soon your goals will start to take shape.

3. Set only positive goals for yourself

Because you want to be growing towards something, write down each of your goals in a positive statement rather than a negative one. For example: "I will save to buy a home" is a positive goal, while "I will not spend money" is a negative goal. By focusing on the positive, you'll be so intent on working towards what you want that you won't feel deprived about the unnecessary things you've stopped spending money on. Using positive language also attracts positive situations and people into your life.

FIVE GOAL-SETTING STEPS – PART II

4. Set a deadline for achieving each of your goals
A goal is not a goal until you set a date for it. We have too many things to do in our lives; that's why so often only those with deadlines get accomplished.

Oil billionaire H.L. Hunt said, "Success requires two things. You must know what you want and you must determine the price you are willing to pay to get it."

Most goals require some sort of sacrifice, whether it is that we spend less time with family and friends in order to further our career, or that we dedicate all of our financial resources to obtaining a university degree instead of travelling or buying an awesome new car. Once we know what we are willing to sacrifice, the only thing left is to put our whole heart and soul into achieving the goal we have set to make sure we get the most out of the choice we have made.

5. Don't try to go it alone; gather assistance
It is important to identify the knowledge you will need to acquire and the people or organizations that could give you essential help as you work towards your goals. No one is successful without the help of others, so don't be afraid to ask for help or advice from those who can be of assistance. There will be plenty of opportunities for you to repay the favour by helping others achieve their goals.

— *The Runway of Life*

MANY PEOPLE GO THROUGH LIFE WITHOUT EVER FEELING
TRULY PASSIONATE ABOUT SOMETHING.
GOALS AND PURPOSE WILL PROVIDE YOU
WITH THE PASSION YOU NEED AND
A REASON TO GET UP AND ON WITH EACH NEW DAY.

PUTTING MORE LIFE IN YOUR YEARS

South Australia's highest-paid public speaker, Peter J. Daniels, who is president and founder of The World Centre for Entrepreneurial Studies, said in his best-selling book *How to Reach Your Life Goals*, that life must be measured in something more meaningful than time.

He also noted that he has noticed that those who retire and have no further goals die or are confined to total medical care within a few short years, while those who retire in a positive way seem to slip into another gear, align their magnetic force to another pole and get a new lease on life, thereby extending their lives even further.

My own father worked until the then-mandatory retirement age at his company — 65. Soon after, I asked him to join me as I was beginning my own company, Canada Wide Media. Talk about a new lease on life! He worked for another 20 very positive years until his death at 85. I was thrilled to have the opportunity to work so closely with my dad and learn from his life experience during those two decades and it was easy to see that having a reason to get up each day gave his life continued meaning and purpose. At a time when many his age were tired and worn out, he excelled at this new challenge and opportunity.

— *The Runway of Life*

YOUNG OR OLD, WE ALL NEED
A MEANINGFUL PURPOSE
TO FEEL TRULY ALIVE. DO YOU
KNOW WHAT YOURS IS?

THE LAST FIVE MINUTES

We all have days when things don't go as we planned — that's life. But when it happens on a regular basis, it's probably time to re-evaluate daily habits and routines.

In his blog at the *Harvard Business Review*, Peter Bregman, author of *Point B: A Short Guide to Leading a Big Change*, explains that there's a simple reason why we often don't realize when things start to go offside. "We rarely take the time to pause, breathe and think about what's working and what's not. There's just too much to do and no time to reflect."

Bregman suggests that we all set aside the last five minutes of each day to review what took place.

"Look at your calendar and compare what actually happened — the meetings you attended, the work you got done, the conversations you had, the people with whom you interacted — with what you wanted to happen," suggests Bregman. "Then ask yourself three sets of questions:

"How did the day go? What success did I experience? What challenges did I encounter?

"What did I learn today? About myself? About others? What do I plan to do — differently or the same — tomorrow?

"Who did I interact with? Anyone I need to update? Thank? Ask a question? Share feedback?"

According to Bregman, the last set of questions is invaluable in terms of maintaining and growing relationships.

"If we don't pause to think about it, we're apt to overlook these kinds of communications," he says. "And we often do. But in a world where we depend on others to achieve anything in life, they are essential."

GIVE YOURSELF TIME TO REFLECT EVERY DAY.
PUT IT IN YOUR CALENDAR — IT'S ONLY FIVE MINUTES,
BUT IT'S TIME WELL SPENT.

TRAIN YOUR BRAIN

E xercising your brain is just as important to your well-being as exercising your body, and there are many long-term benefits. Most importantly, brain exercise helps strengthen your reasoning skills and protect against the loss of mental function caused by things like aging, Alzheimer's and senility. Here are a few suggestions to get you started:

1. Unclutter your mind. Practice ridding your mind of all negative and self-defeating thoughts. Choose a positive thought as your default and use it to refocus your mind whenever it begins to wander into negative territory. You might even want to try meditation, which is an excellent way to train your mind to stay in the moment.
2. Cultivate your reasoning powers. Make a game of putting what you know in new combinations or try some reasoning games (you can find them on the Internet).
3. Feed your mind. The best way to keep your brain healthy is to learn new things. Reading, writing, crossword puzzles and sudoku are all brain-building activities; so is learning any new skill.
4. Cultivate curiosity. Ask questions about things you don't understand. Never be satisfied with what you know. Develop your imagination too.
5. Practice balancing. Balancing on one foot engages many different parts of the brain. Try it with your eyes closed.
6. Be open. Never dismiss an idea as useless. Seek out viewpoints that are different from yours and see how these new ideas contrast with your own.
7. Coordination exercises. When you were a kid, you probably tried writing with your opposite hand for fun. This simple exercise is actually one of the best things you can do for your brain. Try writing, sending a text message or using your computer mouse with your non-dominant hand.

— *Who Dares Wins*

USE IT OR LOSE IT:
EXERCISE YOUR BRAIN EVERY DAY.

WHO DARES WINS

F lying to London on British Airways in the spring of 2000, I found myself listening to an interview with someone from Britain's Special Air Service (SAS) on one of the in-flight channels. In case you don't know, the SAS is an elite anti-terrorist unit that came into being in 1940 and since then has been deployed to almost every major conflict around the globe. As he summed up the philosophy of the SAS near the end of the interview, the fellow mentioned the organization's slogan, which is "Who Dares Wins." At the time, I thought that it would make a great name for a book, so I wrote it down.

Later, as I looked at the note again, I was reminded of all of the amazing people who, by their own example, have inspired me to challenge myself and pursue ever-greater goals. I decided this was a book I had to write and it would be an inspirational collection of stories about people who had succeeded by daring to go after their dreams. In writing it, I hoped that readers would gain insights that they could apply to both their professional endeavours and their personal journey through life.

Among the people featured in the book are Sir Edmund Hillary, whose historic climb up Mount Everest has inspired generations of individuals to reach for their goals, and astronaut Julie Payette, the first Canadian to board the International Space Station and a role model for aspiring astronauts everywhere.

— *The Power to Soar Higher*

TAKE SOME TIME TODAY TO THINK ABOUT WHAT
YOU CAN DO IN YOUR OWN LIFE TO
PROVIDE INSPIRATION AND ENCOURAGEMENT
FOR OTHERS. THINK TOO OF WHO
INSPIRES YOU AND WHAT YOU CAN LEARN
FROM THEIR EXAMPLE.

MONEY WISE – PART I

A few years ago, while listening to CBC Radio, I heard a frightening statistic. A commentator was talking about the sustainability of our economy and noted that by the year 2015, this country will have more citizens over the age of 60 (retirement age) than it will have people of working age. Given that a large number of these people are going to be dependent on the government for pensions, health care and even income assistance, it is just one more reason why, in the course of our career, we need to set a goal of retiring financially independent (i.e., at least $1 million in personal assets).

Once you've accumulated your wealth, the best way to hold onto it, according to a study in the U.S., is to stay married. The study, which began in 1995 and involved 9,000 Americans who were between the ages of 21 and 28 at the time, concluded that staying married for life almost doubles your wealth. By tracking subjects over a 15-year period, assessing their stocks, shares, assets, bank accounts and properties, the study's author, Jay Zagorsky, came to the conclusion that married people ended up much wealthier than their single or divorced counterparts.

The study also found that married people accumulated wealth much faster than single people. Over the course of the study, single people accumulated a median of $1,500 at the beginning up to $10,900 in the 15th year. In the same period, married people gained 93 per cent more than their single or divorced counterparts.

A LOT OF PEOPLE DON'T UNDERSTAND
THE DIFFERENCE BETWEEN INCOME AND WEALTH.
HAVING A BIG SALARY DOESN'T MEAN YOU CAN
AFFORD AN AFFLUENT LIFESTYLE. BUILDING WEALTH
INVOLVES BUDGETING, SAVING, INVESTING,
CONTROLLING DEBT AND SETTING CLEAR
FINANCIAL GOALS.

MONEY WISE – PART II

H ere are some tips to help you be more money wise and build your wealth:

1. Get in the right mindset. How you approach the task of financing your future will have an impact on the results you achieve. Rather than looking upon saving and investing as a burden on your disposable income, try telling yourself, "I am building my personal and family wealth."

2. Set measurable goals. Just as with every other area of your life, you will experience more success with your wealth-building strategy if you set both short- and long-term goals to focus on. Short-term goals could include paying off any unnecessary debt you are carrying (such as credit card debt) personally or within your business. Long-term goals, focused on expansion and eventually retirement, should also have annual targets to keep you on track. It is important to set a realistic timeframe for each goal and then break the cost into manageable chunks based on your income and expenses.

3. Pay yourself. After you've taken care of your debts, start paying yourself and sock some money away in an emergency fund so you can avoid using credit cards to pay for unexpected expenses. Once you've accumulated a cushion, you can put some money into an income-producing investment to get it working for you.

4. Make sure you are calculating your net worth accurately. Although you can list your luxury car, designer clothes and flat-screen TV on the plus side of your balance sheet, keep in mind that they are all depreciating assets and can distort what you think you have. Make sure that you are not spending more on these than you are putting into real estate, retirement funds or your savings account.

MONEY WISE – PART III

5. Train yourself to be a conscientious consumer. Avoid robotically buying things you don't really need just because they are on sale. Also, steer clear of unnecessary banking fees, like ATM fees and late-payment charges, as well as credit cards with high interest rates, and don't be shy about saving big bucks by negotiating the price down when buying a big-ticket item like a car.

6. Make a decision to be wealthy. The power of the mind, once it is made up and focused on a goal, is a powerful force. Unfortunately, most people never decide what they truly want in life; therefore they get little more than they expect. The process of deciding that you will be a success, have a great marriage, strong relationship with your children, or certain type of business or wealth will, in itself, cause you to move forward towards your goal. Your conscious decision will cause your mind to diligently search and create the reality you have chosen.

7. Create a schedule that encompasses your whole life. To create balance in your life, you must factor in time for both your business and your personal life. I have seen far too many professionals sacrifice their family to achieve a goal only to find that when they finally reach it, they have no one to share their success with, or they realize what little importance that goal had compared to the damage it did to their family.

> "MANY PEOPLE TAKE NO CARE OF THEIR MONEY
> TILL THEY COME NEARLY TO THE END OF IT,
> AND OTHERS DO JUST THE SAME WITH THEIR TIME."
> — Johann Wolfgang von Goethe

MONEY WISE – PART IV

8. Define what the high-payoff activities are for you in your business and invest your time in those. Once you have determined these activities, you need the discipline to do them daily. These are the only activities you can do if you want to pay yourself well. The following are examples of high-payoff activities: prospecting for clients, lead follow-up, client appointments, negotiating contracts, developing new products or services and business planning. You must focus, like an attorney does, on billing out hours daily. The more hours you bill, the more income you make. The greater percentage of the day spent on these activities, the more income earned.

9. Invest others with responsibility. In other words, learn to delegate! If you want to focus on high-payoff activities, you need to teach and train your staff to replace you in certain functions. Keep in mind that they are bound to make mistakes as they learn; just as you made mistakes that turned into valuable lessons that helped you develop your skills. Monitor their progress along the way and make sure you provide both constructive direction and praise for improvement.

10. Put good systems in place as soon as you possibly can. Luckily for me, I stumbled across this important lesson early on in my publishing career while attending a conference for magazine publishers. One of the most valuable lessons I learned there was to focus on the top line rather than the bottom line. In other words, determine how much you want to make and then work backwards to figure out what you need to do to make that number a reality.

— *Make Your Life a Masterpiece*

"TOO MANY PEOPLE SPEND MONEY
THEY HAVEN'T EARNED,
TO BUY THINGS THEY DON'T WANT,
TO IMPRESS PEOPLE THEY DON'T LIKE."
— Will Smith

A LITTLE KINDNESS

*"What we have done for ourselves alone dies with us;
what we have done for others and the world remains and
is immortal."* — Albert Pike

A basic, wonderful truth about all people is that through our choices and actions, we can make the world a better place. And we don't necessarily have to do huge things to make a big difference. Yet, there are often times when we don't take action simply because we feel the action is too little or that it wouldn't make a difference. What we need to remember is that what sometimes may seem like the smallest gesture to us, can make a huge difference to someone else.

A little kindness goes a long way. The simplest of things can make the difference. A door being held open, a handwritten note, a kind word, acknowledgement of a job well done, an unsolicited offer of help, an apology; any one of these can be used to help create a bond, bridge differences, increase understanding, transform hurt feelings or generally bring people together.

Kindness is like the oil of life; it makes everything run more smoothly. It is also a magical and contagious thing. Individual acts of kindness and generosity of spirit can create a chain reaction of good feelings. A single smile encourages another to smile; a "good morning" invites a greeting in return, a simple courtesy reminds the recipient how easy it is to do the same. Thoughtfulness, consideration and care enhance our well-being and that of everyone we encounter, so pass it on.

—*The Power to Soar Higher*

IT'S GREAT TO BE ON THE RECEIVING END
OF AN ACT OF KINDNESS, BUT IT FEELS JUST AS
GOOD TO BE DISHING IT OUT.

IT BEGINS WITH A DREAM

No one remembers who says no; we only remember who says yes. Thirteen years before the 2010 Winter Games were held in Vancouver, Bruce McMillan walked down the hall to the office of Rick Antonson, president of Tourism Vancouver, and said, "Why don't we put together a proposal to bid on the 2010 Winter Olympics?"

Antonson said yes, and as they say, the rest is history. On Friday, February 12, the 2010 Olympics opened in front of 60,000 excited fans and three billion viewers worldwide. A monumental dream was realized!

During a pre-Olympic event, Canada's Governor General, Michaelle Jean, O.C., declared, "The very best we have to give, will be given."

And it was, thanks to the organizers, athletes, volunteers, sponsors, supporters and millions of Canadians who welcomed the world with open arms. The Olympics were one of the most inspiring and exciting things that have ever happened in Vancouver.

John Furlong, CEO of the Vancouver Organizing Committee for the Games, immigrated to Canada many years ago from Ireland. Upon his entry into Canada, the immigration officer told him, "Welcome to Canada. Make us better." As leader of the team orchestrating the massive undertaking that was the 2010 Games, John has indeed done his part to make our country better. Following the Olympics, he had this to say about his experience:

"I have an even greater appreciation today about the power of a vision and what happens when people pursue something with the kind of vigour you can. I think something pretty extraordinary has happened in the country and I am glad to have been a part of it."

Let that be said of all of us, that we need to make our lives better and this country better.

— Insight 2011

WE NEED TO BELIEVE IN OURSELVES, BELIEVE IN OUR DREAMS,
AND TOGETHER WE CAN MAKE A DIFFERENCE —
BUT IT BEGINS WITH A DREAM.

IT'S OUR PURPOSE

A lbert Einstein was once asked for his definition of the purpose of life. Surprisingly, or perhaps not, he said: "The purpose of life is to serve mankind."

If I've achieved any form of success in my career, it is due in part to coming to grips with Einstein's statement.

In business, we are, quite naturally, motivated to serve our customers in order to build our client base and be successful, but something that I've discovered during the past 30 years is that my business has also grown in direct proportion to the amount of community and charity work I've undertaken.

Zig Ziglar, one of North America's foremost motivational speakers, said, "You can get everything you want in life if you just help enough people get what *they* want in life."

This is not to say that you need to devote all of your time and effort to a hundred different charities in order to succeed. It is far more beneficial to look for a couple of organizations that would benefit from your expertise, then commit a significant amount of time to helping them reach their goals.

The benefits will astound you and the people you meet will have a profound effect on your life, guaranteed.

Variety Club International has been just such an organization for me. Variety dedicates itself to aiding children with ability challenges. It helps them to fight for independence, to understand the importance of realizing their potential, to establish a meaningful life, to integrate where possible with society and to be accepted and appreciated for who they truly are. After more than 30 years of service, it continues to be an experience that is both humbling and incredibly inspiring.

— *How to Soar With the Eagles*

HOW ARE YOU HELPING OTHERS
GET WHAT THEY WANT?

DON'T FORGET A SINGLE ONE

C had was a quiet little fellow and his mother often noticed that he walked home from school behind the other kids. While they laughed and played, Chad walked alone.

Valentine's Day was approaching and he said to his mom, "I want to make a Valentine's Day card for everyone in my class." Although she wished he hadn't set his heart on the idea (and suspecting that he wouldn't get any cards in return), Chad's mom bought crayons, coloured paper, glue and scissors and painstakingly helped him to make 35 individual cards. It took the whole evening and Chad put the finished cards in a paper bag before he went to bed.

The next morning, Chad bounded out of bed, quickly dressed and had breakfast, then picked up the bag of Valentine's Day cards and ran out the door. He was definitely excited.

His mom decided she had better prepare his favourite cookies for when he came home from school, as she knew he would be upset.

Looking out the kitchen window at 3:15 p.m., the mom saw the kids laughing and joking and there was Chad, as usual, all alone, bringing up the rear.

"Mommy has some milk and cookies for you," she told him as he came through the door. He walked right by her and as he set down his backpack, he said, "Not a one — not even one."

His mother gulped, holding back tears . . . and then Chad added, "I didn't forget a single one."

This Valentine's Day, is there anyone to whom you want to say, "I love you, you're important to me, you helped make my day, you're a key part of the team, I appreciate you," or maybe just "thank you"?

Don't forget a single one — not even one.

— You Can If You Think You Can

EINSTEIN'S LOST TICKET

The great physicist Albert Einstein was travelling on a train from Princeton when the conductor came down the aisle, punching passenger's tickets. When he came to Einstein, Einstein reached in his vest pocket but couldn't find his ticket so he tried his pants pocket. Still no ticket, so he looked in his briefcase. It wasn't there. He checked on the seat beside him. No ticket.

The conductor said, "Dr. Einstein, I know who you are, everyone knows who you are and I'm sure you bought a ticket. Don't worry about it."

Einstein nodded appreciatively. The conductor continued down the aisle. As he was ready to move to the next car, he turned around and saw the great physicist down on his hands and knees looking under his seat.

The conductor rushed back and said, "Dr. Einstein, please don't worry. I know who you are, it's no problem, you don't need a ticket. I'm sure you bought one."

"Young man," said Einstein, looking up at him, "I too know who I am. What I don't know is where I'm going."

DO YOU KNOW WHERE YOU'RE GOING
TODAY AND HOW YOU'RE GOING
TO GET THERE? IF YOU DON'T,
HOW WILL YOU BE ABLE TO TELL
WHEN YOU'VE ARRIVED?

February 16

WHAT IS A MASTERPIECE?

I'd like you to take a moment right now and think about what comes to mind when you hear the term "a masterpiece." Do you imagine some great classical work of art like Leonardo da Vinci's painting of Mona Lisa, Michelangelo's statue of David or Mozart's "Requiem"? Or perhaps the phrase makes you think of someone whom you believe has a rare talent or genius, like Thomas Edison with his invention of the light bulb, Albert Einstein with his *Theory of Relativity* or Henry Ford with his Model T motor car.

What is interesting about the concept of a masterpiece in the modern world is that we tend to think of it as the very best work that an individual could ever produce, the culmination of a life's work or the definitive magnum opus that cannot be topped; and yet, that is not the original meaning of the term.

By its original definition, a "master-piece" actually refers to a specific piece of work created by a journeyman (the next step up from an apprentice) craftsman or artisan who aspires to become a master and gain admittance into a professional guild. Therefore, it is not the culmination of one's life's work, but rather a project undertaken to prove that as a journeyman, one has mastered the basic skills necessary to be considered qualified to practice his profession and offer his services under his own name.

In this way, creating one's masterpiece was both an end and a beginning at the same time.

— *Make Your Life a Masterpiece*

I BELIEVE THAT WE ALL HAVE THE POTENTIAL TO MAKE
OUR MASTERPIECE — THOUGH WHAT THAT IS, IS UP TO EACH
ONE OF US TO DETERMINE FOR OURSELVES.

WHO DO YOU THINK YOU ARE?

Most of the great philosophers that I admire have something to say on the subject of how our thoughts influence what happens in our lives. For example, Marcus Aurelius Antonius, who said: "Our life is what our thoughts make it." Profound? Yes. Original? No.

You have to go back to King Solomon's writings, more than 3,000 years ago in the Old Testament's *Book of Proverbs*, to find what is probably the first time the thought was ever expressed.

Solomon wrote: "For as he thinks within himself . . . so he is."

It seems absolutely clear to me that it is our ongoing and persistent thoughts that make us who and what we are. Therefore, if we are not absolutely thrilled with who and what we are, it is obviously time to change our thinking.

Perhaps the fastest and most effective way to change your thinking and clarify your values is to answer these three questions:

1. How do you spend your energy?
2. How do you spend your time?
3. How do you spend your money?

More than all of our words could ever do, our actions speak volumes about what is important to us and are closely aligned with what we actually think about. So, if you are not thrilled with your life, begin to change by focusing your thoughts on what you truly want — and the rest will follow.

— *How to Soar With the Eagles*

WHAT YOU THINK DETERMINES WHO YOU ARE
AND EVEN MORE IMPORTANTLY, WHO YOU WILL BECOME.
WHO DO YOU THINK YOU ARE?

NINE RULES OF GOAL SETTING

Harvard Business School did a survey of 1980 graduates and their progress today. Eighty per cent of the grads had no stated career or business goals. The remaining 20 per cent, who had stated goals and had written them down, were earning three times as much as the group with no goals.

Here are nine rules that will help you turn your goals into reality:

1. Write down your goals.
2. Prioritize your goals.
3. Personalize your goals.
4. Assess your goals and make sure they are realistic.
5. Get what you need — education, mentoring, etc.
6. Phrase your goals in positive language.
7. Set deadlines, short and long term.
8. Set goals that are consistent with your values.
9. Share your goals with those who will hold you accountable.

Where you will be in three, five or even 10 years will be directly related to the goals you set for yourself today.

— *You Can If You Believe You Can*

TAKE SOME TIME TODAY TO REVIEW
AND UPDATE YOUR EXISTING GOALS OR GET
EXCITED ABOUT SOME NEW ONES.

WHAT ARE YOU HIDING?

The musical *The Phantom of the Opera* is an incredible work that has touched the heart of the world. I have seen it in London, New York, Toronto and Vancouver. In 2011, the London production celebrated 25 years. It is the power and simplicity of the story that always draws me and, I'm sure, so many other fans, back to the show again and again. No matter where it is staged, *The Phantom* weaves a special magic.

At the heart of the story is the mask that hides the Phantom's disfigured face. For the Phantom, the mask doesn't just protect his face, it is also a shield from the harsh scrutiny of a world that can often be cruel. For the most part he hides behind it very well. Andrew Lloyd Webber, the brilliant British musician who wrote *Phantom*, says that he believes the story is an expression of the isolation that all of us feel.

It doesn't matter who we are, each of us has something about ourselves that we are not comfortable with (some ugly truth that we cannot face) and because we do not want the world to judge us for it, we hide that part of who we truly are, from our friends, our family, even ourselves.

As the story evolves, Christine unmasks the Phantom and offers him a brief taste of the love and acceptance he has never known and in that moment he is transformed and responds with kindness in return.

— *How to Soar With the Eagles*

WHAT TRUTHS ARE YOU CURRENTLY
HIDING FROM AND HOW IS IT AFFECTING
YOUR LIFE AND RELATIONSHIPS?

WHAT IF – PART I

Our time on this earth is at once both too long and too short. Too long to spend our time doing something we don't enjoy and too short to waste even a minute on regrets instead of taking action and changing the things that don't make us happy — which reminds me of a taxi ride I took with my wife Kay in Las Vegas. We were on our way from the Mandalay Bay Hotel to a fashion mall, when Kay tried to strike up a conversation with the driver by asking him how his day was going.

"I'd rather be doing anything than driving this cab," the fellow grumbled in response.

Thinking that perhaps he had simply taken the job as a temporary measure to make ends meet or some such thing, Kay asked the driver how long he had been driving a cab.

"Thirty years," came the answer.

Kay and I looked at each other in amazement. Coincidentally, he had begun his career as a cab driver around the same time I started Canada Wide Magazines with one small publication. I thought of all I had accomplished in those 30 years. I couldn't imagine sticking with something I genuinely disliked doing for so long. Yet, judging by his hostile disposition and overall sour outlook, I got the impression he had been sharing his poor attitude with customers for many of those 30 years. It's true that life doesn't always present us with the opportunities that we think we deserve. But that doesn't mean we should just wait around. Opportunity can turn up in the most unlikely of places, if we are willing to seek it out.

WHAT IF — PART II

O pportunity can even turn up disguised as a job that we don't really want. Imagine if this particular cab driver had shown up for his first day on the job 30 years ago with a positive attitude and a desire to be the best darn cab driver in Las Vegas. What if he had taken the time to learn as much as he could about the city so that he could be a knowledgeable guide for his passengers? What if he had chosen to smile as he opened the door for each new customer and helped them into the car before taking care of their luggage and then offering them a free map of local attractions? What if he had developed a reputation as the nicest, friendliest driver in the city and passengers began to ask for him by name . . . and what if, 30 years later he had built a company of his own with a fleet of 30 cars (one for each year he had been in business)?

What if he had only believed in himself . . . what if?

I look at my own life more than 30 years after starting with one little magazine. Today, I enjoy great respect in the city where I live, high regard from other publishers, I have the loyalty and admiration of my colleagues and staff — and I look forward to each new day as an opportunity to do more. The best is yet to come because I am still working on my masterpiece.

— *Make Your Life a Masterpiece*

THERE IS NOT ENOUGH TIME ON EARTH FOR REGRETS.
IF YOU ARE UNHAPPY OR UNFULFILLED,
NOW IS THE TIME FOR ACTION.
DON'T WAIT FOR OPPORTUNITY TO FIND YOU,
GO OUT AND FIND IT.

NO MAN IS AN ISLAND

"Three things in human life are important.
The first is to be kind. The second is to be kind.
The third is to be kind." — Henry James

Like me, you may have come to this realization long ago, but it is almost impossible for anyone to succeed without the help, encouragement and support of others.

The English poet John Donne wrote with great perception several centuries ago that no man is an island, entire of itself. It is an often-quoted line because it is so very true.

"Every man," he said, "is a piece of the continent, a part of the main . . . any man's death diminishes me because I am involved in mankind."

U.S. President Barack Obama offered a similar sentiment in a speech in Cairo in 2009.

"Human history has often been a record of nations and tribes — and, yes, religions — subjugating one another in pursuit of their own interests. Yet in this new age, such attitudes are self-defeating. Given our interdependence, any world order that elevates one nation or group of people over another will inevitably fail. So whatever we think of the past, we must not be prisoners to it. Our problems must be dealt with through partnership; our progress must be shared."

This is as true on an individual level as it is for nations, races and religions. It's impossible to go it alone. We are creatures who thrive only when we are part of the main, actively engaged in the give and take that defines our interdependence as family members, neighbours, communities, societies and as a species.

Look carefully at those who are pushing you onward and upward, and be ready always to extend a hand and to offer them thanks and give others the same kind of encouragement.

— Insight 2011

STILL IN MOTION

Even after 25 years, it is impossible not to be impressed with Rick Hansen, a man who is perhaps best known as "The Man in Motion." With his determined, inspirational, heart-stopping, 34-country, four-continent and 40,000-kilometre wheelchair journey in 1985, he made history and raised $26 million to support research to help people living with spinal cord injuries.

Together with 300 guests at a luncheon, I listened once again to Rick Hansen's amazing story.

Over the years, he has lost none of his humility or passion for his life's mission. Today he is CEO of the Rick Hansen Foundation and has helped raise more than $200 million for projects, awareness programs and resources.

Here are some excerpts from his presentation:

"Focus on things you can do, not the things you can't do. The key is focus."

"It's not a physical limitation, it's a mental limitation."

The highlight for me was when Rick talked about the moments during his journey where he felt as if he couldn't continue.

"Those bitter winter days on the prairies battling minus-50-degree temperatures — asking myself, is this really all worth it? I can't go on, I'm going to quit — asking myself, do I have one more stroke in me and then another and another and seeing the incredible potential each of us has if we don't quit."

Then he turned to the audience to say: "Do you have one more stroke in you?"

As his life journey evolves, Rick just sets the bar ever higher, asking himself and in turn, each of us, "What are you going to do while you're here, with your every breath?"

— *The Power of a Dream*

LIKE RICK HANSEN, WE NEED TO FOCUS ON THE THINGS
WE CAN DO AND KEEP PUSHING THROUGH.

THE PRICELESS PARADOX

*"Things that are given to us for nothing we place little value on.
Things that we pay money for, we value. The paradox is
that exactly the reverse is true. Everything that's really worthwhile
in life came to us free. Our minds, our souls, our bodies,
our hopes, our dreams, our ambitions, our intelligence, our love
of family and children and friends and country — all these
priceless possessions are free. But the things that cost us money
are actually very cheap and can be replaced at any time.
A good man can be completely wiped out and make another
fortune. Even if our home burns down, we can rebuild it.
But the things we got for nothing can never
be replaced."* — Earl Nightingale

Here are just a few of the important things money can't buy:

Time: Each of us only has a finite amount of time to spend in this life and we never know exactly how long that will be. Every time the sun sets, another day is over and all the money in the world will not bring it back. Choose carefully how you will spend your precious time.

Health: Money might be able to buy you health insurance to pay for the best care possible, but it won't bring back your health once it's gone. Leading a healthy, balanced life and taking the time to enjoy the little moments is the best inoculation against disease.

Respect: The kind of respect you can buy with money isn't worth having. True respect must be earned by treating others the way we wish them to treat us.

Happiness: It may be cliché, but true happiness comes from being satisfied with who we are on the inside rather than the money and possessions we have accumulated.

— It Begins With a Dream

FROM THE BOTTOM TO THE TOP

Sometimes it takes hitting the bottom before we find the motivation to do what we know we should have been doing all along.

That's exactly what happened with author J.K. Rowling, leading her to finally sit down and write the Harry Potter series that subsequently turned her into a billionaire. In a moving speech she gave at Harvard on the topic of failure, Rowling described in her own words how hitting rock bottom, being unemployed and living on social assistance finally helped her to fulfill her dream of being an author.

"So why do I talk about the benefits of failure?" she asked her audience. "Simply because failure meant a stripping away of the inessential. I stopped pretending to myself that I was anything other than what I was and began to direct all my energy into finishing the only work that mattered to me. Had I really succeeded at anything else, I might never have found the determination to succeed in the one arena I believed I truly belonged. I was set free, because my greatest fear had already been realized and I was still alive, and I still had a daughter whom I adored, and I had an old typewriter and a big idea. And so rock bottom became the solid foundation on which I rebuilt my life."

Failure has a way of focusing our attention like nothing else because we learn very quickly by experiencing it, what our priorities are. We learn what we can and can't live without, we discover our strengths, our weaknesses and our greatest desires. Essentially, our failures highlight our values and help us to define what is important in our lives.

— *The Power of a Dream*

WHEN YOU HIT THE BOTTOM, THERE'S
NOWHERE LEFT TO GO BUT UP.

JUST DO IT

The Nike slogan, "Just Do It" has got to be one of the simplest and most effective advertising slogans ever invented. It is also the best advice I could give anyone who has a goal.

When I look at my own life and career, I can honestly say it is the times when I acted on my own initiative that I am most proud of. Like when I first met Kay while working as an emcee on a cruise ship. If I hadn't grabbed the opportunity, when that cruise was over, Kay would have sailed out of my life forever. Instead, we're celebrating our 44th wedding anniversary. Likewise, when I got the idea to write a book to elaborate on my speeches and expand my audience. If I had waited to get a publisher, I might still be waiting to publish my first book. Instead, today you are reading my 15th book.

"Just do it" is a reminder for us to get going and to stop procrastinating or fretting over the roadblocks our mind throws up to stop us. It's a reminder to focus on the present moment and the task at hand.

Getting started is often the most difficult part of any new undertaking. It's kind of like trying to learn to drive a car with a manual transmission; the first gear is the hardest, but once you've figured out when to let go of the clutch and you start to move forward, shifting into the next gear is suddenly easy.

Here are three easy steps to help you "Just Do It!":
1. Set concrete, attainable goals and act on them.
2. Commit to your plan.
3. Believe in yourself and be willing to take a few risks.

— *The Power to Soar Higher*

ACTION MAY NOT ALWAYS BRING
HAPPINESS, BUT THERE IS NO
HAPPINESS WITHOUT ACTION.

THE SUPER SIX — PART I

At the turn of the last century, a man named Ivy Lee met with Charles M. Schwab, president of Bethlehem Steel. His objective was to sell his services to Schwab and help his company become more efficient. Schwab's reaction to Lee's proposal was that his people already knew what they should be doing — his real problem was simply one of getting them to do it. As a result, Schwab wasn't buying.

"Just suppose I could give you a tool, an action that would guarantee you'd become more efficient, you'd be interested, wouldn't you?" Lee asked. "Better yet," he continued, sensing Schwab's resistance, "how about if I just give you the idea — let you use it for 21 days and if it works, you share it with your employees. Then send me a cheque for whatever you think it's worth."

"Well, okay, what is it?" Schwab asked.

"At the beginning of every single day, or better yet, the night before, take out a piece of paper and write down the six most important things you need to do to achieve your objectives on that particular day," Lee said. "In fact, go ahead and do that right now for tomorrow."

Schwab thought about it and wrote down six action items.

"Now put them in order of importance, one being the most important," Lee continued. So Schwab did that.

"Starting tomorrow first thing, start on item number one. Do not go on to item number two until you have fully completed item number one. Then continue down the list."

February 28

THE SUPER SIX – PART II

If you get to the end of the day and have not completed your full list of action items, roll over your remaining items to the next day and they become your first priorities for that day. Use this for as long as you like and if you think it is worth something, send me a cheque for that amount."

Less than a month later, Ivy Lee received a cheque in the mail for the then-princely sum of $25,000. Attached was a note signed by Charles M. Schwab that read: "That's the most powerful tool for achievement that anyone has ever taught me and here's a fraction of what it's worth."

Although Bethlehem Steel was relatively unknown at the time, it would go on to become the largest steel producer in the world within five years and Charles Schwab would earn $100,000 on his own, making him the most powerful and famous steel man alive. The $25,000 investment he made in Ivy Lee's idea turned into many millions at a time when the average income in the American workforce was around $2 a day.

Many powerful business people have attributed their success to Ivy Lee's technique and I have to admit that I too have been using it for more than 15 years myself. It is also something that I have shared with everyone who works at Canada Wide Media because it can be used to keep you focused on what's really important in all areas of your life.

I like to call it my Super Six.

— *The Power to Soar Higher*

START TODAY BY WRITING DOWN THE SIX
MOST IMPORTANT THINGS YOU NEED TO ACCOMPLISH
RIGHT NOW . . . AND THEN GET GOING.

MARCH

JOE'S PEARLS OF WISDOM – PART I

My mentor Joseph Segal is a self-made man who believes that experience is a great teacher. "I had a lot of advantages because I never had a business degree," explains Joe. "So I had no preconceived notions about what should be or shouldn't be, about what's right and what's wrong."

Over the years Joe has mentored hundreds of budding entrepreneurs, including Lululemon CEO Chip Wilson, sharing with them his many "pearls of wisdom." Over the next few days, you can benefit from Joe's wise words also:

1. You aren't ready for the answer until you are ready to ask the question

Expecting someone else to solve your problems is unrealistic and you don't learn a damn thing from it. When you figure out what the question is, then you will be ready to find the answer.

2. Too many times in life we see a need, but hesitate to act on it

Believe it or not, the best opportunities don't come in a package with a bow. More often they present themselves in the form of a problem. Successful people are those who are willing to put their neck on the line and take a risk — they see a need and act decisively to find a way to fulfill it.

3. Expect to win

If you believe you'll win, you're already halfway there. The most common thing that holds us back is our own negative thoughts or expectations.

4. If you want to win, you need to have desire, determination and confidence

Desire provides the motivation to get you started, determination keeps you going when you encounter obstacles and confidence gives you the courage to see it through to the end, even when others don't believe in you.

JOE'S PEARLS OF WISDOM – PART II

5. Ultimately, it is persistence that will pay off; forget about perfection
For the most part, there simply isn't enough time in the world for us to worry about perfection. Besides, perfection isn't about doing a good job; it is about being in control and an overbearing need to be right. It is a far better thing to be persistent, find a goal that captures your imagination and strive to achieve it.

6. Most of us will not choose how we will die, but we all choose — every day — how we will live
Free will is a beautiful thing, yet it comes with responsibility and accountability. The sum of your life rests on your shoulders. Only you can decide your fate through the priorities you set, the decisions you make, the efforts you spend, the sacrifices you make. What you choose for today will determine all of your tomorrows. Act accordingly!

7. Success is more a matter of courage than ability
Competing in business in today's globalized world is a battle of wits; more than ability, it requires courage. But don't be mistaken, courage is not the lack of fear, it is fear plus action. Courage comes from deep within the heart and flushes away the paralysis created by fear; it is the willingness to reach beyond one's comfort zone. Courage comes in many forms, not only from thoughts and deeds of greatness, but in the everyday art of being true to your word. It is a skill that can be learned and strengthened through practice and it begins with the question, "What would I be doing if I were 10 times bolder?"

JOE'S PEARLS OF WISDOM — PART III

8. Always play to your advantage; know your strengths — and your weaknesses

Great leaders are those who, when faced with a challenge, can look within themselves, assessing both their strengths and their weaknesses and then take action or make strategic decisions in accordance with what they see.

9. Everything is relative; some things are relevant and some things are not

It's not easy to keep priorities in perspective; however, the ability to do so will be a great factor in determining how quickly you achieve your goals. Just as we must choose one specific career from the many, we must also be discerning about which situations we need to deal with personally, which we should delegate and which we should ignore altogether. Being able to filter out that which is not relevant frees us up to give more attention to what is important.

10. If you haven't experienced the bottom, you won't appreciate the top

Ever wonder why some of the most successful people in business — the ones who manage to stay on top for decades — are those who have, at one time or another, failed magnificently? I believe it is because experience is the best teacher and if you are really going to succeed at anything, you have to know how — when your big plan blows up in your face — to pick yourself up and start building again.

11. Never question who takes more, just give more

If you choose to focus on giving rather than taking — creating a sense that you have more than you need — you will always have an atmosphere of abundance in your life.

JOE'S PEARLS OF WISDOM — PART IV

12. Alone, you are only as good as your reach; you must join hands with others
Remember how as a child, whenever you went out, your parents told you to stick together and hold hands to cross the street? Well, nothing has changed. Joining up with others — sharing both risks and resources — gives us courage and allows us to play to our strengths, accomplishing far more than we could ever do alone.

13. Businesses fail when the person at the top can't see the bottom
Hierarchies work great in the military, not so great in business. Having too many levels of management often means the person at the top — the one making the decisions — has no idea what the people in the trenches are thinking and doing. If you're in charge, make a point of keeping communication flowing in both directions and get the word out that you have an open-door policy.

14. People complicate their own lives
Far too many people complicate their lives by worrying about little things and never choosing a direction or purpose. My philosophy is very straightforward: the simplest way is the best way. Stick to the basics, stay focused on your goals, treat others with respect, speak the truth, be thankful for what you have and don't be afraid to help out others when you can.

15. Do not brood or bottle things up; problems don't disappear, they have to be worked on and worked out
When times get rough, those who make the mistake of withdrawing and trying to hide the problem often simply make the situation worse and end up very depressed. The sooner you come to terms with your problem, the sooner you will be able to get back on top.

— *The Runway of Life*

AN OLYMPIC-SIZED DREAM – PART I

I have had many dreams in my life. One of my most recent dreams involved the Olympics. In 2003, International Olympic Committee chairman Jacques Rogge announced that Vancouver would host the 2010 Olympic and Paralympic Winter Games. In December 2007, I received a letter from John Furlong, head of the Vancouver Organizing Committee, inviting me to be an Olympic ambassador.

Shortly after receiving the letter, I thought, 'There really is nothing bigger than the Olympics; this is a great opportunity. I should find some way to be involved and make the most of what will surely be a once-in-a-lifetime experience.' After thinking about it for awhile, an idea came to me, 'I've got a pretty good voice,' I mused. 'Maybe I could be emcee for the opening and closing ceremonies.'

I talked to fellow governor of the Vancouver Board of Trade, Rick Turner, who was also a director of the Vancouver Organizing Committee and he said, "Go for it, Peter," so I did.

I spoke with John Furlong and let him know of my interest and about a year later, I got an email from Rick Turner asking me if I was, or could be, bilingual in French and English in time for the Olympics. Even though I knew right then and there that there was no realistic chance of me becoming bilingual in such a short time, I didn't give up. Instead, I thought, who do I know that is bilingual? Then it dawned on me. Not only had my daughter Rebecca completed her grade-school education in French immersion, she also attended university in Nice, France. If bilingualism was required, we would make the perfect father/daughter team.

The challenge now was to convince John Furlong that I was the man for the job.

AN OLYMPIC-SIZED DREAM — PART II

I realized that I would have to do something extraordinary. Deciding that a professional demo was the way to go, I hired the local Knowledge Network studio for a few hours and produced a demo video for the opening ceremonies. When I presented the demo to John, he was both surprised and impressed. "I've never seen someone go to so much trouble for a job that doesn't pay," he told me.

By the time I produced my demo, the Vancouver Organizing Committee had already engaged David Atkins from Australia to produce the opening and closing ceremonies. Speaking with David, he told me that it was unlikely I would have a chance at being emcee as it was an off-camera job and one that was generally decided by the television network broadcasting the Games.

"We need to find you something else," he told me, much to my delight.

Many emails and almost two years later (remember, it takes at least 10 tries to make a sale and most people give up after the third try), it was decided that I would give a six-minute motivational address at the very first Victory Ceremony (the medal ceremony) to be held at B.C. Place Stadium during the Olympics. Although it wasn't exactly my dream as I had originally imagined it, I was very proud to be the only motivational speaker — in the entire world — to be invited to speak at the Olympics.

Life doesn't turn out exactly how we expect it to, I never did get to emcee the opening or closing ceremonies, but I did end up playing a role in the Olympics and making some wonderful memories, all because I took action and set my dream in motion.

— The Power of a Dream

WHAT IS YOUR OLYMPIC-SIZED DREAM?

BLAH, BLAH, BLAH

One of the many joys that come from seeing your children grow into wonderful, capable adults is that at some point they too become parents and your life takes on yet another wonderful dimension as a grandparent.

In our family, we are fortunate to occasionally take holidays where everyone comes along. On one such vacation, I sat my young grandson down beside me and told him that I was going to teach him some media speech. "Benjamin," I told him, "Repeat after me: blah, blah, blah."

Recognizing that he comes by the gift of the gab honestly, Benjamin naturally caught on right away and for the rest of the holiday, whenever a family member asked him to give his "speech" he immediately responded with, "Blah, blah, blah."

When the vacation was over, I returned to my busy schedule where I am frequently away from home for weeks at a stretch. As a result, there was a point where I hadn't seen Benjamin for almost three weeks, so I decided to go home early one afternoon to spend some time with him.

When my wife Kay saw me walk through the door, she turned to our little grandson and asked, "Do you remember the speech?" Remembering what I had taught him, his face lit up and he came running toward me shouting, "Granddad, Granddad, blah, blah, blah."

Kay and I couldn't help but laugh out loud as I scooped him up and gave him a big hug.

Having a little grandson to spoil is a real treat and watching him grow and change right before my eyes reminds me how important it is to take time to make memories with those you love.

I hope you will always remember to do the same.

— *The Power to Soar Higher*

MAKE THE MOST OF EVERY MOMENT TODAY
WITH THOSE YOU LOVE.

DON'T FOLLOW THE LEADER, BE THE LEADER

If one of your big goals in life is to be an entrepreneur and own your own business, you must look for opportunity where others see only obstacles and strike out in your own direction. When you achieve a goal that was once thought unattainable, you provide the impetus for others to dream bigger, work harder and go further. For example, Roger Bannister was the first runner to break the four-minute mile at a time when many said it couldn't be done. Today, the four-minute mile is standard in competition simply because he proved that it could be done.

— *The Power to Soar Higher*

WHAT'S YOUR FOUR-MINUTE MILE AND WHAT
ACTION CAN YOU TAKE TODAY TO WORK
TOWARDS BREAKING THROUGH THAT BARRIER?

DRIFTING

How different is a leaf floating on top of a stream from a fish actively swimming in the centre? At first the leaf swirls in the light, but as it drifts further from the centre and the current slows, it gets snagged in twigs and debris at the edge. In contrast, the fish chooses again and again to stay in the flow, gaining strength and momentum from the invigorating current.

Gretchen Rubin, author of *The Happiness Project*, posted a quiz on her blog some time ago about "drifting," which is exactly what the name suggests, letting ourselves be carried away by circumstances rather than taking control of, and responsibility for, what is happening in our lives. But don't be mistaken, drifting isn't about doing nothing. In fact, most people work very hard when they are drifting, often because they are trying to avoid facing up to the fact that they are doing what they think they should, rather than what they truly want to do with their lives.

Here are a few of the questions from Rubin's quiz (if you'd like to take the quiz, visit her blog at *www.happiness-project.com*):

__ I often have the peculiar feeling that I'm living someone else's life, or that this isn't my "real" life, which hasn't yet begun.
__ I spend a lot of time daydreaming about a completely different life as an escape from what I'm doing now.
__ I complain about my situation, but I don't spend much time trying to figure out ways to make it better.
__ There is something in my life about which I used to be passionate, but now I never allow myself to indulge in it. In fact, it makes me uncomfortable even thinking about it.

— *Insight 2011*

IT'S TIME TO STOP DRIFTING AND
SET YOUR OWN COURSE.

EXPAND YOUR ASSET BASE

According to Thomas J. Stanley, PhD, author of *The Millionaire Mind*, you don't need a high IQ or an expensive business-school education to become a millionaire. While conducting research for his book, Dr. Stanley interviewed more than 1,300 millionaires in the U.S. to find out what common traits contributed to their economic success.

Surprisingly, the typical millionaire did not inherit money from family, graduate from an Ivy League college or strike it rich with a stock play. In fact, Dr. Stanley points out that rather than choose a career strictly for the money, millionaires tend to choose careers that match their abilities and then work harder than most people are willing to do to build up their asset base. They also tend to be practical (not prone to a lavish lifestyle) and willing to take calculated risks.

In his interviews, Dr. Stanley asked the millionaires which attributes they thought had contributed to their success. Here are their top four answers:
1. The ability to get along with people   61%
2. Possessing strong leadership qualities   45%
3. Ability to sell my ideas/products   45%
4. Having good mentors   29%

How many of these attributes have you mastered in your own life?

Jim Rohn, who has been a mentor to many millionaires, says the main reason to set a goal to become a millionaire is not for the money, but rather for what you become in the process of achieving the goal. In the book, *Conversations with Millionaires*, Jack Canfield concurs: "You could take away my house, my money, my car, everything, and it wouldn't matter. I know how to create more of those things because of who I've become."

— *Make Your Life a Masterpiece*

IT'S NOT YOUR SALARY THAT MAKES YOU RICH,
IT'S YOUR SPENDING HABITS.

IT NEVER HURTS TO HELP

It's human to want to be liked and in most situations you will be able to accomplish more if people like you. An easy way to build rapport with almost anyone is to offer your assistance in a time of need. That's how I came to know one of Vancouver's most endearing personalities. Here's what happened.

When I returned to Vancouver in 1969 from England, I knew that I needed to re-establish myself with some local gigs. Thankfully, my Vancouver agent Ben Kopelow booked me into Ken Stauffer's Cave Supper Club on Hornby Street as the opening act for the Mills Brothers. Back in those days, The Cave was a very big deal and so were the Mills Brothers.

Unfortunately, I was not really prepared in the sartorial sense and I had no money to buy a new suit. So there I was, set to open at The Cave in seven days, doing two shows a night, with nothing to wear.

Enter character Murray Goldman, one of Canada's premier clothiers and a larger-than-life personality. Murray came to the rescue, inviting me to his Hastings Street headquarters and telling me to pick out five or six outfits: suits, ties, shirts, whatever I needed. He would have them tailored and ready for opening night and I could pay him whenever I was able.

"You have to look good at The Cave and I'll be there opening night to make sure you do," he told me.

I walked onto the stage opening night looking great and feeling confident, thanks to Murray's generosity. What I learned from his example is that when you see an opportunity to help someone, just do it.

— *The Power of Tact*

"DON'T SAY THAT YOU WANT TO GIVE, BUT GO AHEAD AND GIVE!
YOU'LL NEVER CATCH UP WITH A MERE HOPE."
— Johann Wolfgang von Goethe

DEALING WITH PERSONAL CONFLICTS – PART I

In both your business and home life, nothing can destroy your sense of accomplishment and well-being faster than personal conflicts. Upsets between business partners or battles between bosses and staff ruin productivity, reduce income and increase stress levels for everyone — especially those caught in the crossfire.

Conflicts at home, particularly those with a spouse, can spill over into your business life when you show up for work in a bad mood, overtired and distracted. Bad relationships at work are likewise damaging to your personal relationships when you come home feeling fed up and frustrated and take it out on your spouse, children, other family or friends.

Most people have good intentions. They want to get along, do their best and succeed. Yet personal upsets can make otherwise good people difficult to be around. Office politics, backstabbing, rumours, jealousy and revenge all result from personal conflicts and no matter which side of the argument you are on, it can be a major obstacle to your success.

Often, relationship problems are the result of a breakdown in communication and the feeling on the part of one or the other party that they are not being treated with respect. But it's not easy facing up to conflict, for many of us it feels like failure when our interactions with others aren't pleasant or productive. Generally, conflict arises when at least one party feels that they aren't getting what they want or need out of the interaction. The longer this goes on, the more the relationship deteriorates until one party is either too angry to make an effort, or worse still, completely indifferent.

Over the next two days, we will look at four steps that can be useful in resolving personal conflict, whether at home or in the workplace.

March 13

DEALING WITH PERSONAL CONFLICTS – PART II

1. Open up the lines of communication. Often when conflict arises, it is either because one party feels that they are not being heard or they feel that the other party is unapproachable or obstinate. Lines of communication break down; the parties stop talking to each other and everyone becomes much less open about the information they release to the other side. This results in frequent misunderstandings, exaggerated and overly hostile reactions, distrust and fear. Opening the lines of communication is essential to de-escalating the conflict. Just by re-establishing communication, misunderstandings can be corrected, assumptions can be avoided and trust can be rebuilt over time. The first step in opening the lines of communication is to let the other party know in a direct way that you would like to work on improving your relationship with them. Although it may take a third-party intermediary to do this, it is worth the effort to get things back on track.

2. Establish some common ground. With busy schedules and multiple responsibilities, it is easy for miscommunication to happen. Clarifying both parties' assumptions/understanding of the situation is an important step towards resolution. It is also an opportunity to look for points that both parties can agree upon. List these points, share them and use them to establish common ground on which to build.

3. Discover what is wanted and/or needed by both parties and agree on what changes can be made to fulfill those wants/needs. Sometimes we let others down for the simple reason that we don't know what they want or need from us. Likewise, they may not be living up to our expectations because we have not communicated them clearly.

DEALING WITH PERSONAL CONFLICTS – PART III

3. (continued) It is not always easy to express what we want and need from others, especially in situations where others may have authority over us. However, it is essential if we want to have productive relationships. The best way to approach this is to ask the other party to tell you their wants and needs first and then you can reciprocate with your own.

4. Act on fulfilling the agreement. While the three previous steps have been focused on clearing the air and establishing expectations, this is the first one towards rebuilding the relationship. That's why it is so important to follow through on your commitment, making the changes you agreed to and maintaining open communication with the other party.

The above steps can also be used as a proactive approach for establishing rapport with new employees, customers, co-workers, bosses and associates. If you're skeptical about how effective it would be, just imagine how you would feel if the new CEO of the company you worked for invited you into his or her office and said, "Thank you for taking the time to speak with me. I'd really like us to have a good working relationship right from the start, so why don't you tell me what you want and need from the company and from me as CEO."

— *Make Your Life a Masterpiece*

CONFLICT IS A NORMAL, INEVITABLE AND EVEN HEALTHY
ASPECT OF MOST RELATIONSHIPS.
WHEN MANAGED WELL,
IT CAN BE USED TO ENHANCE AND STRENGTHEN
INTERACTIONS WITH FRIENDS, FAMILY MEMBERS,
CO-WORKERS AND PARTNERS.

TACTICAL MANOEUVRES

T act involves addressing how we live our lives and the effect we have on everything and everyone around us. Everything we do matters — and makes either a positive or a negative impact.

Recognizing how your behaviour affects others and holding yourself accountable for your actions is a step in the right direction on the road to developing tact. Even something as simple as offering your chair to another person in a crowded waiting room or giving the right-of-way to another motorist makes a difference. Recall how great you felt when you have done just that and the other person has acknowledged you with a thank you or a wave, or when someone has extended you the same courtesy. It's a nice feeling of connection.

You could also take it one step further and adopt a "pay it forward" strategy whereby you do kind things for others with no expectation of being repaid in an effort to spread goodwill and inspire others to do the same.

We all have a vested interest in making our interactions with others as pleasant and agreeable as possible. Take time to build real connections and that effort will be rewarded.

— The Power of Tact

THINK OF SOME WAYS IN WHICH YOU CAN HAVE
A MORE POSITIVE EFFECT ON OTHERS.
WRITE THEM DOWN
AND THEN PRACTICE THEM.

LEAD US NOT INTO TEMPTATION

S elf-control is something we all struggle with every day. We want to lose weight, but we can't stop eating; we want to be healthy, but we continue to drink too much and not exercise enough; we want to be safe drivers, but we refuse to stop speeding and talking on our cellphones.

These behaviours aren't just embarrassing though, they're actually killing us. According to statistics, more than half of all people who die before they are 65 do so as a result of unhealthy decisions, and children born today may be the first generation in North America to have a shorter life expectancy than their parents.

Jeff Wise, author of *Extreme Fear: The Science of Your Mind in Danger*, offers some tools to help us deal with the temptations we face every day.

1. Admit you have a problem. If you don't like your behaviour and how it is affecting your life, the first step is to own up to it and challenge yourself in a positive way to make a change. "The way you view the task ahead of you determines your mindset and your likelihood of success," says Wise.

2. Focus on one big challenge at a time. You only have so much willpower, so don't try to spread it too thin. Trying to lose weight and quit smoking at the same time is just setting yourself up to fail at both, so pick your battles.

3. Practice, practice, practice. The more you use your willpower, the stronger it gets and the more in control you will feel.

4. Don't overestimate the strength of your willpower. Remove temptation where possible and don't put yourself in tempting situations.

— Insight 2011

THE KEY TO A HEALTHY, HAPPY LIFE IS GETTING
YOUR HABITS UNDER CONTROL.

March 17

LIVE TOGETHER OR DIE ALONE

We humans have achieved quite a lot since the world began, and much of what we have done is commendable. That's the good news. The bad news is that while we often believe our actions are for the betterment of all, more often we are motivated by selfish reasons. Too often we have waged wars, turned away from suffering and done far too much damage to the Earth, wrongly believing that our planet has the capacity and resources to forever serve our wants and needs.

The good news (once again) is that in the nick of time we seem to be recognizing that some massive attitudinal corrections are in order. We can't keep waging wars and allowing suffering. We must also learn to live in closer harmony with the ecosystems that make Planet Earth the amazing life-sustaining place it is — or risk destroying it all.

I could be wrong, but I think more of us have become conscious of the fact that this sharing and giving has to happen if we want to look forward to a better world tomorrow. We have a finite supply of resources and everything we do has an impact. We're slowly learning to pay attention to the environment that surrounds us and to learn lessons from the other species that share this planet. The delicate balance of the natural world is inspiring more of us to think anew about our personal and social responsibilities.

Just as all of the characters on the popular TV show *Lost* eventually had to face the prospect of "living together or dying alone" on an isolated island, we too must decide if we are going to work together to preserve the planet that is our island or suffer the consequences.

— The Power to Soar Higher

LIVE BELOW YOUR MEANS

I'm sure you've heard that old Benjamin Franklin saying, "A penny saved is a penny earned." Well, it turns out that when you factor in all of the taxes we pay (federal tax, provincial tax, gas tax, environmental tax, excise tax, GST or HST, etc.) from the time we earn our money to when we spend it, it's actually closer to "a penny saved is two pennies earned."

In his book *The Only Investment Guide You'll Ever Need*, Andrew Tobias talks about 50 per cent money and how we really need to earn two pre-tax dollars for every dollar we want to spend. Therefore, the most practical way for us to save money, particularly if we aren't in a position to increase our earnings, is to actually save our money by spending less of it. It's a radical concept, but one that I'm sure your parents and grandparents are familiar with, especially if they were alive before the era of easy credit.

As with most things in life, Tobias's strategy for saving is simple, but not easy. There will always be temptation to forsake the future for immediate gratification. We all want to buy that new piece of technology, treat ourselves to an expensive night on the town, or take out a loan for the flashy car we can't afford. And while it might feel great at the time, rash spending hurts a lot later on (something most of us learn the hard way).

Learn to enjoy life's simple pleasures and save as much as you can. Expensive things don't create lasting happiness and security. Careful spending will bring you greater leisure and enjoyment in the long run.

— *Insight 2011*

IF YOU WANT TO RETIRE RICH,
LIVE BELOW YOUR MEANS.

BACK TO CAPISTRANO

On several occasions I have driven down Southern California's Interstate 5 and every time I do, as I near San Juan Capistrano I can't help but think about the swallows. I've never been there on March 19, St. Joseph's Day, the date when residents of Capistrano celebrate the return of the swallows from their winter home in Argentina. Yet, every year, just like clockwork, huge clouds of swallows descend to spend the summer months in and around the old Mission, which is a protected bird sanctuary.

For those of us who fly the international air routes with any regularity and appreciate the great distances, this migratory achievement seems all the more miraculous when you consider that in any given year, each of these small birds will fly 12,000 miles roundtrip. Most of those miles are over water. That's a lot of flapping.

Unlike a 747, swallows can't make the entire trip without a break. So how do they manage? While it sounds incredible, I've been told that each swallow carries a small twig in its beak. When the bird gets tired, the twig becomes the "boat" on which it rests while bobbing about on the water until it is ready to continue the journey.

I have no idea if this is true or just a legend, but I like to believe it for the simple reason that it is an inspiring thought. Of course, twig or no twig, the fact that these birds are committed to make the journey year after year is truly amazing. We can learn a lot about courage and stamina from these little swallows.

— *The Power to Soar Higher*

IS THERE SOMETHING IN YOUR OWN LIFE
THAT YOU HAVE BEEN TRYING TO BUILD UP
THE COURAGE TO DO? TAKE A CUE
FROM THE SWALLOWS OF CAPISTRANO AND
BEGIN YOUR JOURNEY TODAY.

WISHING WON'T GET YOU THERE — PART I

B logger Chris Guillebeau talks about how his choice to become a "travel hacker" (someone who travels the globe without spending much money to do it) has meant that he had to make choices about what is important to him. He doesn't have a car or a house; instead he takes transit or rides his bike and rents an apartment so that he can spend his money on travel. He also doesn't have a "job"; instead he earns his income from products and services offered through his website and blog, *The Art of Non-Conformity*.

A couple of years ago, Chris decided to fulfill one of his big dreams, which was to visit every country in the world within a period of just a few years.

When Chris — who calls Portland, Oregon, home — travels overseas, the people he meets are always fascinated by what he is doing and invariably make a comment such as, "That sounds amazing, I wish I could do that."

"What's keeping you from it?" is his standard response.

It's an excellent question and one that we should all ask when we find ourselves wishing we had something different than what we have or making rationalizations for why we aren't living our dreams.

Perhaps the most common rationalization for not taking action is a familiar one: "I don't have the money to pursue my dream."

Chances are if you live in North America, you have more than enough money to meet your basic needs and plenty left over for the things that you want, such as your own house or condo (complete with a big mortgage payment), a car (or two or three), a cellphone, cable television and high-speed Internet service, just to name a few recurring expenses that can add up very quickly.

WISHING WON'T GET YOU THERE — PART II

The truth is that beyond basic food, shelter and transportation, everything else that we choose to spend our money on is exactly that, a choice, our choice. We choose what we value when we decide how to spend our time, money and other resources.

Are you willing to sacrifice your dream in order to continue to live the life you have or are you willing to sacrifice a few comforts and do what it takes to have your dream?

Here are two questions that Chris suggests people ask themselves to help determine if they are on the right path to fulfilling their dreams.

1. Am I satisfied with my job or career?

Your job should do more than simply provide income for the rest of your life. Ask yourself, what am I working for? Am I working to make a living or to make a life? If your work supports your goals, that's great. If it doesn't, maybe it's time to change.

2. What are my financial priorities?

If you have difficulty answering, there's an easy way to tell. Check your credit card statements and receipts from the past six months. Where you've been spending a lot of money is where your priorities are.

Once you fully understand what you want, it's not usually that difficult to get it.

Chris's advice for dealing with critics and naysayers? "At all stages of life, people will gladly offer you unsolicited lists of things you 'must' do, be or have. Most of the time you can nod your head, walk away and ignore them."

— *The Power of a Dream*

WISHING WON'T GET YOU ANYWHERE.
THE LIFE YOU HAVE IS THE ONE YOU'VE MADE
FOR YOURSELF. IF YOU WANT SOMETHING
DIFFERENT, YOU'RE GOING TO HAVE TO
DO SOMETHING DIFFERENTLY.

A PURPOSEFUL LIFE

People who love what they do are more apt to be successful. When your purpose and your talent intersect, the sky is the limit for your achievement in life.

The philosopher Joseph Campbell once said, "If you follow your bliss, you put yourself on a kind of track that has been there all the while, waiting for you and the life that you ought to be living is the one you are living. When you can see that, you begin to meet people who are in your field of bliss and they open doors for you. I say, follow your bliss and don't be afraid and doors will open where you didn't know they were going to be."

Unfortunately, many people have never experienced that feeling of being plugged into the world around them. Instead, they get up every morning and go through the motions, feeling tired, frustrated and even resentful about the work they do every day.

William Bridges, author of *Managing Transitions*, says, "Nothing less than finding what you were meant to be and do will give you the motivation and the capability that today's work world demands. Identifying your life work is no longer an escapist fantasy. It is a condition of being successful."

So, let's get started. Small steps taken today can lead to big changes tomorrow. Over the next five days, we will explore some helpful steps to get you on the way to finding your purpose.

— *The Runway of Life*

"LIFE IS WHAT YOU MAKE OF IT,
ALWAYS HAS BEEN, ALWAYS WILL BE."
— Grandma Moses

A PURPOSEFUL LIFE – GET A GRIP ON YOUR FEAR

We all know that fear has its place. What's more, it can play a useful role in helping us find our purpose.

So what is useful about fear? First off, fear highlights our weaknesses. We are no good to ourselves and our dreams if we don't recognize and deal with our weaknesses. One way to do so is to look for areas in your life where you don't seem to be making progress (fear of failure may be stopping you from taking on new projects or fear of criticism may hold you back from sharing your best ideas). Walk through your fears. Trace where they began and how they have progressed and you will find the weaknesses that need to be addressed.

In addition to showing our weaknesses, overcoming our fears makes us stronger. Have you ever stopped to consider that you have survived and maybe even triumphed over the difficult experiences that led you to this point in your life? What strengths did you discover within yourself as a result? What character traits were you forced to develop to deal with tough situations? Fear served you.

Now that we understand how fear can be useful, it's important to put it in its place so we can do what we need to do. In her book, *Feel the Fear and Do It Anyway*, Susan Jeffers says, "Ultimately, fear is what's holding you back from going after your dream. Let's face it, shaking up your life is scary. So go ahead and indulge in your worst-case fantasy. Then get busy figuring out what steps you can take to prevent it from happening."

— *The Runway of Life*

ALLOW FEAR TO MAKE YOU AWARE OF YOUR
WEAKNESSES, CONFIDENT IN YOUR STRENGTHS AND
EXCITED TO EXPLORE YOUR POTENTIAL.

A PURPOSEFUL LIFE — GET REAL

You've seen the ads for easy-money jobs: "Local mom earns $500 a day on the Internet; you can too." Sounds great, right? The problem is, if it sounds too good to be true, it most likely is. Legitimate companies pay people according to the level of skill and ability they bring to the job. Get-rich-quick schemes are just that, schemes, and more likely than not, you will be the one who gets scammed. As my mentor Joe Segal often says, "There's no free lunch, even when someone else is buying."

So snap out of it! Finding your purpose, like everything else worthwhile, takes time and effort. Here's an exercise to help you discover what inspires and motivates you.

Grab a piece of paper and make a list of people you admire and why you admire them. For example, you might admire Patch Adams for choosing to step outside the traditional role of medicine and invent new ways of healing and connecting with his patients while also having fun. You might admire the band Green Day for creating the music they love and also speaking out about political and social issues. You might admire General Romeo Dallaire for revealing the truth about the genocide in Rwanda in a culture where concealing is the norm. List as many as you can think of. When you're done, look at the list and consider that you are attracted to these qualities because they speak to you and represent values that are important to you. If this were your list, stepping out of the box, social activism and telling the truth would be action steps that would help you to define your purpose.

— *The Runway of Life*

TRAITS YOU ADMIRE IN OTHERS CAN HELP YOU
DEFINE YOUR PURPOSE.

A PURPOSEFUL LIFE — GET A NEW PERSPECTIVE

"Every man mistakes the limits of his
own field of vision for the limits
of the world." — Arthur Schopenhauer

Family aside, nobody knows you better than your friends and close associates, which means they are a potential source of great insight into your purpose. Put together a questionnaire and send it out via email to at least 10 people you know. The purpose of the questionnaire is to help you gain a new perspective on yourself.

You can pose such questions as:

What do you think I am good at?

Do you notice any natural talents in me that you think I could develop into a career?

What impresses you most about me, what are my biggest strengths?

How am I getting in my own way when it comes to the ideal job search?

Within a few days, you should have enough feedback to discover some trends — for example, you may notice the majority of your friends/associates think you would be a great event organizer even if you have always taken your planning skills for granted. At the very least, at the end of this exercise you will have some objective ideas about your strengths and any behaviours that might be holding you back.

— *The Runway of Life*

GAIN A NEW PERSPECTIVE ON YOURSELF BY LOOKING
THROUGH THE EYES OF OTHERS.

March 26

A PURPOSEFUL LIFE – GET FOCUSED

In my experience, most of us are not aware of what we want in each moment. Too often, we haven't even thought about it. Instead, we are too busy reacting — in fight, flight or freeze mode — which means that most of the time, particularly when we are faced with challenges or difficulty, we are focused on what we don't want and we don't even know it.

For example, when we are experiencing fear, self-doubt, worry, anger, frustration, anxiety, negativity or other disempowering thoughts, we are not focused on what we want.

Likewise, when we are complaining about the job we lost, the skills we lack, the money we don't have, the payments we can't afford and the sacrifices we've had to make, we are focused on what we don't want.

But here's a novel idea, instead of feeling bad or complaining, all of which keeps your attention on what you don't want — meaningless work, office politics, an endless commute, someone else calling the shots — zoom in on the life you do want. Five minutes a day spent visualizing your ideal work-life and fashioning a plan to get there will move you far closer to your goal than 30 minutes of complaining.

— The Runway of Life

SPEND SOME TIME EVERY DAY VISUALIZING
WHAT YOU DO WANT IN YOUR LIFE.

A PURPOSEFUL LIFE – GET INVOLVED

In 2005, the co-founder and then-CEO of Apple Computers, Steve Jobs, delivered the commencement address to the graduating class at Stanford University. Interestingly, Jobs himself was not a college graduate, although that had never gotten in the way of his success. In his address, Jobs focused on the importance of finding a purpose. Here is part of what he had to say: "Your time is limited, so don't waste it living someone else's life. Don't be trapped by dogma — which is living with the results of other people's thinking. Don't let the noise of others' opinions drown out your own inner voice. And most important, have the courage to follow your heart and intuition, they somehow already know what you truly want to become. Everything else is secondary."

From the time we are young until we choose a career, one of the most common questions we get from friends and strangers alike is, "What do you want to do with your life?" You have probably racked your brain trying to figure out what your ideal career is. But chances are you've never even heard of the type of work that would be a perfect fit for you. In fact, many people who follow their passion find that it leads them into uncharted territory and eventually they "invent" a career that is custom-fit to them.

Let your natural curiosity guide you and look for ideas in the "world" of your interests. Make it a point to simply do things you like, without trying so hard to figure out how they could turn into a career. This process will also bring you in contact with others who share your passions.

— *The Runway of Life*

DO THE THINGS YOU LIKE
AND LET YOUR CURIOSITY GUIDE YOU.

LOVE'S LABOUR FOUND

I'll admit to you right now that I have never been very good with my hands. While some people can pick up a piece of wood and with just two or three tools turn it into a beautiful piece of furniture, I have not been so blessed.

When I was just 16 years old, I got a summer job at Fraser Mills in Surrey, B.C., working the midnight to 8 a.m. shift feeding the dryer to help make sheets of plywood. It took two of us to feed this big machine.

My co-worker was 40 years old and making essentially the same money as I was. After eight weeks of labouring, I decided I would never work with my hands again.

Now, I'm not telling this story because I want to put down people who do physical jobs to earn their living. The reason I am telling you this is because it is important for each one of us to decide what we want out of life and to go with what works for us.

What I really thought to myself is that I am not going to make much of my life working at a mill for an hourly wage. In my mind's eye, I saw myself at 40 still feeding that dryer and I knew that my talents lay elsewhere. I also knew that I needed to keep trying different things until I discovered what those talents were.

Eventually I did find my talent, and I hope you do too.

— *The Runway of Life*

MAKE IT YOUR GOAL TO DISCOVER ALL OF YOUR TALENTS
AND USE THEM TO FULL ADVANTAGE.

WHY DO WE NEED GOALS?

Here you are setting off on your very first cross-country trip. You've packed up the car and you're ready to go. From the windswept beaches of Tofino to Newfoundland's Cape Spear, you want to see it all.

You back the car out of the driveway and you're off. You've already planned your first stop, visiting the giant red cedars of Cathedral Grove on Vancouver Island.

Not far into your trip, you realize you need to check your map because it seems you've missed the on-ramp to the highway. You check the glove box and for a moment you panic because you realize you've forgotten it.

After considering the problem for a few moments, you say the heck with it. You don't need a map, you know where you're going and you can always stop and ask others for directions along the way. You take a right, turn on the radio for company and keep on going. Unfortunately, you never reach your destination. You were headed the wrong way, but you were making good time.

Too many of us take this same approach to goal setting; we dream about where we want to go, but we don't have a route mapped out to get there.

What is a map? Essentially, it is the written word. What is the difference between a dream and a goal? That's right, the written word.

Of course, just as with a map, we need to do more than simply jot down some ideas on a piece of paper. Without putting some real thought and energy into formulating each goal, we are simply making a wish. Our goals need to be clear, complete and focused.

— *The Runway of Life*

GOALS GIVE LIFE ITS FLAVOUR. THEY ALSO PROVIDE
A SENSE OF DIRECTION AND PURPOSE.

TAKE CARE — PART I

*"Everyone thinks of changing the world,
but no one thinks of
changing himself."* — Leo Tolstoy

As my friend Dr. Art Hister, who is a regular on radio and television in Vancouver, is fond of saying, "If you don't make the time to take care of yourself now, you better make time for illness later."

These days, I am much more proactive in my health regime and I attribute it to two things. The first is the stroke I had a few years ago, which was a real wake-up call about how I was treating my body, including my habits around eating, sleeping, working and most of all, exercise. The rest of the credit goes to my book, *The Runway of Life*. As I was writing that book, I started thinking about how my own runway would someday end and of all the things that I still want to accomplish.

Although it is not always easy to fit a healthy lifestyle into running a business, there are some basic habits to which I always try to adhere.

First of all, no matter if I am at home or away, I usually get to bed by 10 o'clock every evening. Sometimes this can be a challenge when I have evening engagements to attend, but whoever said you have to stay until the end of every party? Not me. When I go to a cocktail party or reception, I focus on three important tasks: first, I show up (in a timely fashion); secondly, I seek out the person who invited me and thank them for their hospitality; thirdly, I mingle and meet a few people (exchanging business cards), and then I'm done.

My second habit involves exercise. Maintaining a regular exercise regimen has always been one of my biggest challenges.

TAKE CARE – PART II

I've been much more successful at getting regular exercise since I dedicated room in my home as a gym. I've been able to discipline myself to exercise at least four days a week for 30 to 45 minutes, in addition to regular long walks.

My last habit focuses on eating more sensibly (i.e., cutting out the crap!). For me, it's the little changes that make the most difference over the long term, mostly because they are the ones that I can actually stick with. One such change I've made is to eat oatmeal for breakfast. This has had a very positive effect on my cholesterol level and by allowing myself one day a week to still have more indulgent foods such as bacon or eggs benedict, I don't feel I'm being deprived.

Most importantly, I have changed the way I eat at business functions. Some people see a meal out as an excuse to break their diet, but I have learned it is possible to have a good meal without overindulging. Likewise, if decadent sweets are your weakness, before the main course is over, ask the server to bring you a fruit plate. That way it will be in front of you when it's time for dessert and a gentle reminder of your healthy eating strategy.

Something else that is important for everyone (especially when you reach a certain age) is to make time for an annual medical examination. Although it's easy to let these slip (after all, who likes being poked and prodded?), remember that the majority of serious medical conditions can be successfully treated if the early warning signs are detected and acted upon.

— *Make Your Life a Masterpiece*

IT'S NOT EASY TO START LIVING HEALTHIER,
BUT IT IS IMPORTANT IF YOU WANT TO BE AROUND
LONG ENOUGH TO ACHIEVE YOUR DREAMS.

APRIL

1. The Duke
2. Choose to Be a Positive Influence
3. Exercise Your Mental Capacity — Part I
4. Exercise Your Mental Capacity — Part II
5. Frank Rethinks Life
6. Money Talks
7. If You Don't Need It, Let It Go — Part I
8. If You Don't Need It, Let It Go — Part II
9. Kissing Frogs — Part I
10. Kissing Frogs — Part II
11. The Balancing Act
12. The Silver Lining
13. The Real Reasons We Resist Change — Part I
14. The Real Reasons We Resist Change — Part II

15. Unforgettable
16. Not a Day to Waste — Part I
17. Not a Day to Waste — Part II
18. Be a Hard Worker
19. The Worry Clinic
20. What I Learned From Jack
21. Snake Charmers
22. Lessons on Leadership
23. Leadership Law No. 1
24. Leadership Law No. 2
25. Leadership Law No. 3
26. Leadership Law No. 4
27. Leadership Law No. 5
28. Leadership Law No. 6
29. Leadership Law No. 7
30. Muster Your Courage — Do It Now

THE DUKE

Hollywood tour guide Stephen Schochet (who, by the way, loves his job and it shows) tells a funny story about the late actor, John Wayne, who was well-known for his easygoing nature.

Schochet notes that for the last 30 years of his life, John Wayne often had a profound effect on people who crossed his path. Meeting him in person for some was like meeting Abraham Lincoln or George Washington. Yet the Duke (as he was known) usually stayed humble and kept his sense of humour.

On one such occasion when he was out with a group of friends in a restaurant, the Duke excused himself to go to the men's room and when he came back his pant leg was wet.

"Hey Duke, what happened?" one of his friends asked.

"Nothing," replied Wayne. "Happens all the time, I'm used to it."

"What happens?" the friend persisted.

The Duke, looking slightly embarrassed, explained. "All right, if you must know, I'm standing in the men's room taking care of business and there's some guy right next to me. At first, he just kind of glances over, but then I can see this look of recognition come across his face and he yells out, 'Oh my god, you're John Wayne!' and suddenly he whirls around towards me . . ."

It takes a big man to laugh it off when people keep peeing on him. How we choose to deal with things says a lot about our character and it goes a long way in determining whether our experiences end up being positive or negative.

— *Make Your Life a Masterpiece*

IT'S IMPORTANT TO TAKE YOUR SENSE OF HUMOUR
WITH YOU, WHEREVER YOU GO.

CHOOSE TO BE A POSITIVE INFLUENCE

O ne of the top two reasons people resign from their job is their relationship with their boss. The thing people are most likely to complain about when they come home from work at the end of the day is their uncooperative, difficult, dim-witted colleagues.

Sound familiar?

Organizations are relatively simple things; what makes them complex is the network of human relationships within them. To be effective, we need good working relationships with our bosses, colleagues and subordinates, but how do we achieve the results we want and build positive relationships without being manipulative? How do we gain others' commitment when they are being less than cooperative, even difficult?

One word: Influence.

Here are some tips:

Lead by example. Act the way you want others to act and treat people the way you want to be treated. Before you act, think about how it will impact those around you. Make good decisions that can be emulated.

Make your words irresistible. Instead of saying, "What's taking so long with that project?" say, "I can hardly wait to see what you've come up with." It's all in the phrasing.

Be a leader, not a follower. Don't do things you'll regret or get talked into doing something you don't want to do. You are the only person in control of you. Respect yourself.

Block out negativity. Never repeat negative comments; it only adds to the negative environment. If you can't ignore negative comments, twist them into positive ones. If someone says, "I hate her, she's loud, stupid and irritating," counteract with, "I think she's got some great ideas and she's always helpful." After a while, people will stop coming to you with negativity because they know you don't play that game.

— Insight 2011

TODAY, CHOOSE TO BE A POSITIVE INFLUENCE.

EXERCISE YOUR MENTAL CAPACITY – PART I

In 2001, I had a stroke. At the time, I was speaking for the American Mental Health Association at the Bayshore Hotel in Vancouver. With about 20 minutes to go in my session, I couldn't remember my stories, I couldn't find my place in my speech, I felt hot, sweaty and disoriented. Worst of all, I had the sensation that I was falling off the stage.

Not knowing any better and not even imagining there could be anything wrong with me, I simply chalked it up to a stuffy room and continued on with my talk. After I finished, I moved to the back of the room where I generally sell my books and again noticed that something was a bit odd when I couldn't sign my name properly. However, I brushed this off as a side effect of fatigue and carried on. What I didn't recognize then was that I was experiencing the classic symptoms of a stroke, which include: sudden weakness and numbness, difficulty speaking, vision problems and severe headache or dizziness.

Before leaving the hotel, I met with the client to talk about the session and then drove myself home.

The next morning when it was time to get up, I discovered I had lost a considerable amount of control over my coordination and movement. By sheer force of will I managed to get out of bed, shower, shave, drive myself to the office and make it to my chair. That's where I was when Heather Parker, then vice president of Canada Wide Media, walked in. She took one look at me and said, "There's something wrong with you. You need medical attention." Heather took me to a nearby clinic where they quickly determined that I had had a stroke. I was shocked.

April 4

EXERCISE YOUR MENTAL CAPACITY — PART II

Following my stroke, it took me more than an hour to walk one block with a cane, holding my wife's arm. Most doctors agree they can't do much about a stroke that you have had (they can only help prevent a future stroke), so I am absolutely thrilled at the recovery I have made. I was also happy to learn that a habit I have maintained for many years played a positive role in that recovery.

Six weeks after my stroke, I went for a brain scan at Royal Columbian Hospital. After the technician had completed the scan, he displayed the pictures of my brain on two screens. Although he knew I was 60 years old, he didn't have any other information about me. So, after pointing out a little "Z" shape where the stroke had left its mark, he turned to me and said, "If I didn't know you were 60, I'd think I was looking at the brain of a 40-year-old."

He then turned to my wife and asked, "What does he do for a living?"

"He's in publishing," Kay replied.

"No, it's not that," he said.

"He's also a professional speaker," Kay offered.

"No, it's not that either," the technician said, shaking his head. "He must do something else."

Kay then told him how I had a habit of reading at least one book a week.

"Aha, that's it!" he exclaimed.

He asked how long I had been doing this and I told him 20 years.

"That's definitely it. Your habit of reading is keeping your brain young and as long as you continue to exercise your mental capacity, your mind will remain agile."

— *Make Your Life a Masterpiece*

"A MIND THAT HAS BEEN STRETCHED WILL NEVER RETURN TO ITS ORIGINAL DIMENSION." — Albert Einstein

FRANK RETHINKS LIFE

Something we learn as we grow older, and hopefully wiser, is that almost everything changes. Change is why things like running your own business or maintaining a happy marriage are such a constant challenge. At 40, 50 or 60, we are not the innocents we were when we headed out into the business world or walked down the aisle. It's important to embrace the lessons that come with experience and make changes when necessary.

Like many people of my generation, my friend Frank Palmer, the founder of Palmer Jarvis Advertising (which eventually became the advertising powerhouse DDB Canada), put his work and building his business above everything else. Here are a few items included in a recruitment ad that Frank wrote in the late '80s listing what makes a Palmer Jarvis partner. It's pretty tough stuff:

"The years without a holiday.
Late nights in the office when your contemporaries were in the pub.
The school sports days you never saw.
The friendships you had to leave behind.
Risking your health for the health of your business.
Handicapping your golf game instead of your business.
Missing your children's first steps into the world."

A few years later, I saw another ad for Palmer Jarvis signed by Frank. It simply said, "We respect the power of change. We've learned how to deal with it positively and we're turning it into success for our clients." That was it.

I'm glad he said that and I'm even happier that Frank decided to shift his priorities. I just hate the thought of someone missing their children's first steps, not to mention some regular rounds of golf.

— *How to Soar With the Eagles*

WHAT CHANGE COULD YOU MAKE TODAY
THAT WOULD IMPROVE YOUR LIFE?

MONEY TALKS

The old saying, "money talks" is correct, but the only thing it knows how to say is goodbye. Napoleon Hill once said that if you don't have the habit or discipline of saving money, the seeds of success are not within you.

In our consumer society, with so much focus on instant gratification, it's not surprising that the habit of regularly saving a portion of our income requires a great deal of discipline and self-control. It's something that many of us struggle with. The credit analysis firm TransUnion reported in the fall of 2010 that the average amount of non-mortgage household debt in Canada is more than $25,000.

We're living far beyond our means when we should be living beneath them.

How many of the following lies have you told yourself to justify why you're still not saving regularly?

• I don't spend more than I make; therefore I don't need to budget and track my spending.

• I make good money and my job is secure, so why do I need to save?

• I'm still relatively young and healthy, and nothing's going to happen to me.

• I'm free of debt; I don't need to save.

• I work hard and I want to enjoy myself instead of living like I'm poor.

Who are we kidding? If we should have learned one thing from the recent global financial crisis, it is that no one is immune to financial difficulties. The good news is that the more proactive we are in getting our financial house in order and developing a safety cushion (through savings), the more likely it is that we will weather such storms.

IF YOU DON'T ALREADY HAVE A REGULAR
SAVINGS PLAN IN PLACE, TAKE STEPS TODAY TO GET
STARTED WITH A SIMPLE STRATEGY TO
SAVE AT LEAST 10 PER CENT OF WHAT YOU EARN.

IF YOU DON'T NEED IT, LET IT GO – PART I

*"The physics of clutter is that it will come into
your life without your assistance, but will not go away
without your assistance."* — Julie Mahan

I t's important to keep our lives free of unnecessary things. Og Mandino puts it beautifully in the following quote that speaks of our actions as well as the possessions we accumulate, "Never again clutter your days and nights with so many menial and unimportant things that you have no time to accept a real challenge when it comes along. This applies to play as well as work. A day merely survived is no cause for celebration. You are not here to fritter away your precious hours when you have the ability to accomplish so much by making a slight change in your routine. No more busy work. No more hiding from success. Leave time, leave space, to grow. Now. Now! Not tomorrow!"

My mentor Joe Segal once told me, "If you don't need something, rather than hold onto it, give it to someone who does." For many of us, it's easy to say but hard to do. It's amazing how attached we have become to all of "our stuff," as the late comedian George Carlin was famous for joking about. The scary part is that for many people it is really getting out of control.

In June 2008, *Maclean's* magazine did a story on North America's fastest-growing real estate segment, the storage business, which generates $22 billion per year in revenue. In fact, in the span of just one decade, the amount of this kind of storage in the United States has more than doubled to an area larger than Manhattan and San Francisco combined!

IF YOU DON'T NEED IT, LET IT GO – PART II

Interestingly, the article noted that many of the people who rent these storage lockers have a greater volume of "stuff" in storage than they have in their own homes and they are paying money to keep it there because they don't have room for it anywhere else — because of all their other "stuff." Imagine how much easier and less complicated their lives would be if they just got rid of some of that stuff.

So, here's the question you knew I was eventually going to ask, "What part of your life needs tidying up?" Is it your basement, your car, your desk at work, your computer hard drive, that drawer or closet where you put everything that doesn't have a place? Maybe it's all of these.

Clearing out the stuff in your life that you no longer need or use doesn't just get rid of old junk that's getting in your way; it also frees up your mind and creates room for you to move forward with important plans and goals. So don't store your stuff, make a decision on what can stay and what needs to go and take action.

Here are a couple of tips to help you along:

1. If you're worried about getting rid of documents with personal information on them, get a paper shredder or hire a shredding service to dispose of them.

2. Gather all of your product warranties and instruction manuals in one place (an expandable file works great) to keep them organized and on-hand when needed.

— *The Power to Soar Higher*

WHEN YOU'VE RID YOUR LIFE OF UNNECESSARY THINGS,
SUDDENLY YOU'LL HAVE A MUCH CLEARER VIEW
OF EVERYTHING THAT YOU DO HAVE AND FEEL INFINITELY MORE
PRODUCTIVE WITH MORE ROOM TO THINK AND BREATHE.

KISSING FROGS – PART I

M y good friend Darcy Rezac retired earlier this year. For 24 years, Darcy was the managing director and chief engagement officer with the Vancouver Board of Trade. In addition to coining the phrase "Connecting for Good," Darcy wrote the book on networking — literally (together with co-authors Gayle Hallgren-Rezac and Judy Thomson). It's called *Work the Pond*. With Darcy's permission, I would like to share with you The Seven Secrets of Networking to help you get out into the pond and expand your network:

1. You have to kiss a lot of frogs to find a prince. Make it a habit to put yourself in situations where you will meet new people.

2. Networking is not all about you; it's discovering what you can do for someone else. Relationships are created and sustained when we discover something that we can do for someone else. For some, this is a new way of viewing the world, but it works.

3. Introduce yourself by name, always carry business cards and give them out. Too many people don't follow this simple advice. Grab the advantage, be someone who does.

4. Treat everyone as equals. This makes life a whole lot easier than trying to figure out who's who. One person's frog may be another person's prince or princess.

5. Give everyone the password to the network: permission. Give yourself — and everyone you come in contact with — permission to network. The multiplier effect of this simple secret is astonishing.

6. Harness the power of asking questions. Great icebreakers, questions let people know you are interested in them.

7. Show up and share something. Networking is a contact sport, but there's no reason to show up if you have nothing to contribute. Read, listen, seek out knowledge and share it.

— *The Runway of Life*

KISSING FROGS – PART II

Now that you know how to network, let's talk about following up. *Work the Pond* dedicates an entire chapter to this important aspect of building your network. It really is the only way you are going to turn that stack of business cards you've collected into a valuable network of people who can, in turn, connect you with their networks.

Following up doesn't have to be time-consuming or elaborate. Remember networking secret No. 2? Find out what you can do for someone else. Often the "what" is information or a contact. A quick email can usually take care of business and not only will the person be grateful, they will also be sure to put you on their list of people who can be counted on to follow through.

Even if you haven't kept in touch with someone and you're feeling a bit guilty, don't be too quick to throw out their business card. Every year there are several opportunities for redemption — we call them holidays. Thanksgiving, Christmas, New Year's or other special occasions are a good time to restart a connection. You don't even need a reason; the holiday itself is reason enough.

Other opportunities to follow up are when you read or hear about something connected to a person or the business they are in, such as a promotion, career change or new product launch.

And one final tip before you hop into the pond. To ensure that you can follow up, when you get a business card from someone and especially when you have promised to do something, write it down so you don't forget. Memory can be a tricky thing, especially after a few glasses of wine or your 50th introduction of the evening.

— *The Runway of Life*

GET OUT THERE AND KISS SOME FROGS.

THE BALANCING ACT

*"My private measure of success is daily. If this were
to be the last day of my life, would I be content with it?
To live in a harmonious balance of commitments and pleasures
is what I strive for."* — Jane Rule

When CNN asked Shelly Lazarus, chairman and CEO of Ogilvy &
Mather Worldwide, to share the golden rule that she lives by, she
said quite simply, "Business can't trump happiness."

She went on to explain, "Unless you love your work you won't find
balance. How can you, if you resent time away from family spent at a
tedious job? I fell into a job and a company I loved. I never wanted to leave
and never worried that my family suffered for it. Finding fulfilling work
should be an early priority on everyone's career path. This may sound soft
and mushy, but happy people are better for business. They are more creative
and productive, they build environments where success is more likely and
you have a better chance of keeping your best players."

Former U.S. secretary of state Colin Powell agrees. "Have fun in your
command," he says. "Don't always run at a breakneck pace. Take leave when
you've earned it. Spend time with your family and surround yourself with
people who take their work seriously, but not themselves, those who work
hard and play hard."

Achievement and enjoyment are the front and back of the coin that
depicts value in life. You can't have a worthwhile life with one and not the
other. Trying to live a one-sided life is why so many "successful" people are
not nearly as happy as they should be.

— *Make Your Life a Masterpiece*

WHAT ARE YOU DOING TO CREATE A
HEALTHY BALANCE IN YOUR LIFE?

THE SILVER LINING

During the 1940s, a young Jewish boy chose to skip university in order to pursue his dream of becoming the next Benny Goodman. Going against his parents' advice, he began playing in a jazz band. Unfortunately, his musical abilities weren't substantial enough to pay the bills and he soon realized that he was just another musician teetering on the brink of unemployment. However, unlike many of his fellow musicians, he was very good at managing his money, which meant that those periods of unemployment weren't nearly as devastating for him as they were for others.

Recognizing his talent for money management, his musical colleagues began to pay him to manage their finances as well. This led the young man to rethink his career goals and it also changed the course of his life.

That young man's name was Alan Greenspan and he went on to serve as long-time chairman of the United States Federal Reserve (1987-2006). His failure as a musician not only taught him resilience and self-reliance (important skills that we can all use), it also taught him that he had other, significant talents, to share with the world.

Just like Mr. Greenspan, our failures can help us to discover hidden talents we never knew we had. It's the silver lining that helps us get past our failures and on with the rest of our life.

— *The Power of a Dream*

EVERY FAILURE IS AN OPPORTUNITY
TO DISCOVER SOMETHING
NEW ABOUT OURSELVES.

THE REAL REASONS WE RESIST CHANGE — PART I

Having struggled with maintaining a healthy weight most of my life, I know what it's like to want to make a change and yet, despite my best intentions, it doesn't happen. What I've learned from my own experience is that despite our good intentions, the most common reason we don't succeed is self-sabotage.

See if you recognize any of these five scenarios?

We don't really want to change.
Maybe you think you want to change something, but is it really your idea? Maybe you are simply feeling pressure from your spouse, family members, boss or friends.

It's difficult to make a significant change in your life if your heart really isn't in it. It takes real motivation to change. If you find that you don't feel an inner motivation, it's time to ask yourself who you're trying to please and whether or not the change is in your best interest.

Our environment doesn't support the change we want.
It's difficult to let go of an old habit without changing the environment that has supported it. For example, if your goal is to lose weight, it's much harder to do if you continue to hang out with people who only eat junk food. Likewise it is difficult to motivate yourself to be more active if the TV is always on, playing your favourite shows and giving you an excuse to sit on your butt.

Make adjustments to your environment that will support the goal you've set for yourself. Unplug that TV for a while, seek out people who share your commitment to eating healthy (even if it is through an online forum), look for support from positive influences and make it as easy as possible for yourself to succeed.

THE REAL REASONS WE RESIST CHANGE
— PART II

We let fear take over.
Change can be scary, even when we have the help and support of those around us. Fear of the unknown and fear of failure are just two reasons that change can be frightening.

Sometimes you just have to take action, feel the fear and do the thing that scares you anyway. The good news here is, the payoff will be worth it. Moving out of your comfort zone helps you to build strength, courage and confidence in a way that stays with you and makes you stronger.

We don't know how to practically make the change.
This is a common obstacle and big changes can be overwhelming.

Fortunately, with the Internet it's a lot easier to share information and get practical guidance. Just make sure you are actually getting your advice from people who have successfully accomplished whatever it is you want to do. You may not find success with the first method or approach you try and you may need to break your big goal into smaller ones to make it more manageable, but the important thing is to take that first step and get started.

We're too quick to believe we've failed.
Do you remember when you were young and just learning to do new things on your own, like tying your shoes or riding a bike? At that age, failure wasn't an option, you just kept picking yourself up and trying again until you mastered the skill.

It takes time, dedication and patience to learn something new and most old habits can't be changed in the blink of an eye. We could all take a lesson from our five-year-old selves and remember the old adage, "If at first you don't succeed, try, try again."

UNFORGETTABLE

I loved what the King of Siam said in the movie *Anna and the King*. I even wrote it down in the dark so that I wouldn't forget it: *"It is always surprising how small a part of life is taken up by meaningful moments. Most of them are over before they start. Yet, they cast a light on the future and make the person who originated them unforgettable. Anna has shed such a light on Siam."*

What are some of the traits that make a person unforgettable? Here are a few that come to mind when I think of the people I admire:

Selflessness — We live in a self-indulgent world, so when we meet someone who puts others before themselves, they stand out. Whether it is by offering their time, their attention or much-needed assistance, selfless people make others feel loved, appreciated and special.

Compassion — When we are focused on our own needs and priorities, we can forget about those around us. Compassion is the ability to see and respect things from the perspective of others. Compassionate people are self-aware and mindful of the impact their words and actions have on others.

Authenticity — Being true to one's self and feeling comfortable in one's own skin is one of the traits I can admire most. To have a real relationship with anyone requires honesty and the strength to speak from the heart even when the truth may be uncomfortable.

Tolerance — Those who practice tolerance show both an interest and concern for ideas, opinions and practices that differ from their own. Cultivating this ability to accept people for who they are — without fear — and not expect them to conform to who we want them to be contributes both to our happiness and the health of our relationships.

— *Who Dares Wins*

NOT A DAY TO WASTE — PART I

I truly enjoy meeting and learning from people who have found their own way to pursue a particular passion. I was in Cardiff, Wales, recently visiting family following a business trip to London. I booked my return trip from Cardiff to London on the train and the morning of my departure, I was enjoying breakfast at the Cardiff Marriott Wales, just down the block from the train station. As I sat eating, I noticed that the walls were covered with photographs of famous Welsh folks including singers Tom Jones and Shirley Bassey, Manchester United football player Ryan Giggs, Cardiff City football coach John Toshack and Olympic runner Colin Jackson. In between the pictures were quotations, nicely framed. One that caught my eye was from Charles Dickens, "A day wasted on others is not wasted on self."

I copied it down in my notebook, sure that I would use it somewhere in the future. Having finished my meal, I gathered my bags and walked over to the Cardiff Central Station. Arriving with my ticket for the noon train in hand, I was ushered into the first-class lounge, which is part of the 1934 rebuilt station. Now, don't be misled, it may have been called a first-class lounge, but in reality it was a small, unimposing room whose most important function was to provide passengers with shelter from the inclement Welsh wind and rain.

As I walked in, the congenial hostess, Lena McSorley, asked if I would like coffee, juice or a muffin before checking my ticket and confirming the departure platform and time.

"Just relax," she told me. "The train will be here in 45 minutes."

Being the only passenger in the lounge, I settled into a comfortable chair and surveyed my surroundings.

NOT A DAY TO WASTE – PART II

O n the wall beside me was a certificate stating, "Lena McSorley has been voted Cardiff's Best Ambassador for 2009." Looking over at Lena, I saw nothing more than a regular, straightforward, simply spoken person, but eventually my curiosity got the better of me, so I asked her how this came about.

With a sense of humility, she produced a certificate from the Prince's Trust congratulating her on having raised £1,221.19 in 2005. She then produced a certificate from the Velinare Cancer Treatment Hospital for which she raised £5,800 in 2006. In 2007, she raised £500 for the Alzheimer's Society of Wales. In 2008, she raised £3,868.14 for children suffering from cancer and leukemia. In 2009, she raised £2,000 for sexually abused children in Cardiff and in the same year, a further £4,068.75 for the Children's Therapy Clinic in Wales. That's almost $30,000 Canadian.

My next questions were why and how? Her response: "I've been married for 16 years, my husband is retired and I feel very lucky with life. I've had no health problems or family problems and it's a privilege to be running this first-class lounge at Cardiff Central Station."

As for the how, Lena simply asks those who come into the lounge if they could help her current project. No big campaigns, no elaborate brochures and no overhead, just a friendly, genuine woman who cares for her community. Maybe she too has read the Charles Dickens quote on the wall at the Cardiff Marriott and taken it to heart, because she's certainly not one to waste a day on herself and in so doing, Lena has discovered her true passion: helping others.

— *The Power of a Dream*

TIME SPENT HELPING OTHERS
IS NEVER WASTED. IT ALSO PUTS OUR
OWN TROUBLES IN PERSPECTIVE.

BE A HARD WORKER

I spent my early years in a small English town called Greenford, just outside of London, where the local theatre was the major source of entertainment in those post-war years for people of all ages. My mother would often take me to the movies and in those days, the seats were priced according to where they were located within the theatre.

The majority of the seats on the main floor of the theatre were the sixpenny seats. These were the least expensive seats and there was always a huge lineup for them, which meant that you had to wait outside no matter what the weather was doing. The most expensive seats were called 2/6's (which cost the equivalent of 50 cents each). Besides the fact that they were the best seats in the theatre, just by paying a little more, you didn't have to wait outside in the sleet or snow.

If it was too hot, too cold, raining or snowing outside, my mother would spoil me and we would sit in the 2/6's. Whenever we did, she made a point of telling me that she did this so that I would know what it was like to have the very best that life had to offer (despite the fact that she had to sacrifice something else to pay for it). The lesson, which was not lost on me, was that it was possible to obtain the finer things in life, but you had to be willing to work for them.

Here in North America, we are so fortunate that those things that are considered luxuries for most people in the world (a comfortable home, a nice car, a good education for our children) are readily available to anyone who is willing to work hard to obtain them.

— *Make Your Life a Masterpiece*

"I CAN" IS 100 TIMES MORE
IMPORTANT THAN IQ.

THE WORRY CLINIC

D r. George W. Crane was a psychologist and physician who wrote a syndicated newspaper column, and the following story first appeared there:

One of the older staff doctors at Wesley Hospital told me of this case. It occurred in the year 1910 when blood transfusions and other medical miracles were not yet common.

Jimmy, age 10, was devoted to his six-year-old sister. One day, Jimmy's little sister fell off her bicycle and cut a large artery in her leg. Bleeding profusely, by the time the doctor arrived at their house, she was failing fast. Although the doctor quickly managed to clamp the artery, the girl's heart was failing. In desperation, the doctor turned to her brother and said, "Jimmy, will you give your blood to help save your little sister's life?"

Jimmy swallowed hard, then nodded his head, so the doctor lay him on the kitchen table and began withdrawing blood which he injected directly into the little girl's vein.

For the next 30 minutes, the doctor and the family watched the little girl anxiously and prayed. When it was finally clear that she was over the crisis, he wiped the perspiration off his forehead and turned around only to see Jimmy, still stretched out on the kitchen table, tense and trembling.

"What's the matter, Jimmy?" asked the doctor.

"W-w-when do I die?" Jimmy responded through clenched teeth.

That's when the doctor realized that Jimmy had misunderstood what the request for his blood really meant. In his young mind, he imagined his sister was going to need all his blood, which meant that Jimmy, though hesitating a moment and swallowing hard at the request, had silently agreed to die for his little sister.

— Insight 2011

PEOPLE DON'T CARE HOW
MUCH YOU KNOW, UNTIL THEY KNOW
HOW MUCH YOU CARE.

WHAT I LEARNED FROM JACK

In 2006, my company produced the official program for the Telus Skins golf tournament, which was held at the Nicklaus North golf course in Whistler, B.C. During the tournament, my wife Kay and I had the opportunity to walk in the crowd that was following the legendary PGA champion Jack Nicklaus.

As he prepared to take his second shot on the 12th hole, Nicklaus turned to his caddie and asked, "How far to the green?" Glancing down the fairway, his caddie responded, "About 91 or 92 yards." Jack quickly turned to him and said, "Well, which is it, 91 or 92 yards?"

Talk about precision.

Thinking about it later, I realized that while it wouldn't make that much difference to you or me if we judged the distance to the pin that precisely, Jack's entire career as a champion was built on his ability to get that ball as close to the pin as possible. In his world, one yard could be the difference between sinking that all-important putt to win the tournament or having to take another stroke and end up being out of the money.

There are times in all of our lives when we need to perform like a champion, where "close enough" just isn't good enough and we have to be more, do more and deliver more than the competition to be successful. At those moments, we need to be ready to step up and get in the game.

— *The Power to Soar Higher*

IF YOU WANT TO BE A CHAMPION,
YOU HAVE TO BE ON TOP OF YOUR GAME.

SNAKE CHARMERS

Before I became a speaker, I tried my hand at stand-up comedy in England. Following a successful nine-week run on a BBC variety show, I hit the road as a headliner on a seven-week tour of big nightclubs in Birmingham, Leicester and Manchester.

The first week I was booked at a nightclub in downtown Birmingham. Following the dress rehearsal with the orchestra and the MC, I asked the nightclub manager who else would be on the bill. He told me there would be a young female singer and then, pointing to an elderly couple in a dark corner, he said, "Those two people as well."

I asked what they did and he said, "They're snake charmers."

"Real snakes?" I asked incredulously.

"Yes, including pythons and lizards."

In my weirdest dreams I hadn't imagined working with snake charmers and as I gazed across the room I saw myself as a 60-year-old performer, having spent years on the road and still struggling to make a living in dimly lit clubs, the third act on the bill. All of a sudden, the light went on and I could see that this was not the business for me. At that precise moment, I could feel my once-big dream of being a comic begin to die, and I knew it was a major turning point in my life.

I didn't even wait to perform that night (an unpardonable sin in the business). Instead I rushed to a phone box and told my wife that I was quitting and coming home. Little did I know that my experiences on the comedy circuit were preparing me for my future on stage as a motivational speaker.

— *The Runway of Life*

WHEN YOU'RE HEADED IN THE WRONG
DIRECTION, IT TAKES COURAGE TO PUT ON
THE BRAKES AND CHANGE COURSE.

LESSONS ON LEADERSHIP

O n January 15, 1942, the day I was born, General George Patton arrived in Indio, California, to take command of a desert training centre. And while I came into the world with a gentle squawk, Patton rolled into town in a sirens-screaming motorcade.

Waiting expectantly for a traditional motivating speech, Patton's officers and men watched him dismount his car at 11 a.m., the precise moment he was scheduled to take command. He saluted the troops and said: "I assume command of the First Armored Corps. At ease!"

Never one to pussyfoot around, Patton got right to the point. "We are at war with a tough enemy. We must train millions of men to be soldiers! We must make them tough in mind and body . . . We will start running from this point in exactly 30 minutes. I will lead!"

Good leaders inspire people to have confidence in their leadership. Great leaders inspire people to have confidence in themselves. If you plan to lead, you can't sit around waiting for something to happen. Leaders make bold moves. Leaders take risks. Leaders make use of their own ingenuity and do what has to be done. Even the best leaders make mistakes; it's how we move on from those mistakes that determines our success.

For 35 years, I have led Canada Wide Media in good times and bad through an ever-changing business climate. Our staff of 130 great people produce over 50 quality products including magazines, trade publications and websites, making us the largest independently owned magazine publishing company in Western Canada.

What leadership skills do I use to propel Canada Wide forward? I'm no General Patton, but I do have seven basic principles that I employ to assure the company's success. Over the next week, I will share those principles.

— *Who Dares Wins*

LEADERSHIP LAW NO. 1

S ometimes being a leader means you don't do what's popular, you do what has to be done. You can't marry all the girls and you can't give your employees everything they want. Businesses thrive when tough calls are made and leaders have to make those tough calls. Leadership can be a lonely, distasteful job, but once the choice has been made, the job has to be done. Leaders have to lead. Period.

According to Sir Adrian Cadbury, being able to make unpopular decisions is a key aspect of ethical leadership. Cadbury is the former chairman of Cadbury Schweppes PLC, one of the world's largest food and beverage companies. He was also a pioneer in raising awareness and stimulating debate on corporate governance and he produced the *Cadbury Report*, a code of best practices that served as a basis for reform of corporate governance around the world.

Sir Adrian said: "The company that takes drastic action in order to survive is more likely to be criticized publicly than the one which fails to grasp the nettle and gradually declines. There is always a temptation to postpone difficult decisions, but it is not in society's best interest that hard choices should be avoided because of public clamour."

Good leaders won't always win popularity contests, but that shouldn't stop them from doing what they know to be right, for their customers, their employees, their shareholders and the future of the company. They also lead by example, being visible to everyone in the company so they can see and emulate that example.

— *Who Dares Wins*

IF YOU WANT TO LEAD, YOU MUST
BE WILLING TO MAKE DIFFICULT DECISIONS
AND STAND BY THOSE DECISIONS.

LEADERSHIP LAW NO. 2

S uccessful leaders know how to stay focused on the big picture, the details of which should be spelled out in your mission statement.

My company's mission statement is proudly displayed in the front lobby of our office. Here are a couple of items from that document:

Honesty and integrity in all of our dealings,
both inside Canada Wide and outside the company,
are cornerstones of our business.

We are committed to thoughtful planning and
responsive management in all sectors of the company
to ensure the company's ongoing financial success.

Renowned author Stephen Covey believes that one reason it's difficult for today's business people to stay focused is that we waste our energy on "urgent and unimportant" events. We do this, he says because anything that is urgent tends to be seen as important. Phone calls, emails, text messages and other interruptions — all create a sense of urgency, no matter how unimportant their content might be. Think about how much of your day is taken up with these rather than getting on what's in your mission statement.

Canada Wide Media doesn't own a restaurant, or a pub, or a newspaper. We have stuck to what we do best by rereading our mission statement and becoming experts in the magazine publishing field in Western Canada.

In the Jewish tradition there is a holiday — Simchat Torah — that celebrates the completion of the cycle of one full reading of the Torah — the Five Books of Moses. When the readers finish, they roll the scroll all the way back to the beginning and start again. By continually reading the Torah they stay in touch with the original core ideas they value.

— Who Dares Wins

TAKE YOUR OWN COMPANY MISSION
STATEMENT AND ITS CORE VALUES AND
REREAD IT AT LEAST ONCE A MONTH.

LEADERSHIP LAW NO. 3

L eaders are always learning. It has been said that education and a dedication to lifelong learning is the great equalizer. Exceptional leaders thrive by continually developing themselves.

Peter Drucker, author of more than 20 best-selling books on management, said that a leader's role is to teach everyone in the organization to be devoted to his or her work. The leader must first lead. All employees have to see themselves as executives. You can't take anybody any further than you have been yourself — that is why a leader must always be learning.

The mind needs food as much as the body does. If a leader is not feeding their mind, their ideas become stagnant and outdated.

— Who Dares Wins

ASK YOURSELF THESE TWO QUESTIONS:
WHAT HAVE I LEARNED IN THE PAST YEAR
TO INCREASE MY BOTTOM-LINE PERFORMANCE?
WHAT DO I PLAN TO LEARN
IN THE NEXT YEAR TO FURTHER
IMPROVE MY PERFORMANCE?

LEADERSHIP LAW NO. 4

L eaders are visionaries. One of the Proverbs of the Old Testament says that when there is no vision, people perish. In business, as in every other endeavour, there must be vision.

H.G. Wells, reflecting on how every human being can determine whether he or she has really succeeded in life, said that the true measure of success is the difference between what we made of ourselves and what we might have made of ourselves.

Correct me if I'm wrong, but I maintain that you are a better, more capable person than you have demonstrated so far and I challenge you to dare to be your best. Once you stop drifting with the crowd and develop a vision, life takes on a new significance and new forces take shape within you.

Throughout history, great leaders have demonstrated that a gripping vision of the future is at the very heart of exceptional leadership. In the early 1940s, in the heat of the Second World War, a poster of Winston Churchill was plastered all over England. The bold words accompanying Churchill's image simply said, "Deserve Victory." It's a message that was an integral part of Churchill's life philosophy and a nation was inspired.

Churchill said, "What is the use of living if not to strive for noble causes and to make this muddled world a better place to live in after we are gone."

A true leader inspires the people in his/her organization with a vision — a purpose — for why the company does what it does — something much greater than simply just providing a service or making a profit.

— *Who Dares Wins*

THREE THINGS LEADERS MUST DO
TO MAKE A VISION REALITY:
DEFINE IT, LIVE IT, CELEBRATE IT.

LEADERSHIP LAW NO. 5

Too often, people go about their business in a headlong way, never pausing to think of the potential results. One great need in our world is for more sober, profitable thinking. It takes more than good intentions and dreams to make a business successful. Good leaders plan ahead.

A great mathematician said that if he had but three minutes to work at a problem on which his life depended, he would spend two of those minutes considering the best way to approach it. Likewise, if you have a garden, the planning must come before the planting, as it makes much more sense to work it all out with a pencil than it does with a shovel.

The former head coach of the San Francisco 49ers, Bill Walsh, was considered an eccentric because of how extensively he planned his football team's plays before each game. While most coaches would plan a few opening plays then wait to see how the game unfolded before responding with plays that seemed appropriate, Walsh was determined to have the game respond to him rather than the other way around. Walsh won a lot of Super Bowls with his "eccentric" approach. As a leader, he understood the value of planning ahead.

Carefully plan ahead. Success in all things needs preparation.

— *Who Dares Wins*

GOOD PLANS SHAPE GOOD DECISIONS.
THAT'S WHY GOOD PLANNING HELPS TO MAKE
ELUSIVE DREAMS COME TRUE.

LEADERSHIP LAW NO. 6

Leaders pay a price to be successful. Great leaders pay a price to stay. What qualities, habits, disciplines got you where you are today? What leadership skills did you employ and what price did you pay for your success? Now, are you ready to go higher?

If you truly want to develop beyond your present level, here are three questions to ask yourself:

1. How far do I want to go? Look at the job of your immediate boss and all that it requires. Could you do it? Answer honestly. Now, go a step further — what about the most senior leader in your sightline (maybe it's the CEO)? Consider the time, energy and skills it would take to do that job. What would it require that you don't have now? What would you have to give up? What parts of that job would you struggle with or dislike doing?

2. What am I willing to sacrifice? Being a leader requires commitment and sometimes that means business priorities take precedence over everything else, even family. Finding the right balance between career and personal life is a challenge all leaders must face.

3. How will I invest in my future? Leadership is a long-term proposition that requires intellectual, emotional and physical stamina. As a leader, you will be constantly tested and expected to rise to the challenge. Leadership is a continual process of development and great leaders are those who are able to innovate and adapt.

Zig Ziglar once said, "Be a meaningful specific. Most people are meaningless generalities. Remember what got you where you are and keep daring to build on those qualities so you can stay on top."

— *Who Dares Wins*

SUCCESS COMES AT A PRICE.
ARE YOU WILLING TO PAY IT?

LEADERSHIP LAW NO. 7

P ositive attitude is everything. It was W. Clement Stone who coined the phrase Positive Mental Attitude (PMA). He also coined the phrase Negative Mental Attitude (NMA). He said, "I can't absolutely guarantee you will be successful with a positive mental attitude. But I can guarantee you won't be with a negative mental attitude."

Dr. Thomas J. Stanley, who wrote the best-selling book *The Millionaire Mind*, interviewed a thousand millionaires and discovered that a whopping 62 per cent of those he interviewed claimed that the ability to get along with other men and women was the single most important quality they attributed to their enormous success.

Having a negative attitude always costs us, whether it is at home with family, in the community with friends and neighbours, or most definitely in business with colleagues, customers and employees. People want to do business with people whom they like and respect.

Helen Keller once said, "If life is not an adventure, life is nothing." I say, if life is not lived with a positive attitude, life is nothing.

If you're having difficulty maintaining a positive attitude, try these ideas:

Check in with your internal dialogue. Divide a sheet of paper into two columns and, for a few days, jot down on one side all the negative thoughts that come into your head. In the second column, rewrite each thought in a positive way. Next, practice doing this in your mind until it becomes a habit.

Learn to communicate more effectively. Not saying the things we feel can lead to a sense of frustration, hurt, anger or anxiety. If you find communicating difficult, or are afraid of arguments or hurting others' feelings, take a course to improve your skills.

— *Who Dares Wins*

DARE TO HAVE A POSITIVE
ATTITUDE AND YOUR WILDEST
DREAMS ARE POSSIBLE.

MUSTER YOUR COURAGE – DO IT NOW

"Be your name Buxbaum or Bixby or Bray
or Mordecai Ali Van Allen O'Shea,
you're off to great places! Today is your day!
Your mountain is waiting —
So . . . get on your way!" — Dr. Seuss

There's a story I like to tell about a painfully shy man who fell in love with a young woman. He sensed that she felt the same way, but he couldn't find the courage to ask her out. Finally, he decided he would mail her a love letter every day for one year and then ask her on a date. Faithfully, he followed his plan and at year's end he was courageous enough to call her — only to discover that she had married the mail carrier.

If there is something you want to accomplish, muster up your courage and do it now! Start today! If there is something that you have been meaning to do or something you've been putting off, waiting for the perfect time to do it — today is that day.

When I had a stroke some years ago, I suddenly realized that I just don't know what the future holds and I can't take the chance that my body will be healthy, strong and capable forever. That's why I don't put off anything important that I want to accomplish . . . and you shouldn't either.

As Dr. Seuss said, "Today is your day" and right now is the time to make that first step. Don't wait any longer.

— Make Your Life a Masterpiece

"THE HABIT OF ALWAYS PUTTING OFF
AN EXPERIENCE UNTIL YOU CAN AFFORD IT,
OR UNTIL THE TIME IS RIGHT, OR
UNTIL YOU KNOW HOW TO DO IT IS ONE OF
THE GREATEST BURGLARS OF JOY. BE
DELIBERATE, BUT ONCE YOU'VE MADE UP YOUR
MIND, JUMP IN." — Charles R. Swindoll

MAY

May 1

DRESS SMARTLY — PART I

"She wants me to dress smart-casual.
What is that?"
"I don't know, but you don't have it."
— Characters George and Jerry in
a scene from the TV show *Seinfeld*

A number of years ago, a teenager by the name of Jacqueline Rogers took a job at Canada Wide Magazines working with the editor of *BCBusiness* doing filing, research and circulation work. Although she always wore jeans and a T-shirt, from the outset I was impressed with her positive attitude, boundless energy and enthusiasm and often wondered how she would fare in sales. One day I decided to find out, so I asked Jacquie if she would make a couple of sales calls.

Her answer was a very firm no, and at the time I didn't understand her reluctance.

It wasn't until a few weeks later that I discovered the real reason. The only clothes that Jacquie owned were jeans and T-shirts and she didn't feel that this was a suitable wardrobe for someone who was making sales calls. I also discovered that she had absolutely no money to buy new clothes, so I handed her a cheque for $1,000 and asked her to go to the mall and buy three or four inexpensive but smart outfits.

Jacquie bought the clothes that she needed and went on the sales calls. Just as I suspected, she was a natural and it was the beginning of a whole new career for her here at what is now Canada Wide Media. Jacquie Rogers eventually became general sales manager of *TV Week*, bringing that same energy, passion and excitement that I first recognized to all that she does.

— *Make Your Life a Masterpiece*

DRESSING SMARTLY GIVES US THE CONFIDENCE
TO PUSH BEYOND BOUNDARIES AND OPENS DOORS
TO NEW OPPORTUNITIES.

DRESS SMARTLY — PART II

How you dress defines your business presence and to those who don't know you, you are how you dress. As a general rule, in new situations you have just four seconds to make a first impression.

According to Michelle Sterling, image consultant and founder of Global Image Group, the process works like this:

• If you appear to be on a comparable business or social level, you are considered suitable for further interactions.

• If you appear to be of higher business or social status, you are admired and cultivated as a valuable contact.

• If you appear to be of lower business or social standing, you are tolerated but kept at arm's length.

• If you are in an interview situation, you can either appear to match the corporate culture or not, something that will ultimately affect the outcome of your career path.

Which of these categories do you want to be in?

Knowing how to dress in an ever-changing business world can be challenging and searching on the Internet for clarification about dressing for business occasions is like trying to file your own income taxes. One site that claimed to demystify the term "business casual" offered no fewer than six categories of dress. Among them: active casual, smart casual, dress casual and my favourite, power casual. However, in reading the descriptions for each category, the distinction between one "casual" and another was lost on me.

That's why, when it comes to deciding how to dress for any business occasion, I like to keep it simple. My rule of thumb is to dress just a little bit better than the person I am meeting.

— *Make Your Life a Masterpiece*

YOU DON'T DRESS FOR THE JOB YOU HAVE NOW.
YOU DRESS FOR THE JOB YOU WANT TO HAVE.

DRESS SMARTLY – PART III

A survey conducted by The Ladders, a U.K. management consulting firm, found that more than 37 per cent of senior executives (both male and female) had, at some point, decided against hiring a candidate due to the way they dressed. The most common complaints being that their clothes were too casual, inappropriate or poorly coordinated.

Here are five tips to help you dress smartly:

1. Too many patterns or textures can mess up your look, so don't wear stripes or checks on both your shirt and pants. Reserve a texture or pattern either for your top or bottom and keep the other plain. Team a patterned tie with a plain shirt.

2. No matter what you wear, your clothes should always be neat, clean and in good condition. Remember, even casual attire should never look sloppy or worn out.

3. Don't forget to look down. Your shoes should be in good condition and of a type that is appropriate to the situation. Also, check that your heels are cleaned and in good condition. After you say goodbye, people will look at them as you walk away.

4. Invest in a good-quality wardrobe. If you don't have a lot of money to spend, focus on the basics first — slacks (skirts), dress shirts (blouses) and shoes — and remember that you can never go wrong with black. It's always appropriate, versatile for all seasons and it works with all other colours.

5. You're not dressed for business unless you have your business cards on you. Always try to have a small pocket somewhere on your person to carry a few business cards that are easily accessible — because you never know who you're going to meet.

— *Make Your Life a Masterpiece*

NO ONE EVER LOST A SALE
FOR LOOKING TOO PROFESSIONAL.

DARE TO BE UNCONVENTIONAL

Making the most of every moment and every opportunity isn't just about the time we spend on our career. It also applies to our personal life and our relationships with those we love. I have learned that sometimes you have to step outside the box of conventionality in order to make the most of the opportunities that life presents to you. That's exactly what I decided to do when my daughter announced she was getting married.

When my eldest daughter Samantha got engaged, my wife and some of Sam's closest friends put on a number of showers for her and although I was probably reluctantly invited to them, it is virtually a women-only club and therefore I would have felt out of place attending. Still, I too wanted to do something with Sam to celebrate.

I thought about it for a long time before it dawned on me that I wasn't the only man being left out in the cold by this tradition. Because Samantha worked at what was then Canada Wide Magazines with me, I happened to know that many of her associates in the advertising agencies, PR companies, television stations and hotels we do business with are of the male persuasion.

I decided to throw my own wedding shower for Sam and invite all of these men. I rented Dario's Italian Restaurant in Vancouver and put on a luncheon for 100 of her male business associates. Each guest was asked to bring a bottle of wine as a gift. The shower was a great success, Sam loved it and all the guys were thrilled to be invited to what may have been their first — and only — wedding shower.

— *Make Your Life a Masterpiece*

DON'T LET CONVENTION STAND IN
THE WAY OF CELEBRATING THE IMPORTANT
MOMENTS WITH THOSE YOU LOVE.

CLAIM YOUR POWER

"When we have begun to take charge of our lives, to own ourselves, there is no longer any need to ask permission of someone." — George O'Neil

Sometimes it is easier to believe we are powerless in a situation when we don't want to take responsibility for making a decision. Perhaps it is because secretly, we like the idea of a force we cannot resist or a situation we cannot prevent from developing. Likewise, if we believe the situation is beyond our control, we don't have to take responsibility for the outcome.

Being powerless also gives us an excuse to let events happen that we wouldn't publicly express a desire for — perhaps in a situation where someone's feelings might be hurt or what we want is in conflict with what our family or community expects of us. When you think about it, it may be easier to cast yourself as a victim of circumstance rather than declare yourself an architect of transformation. But ask yourself this, which one do you want to be known as?

The first step to claiming your power is to give yourself permission to live the life you want. Although others may express disappointment or disapproval at the choices you make, it is only you, not them, who have the power to make you feel bad. If you don't give away your power, no one can make you feel bad about your choices and decisions.

— *The Runway of Life*

GIVE YOURSELF PERMISSION
TO LIVE THE LIFE YOU WANT AND
CLAIM YOUR POWER.

BRIAN DYSON'S 30-SECOND SPEECH

"Of the five balls you juggle in life,
you can drop only one," so says
the former CEO of Coca-Cola

Imagine life as a game in which you are juggling, trying to keep five balls in the air. Those balls are: work, family, health, friends and spirit and it's your job to make sure that they all stay in motion and none of them falls.

But what if you did drop one, which would bounce and which would break?

Out of all of them, work is the only ball that is made of rubber, the only one you can afford to drop. If you drop it, it will bounce back. The four others — family, health, friends and spirit — are made of glass. If you drop one of these, at the very least it will be cracked, chipped and damaged. In the worst-case scenario, it will shatter. Either way, it will never be the same.

Although work and career are important, they will never provide you with the quality of life that comes from investing your time and energy into family, health, friends and spirit. So work as efficiently as possible during business hours and leave on time. Give proper attention to your family and friends and take a decent rest to revitalize your energy. You deserve it and so do the people you care about.

— Insight 2011

VALUE HAS A VALUE ONLY IF
ITS VALUE IS VALUED. WHAT DO YOU PLACE
THE MOST VALUE ON IN YOUR LIFE?
DON'T DROP THE BALL.

BE A FIRE HYDRANT,
NOT A FLAMETHROWER

For most of us, it's all too easy to take sides in an argument or fan the flames of disagreement. But whether it's a discussion about which hockey team deserves to win the Stanley Cup or what to do with violent repeat offenders, if you overdo it, you're asking for trouble. When arguments become heated, people tend to shut down their listening skills and instead focus on driving their own point home — which, if you're not careful, can easily escalate into a shouting match.

And while a million angry and insulting things may be bubbling up in your throat and threatening to burst out of your mouth, you don't have to let the dam break. Before you get into a situation that could do permanent damage to your relationship with the other person, take a moment to consider whether the point you are arguing about is worth the trouble. If it's not, take a step back and attempt to cool down the situation.

Saying something like, "I guess I got a little carried away, but it's important for me to understand your point of view so maybe we could discuss this another time," lets the other party know that not only are you not looking to get into a fight, but that the relationship is more important to you than being right.

— *The Power of Tact*

IT'S HOW WE DEAL WITH CONFLICT
THAT DETERMINES THE OUTCOME. LEARN TO FIX
ARGUMENTS AND SOOTHE HURT FEELINGS
INSTEAD OF SAYING THINGS THAT WILL ONLY
ADD FUEL TO THE FLAMES.

ANOTHER BRILLIANT IDEA

I deas are powerful things. The good ones come around again and again; that's because they are constantly being recycled.

In my business (that of motivation), we are known to be excellent recyclers. We read each other's books, catch each other's presentations, share thoughts at conventions and gain valuable insights by watching closely what has worked and what hasn't for others. With each idea, we give it our own special kick, hone it and try to make it better.

It's nothing new. Entertainers do it, lawyers do it, politicians do it. It just makes sense that when we see someone in a successful niche that we observe and pick up some good pointers to incorporate into our own endeavours.

The best ideas and the best books are quoted often. I'm a great reader of the Bible, not only because I'm a practising Christian, but because I believe that within its sometimes convoluted messages, there is endless wisdom.

Proverbs 12, for instance, says that as a man thinks in his heart, so he is. Pretty simple stuff, but what an incredible truth.

James Allen, who lived from 1864 to 1912, was a writer who inspired a generation of motivational speakers, me included. We love his stuff and use it often. Allen wrote a book called *As a Man Thinketh*. It was the theme of Proverbs 12 refined for the 20th century. Motivator Earl Nightingale picked up on it and sold more than a million copies of a recording he called: "You become what you think about most of the time."

Despite all of this recycling, it's a thought that doesn't go stale and I continue to share this powerful bit of wisdom in almost every presentation I do.

—You Can If You Believe You Can

WHAT GREAT IDEAS
CAN YOU RECYCLE?

THE WEIGHT OF WATER – PART I

A lecturer, when explaining stress management to an audience, raised a glass of water and asked, "How heavy is this glass of water?" Answers called out ranged from 20g to 500g. The lecturer replied, "The absolute weight doesn't matter. It depends on how long you try to hold it.

"If I hold it for a minute, that's not a problem.

"If I hold it for an hour, I'll have an ache in my right arm.

"If I hold it for a day, you'll have to call an ambulance.

"In each case, it's the same weight, but the longer I hold it, the heavier it becomes." He continued:

"And that's the way it is with stress management.

"If we carry our burdens all the time — whether they are the responsibilities of our job, our commitments to our family, the burden of a major illness, or anything else — without setting them aside now and then to take a break; sooner or later, as the burden becomes increasingly heavy, we'll come to a point where we won't be able to carry on and then we'll be no good to anyone, least of all ourselves. As with the glass of water, you have to put down your burdens and responsibilities from time to time and rest before taking them up again. When we're refreshed, we can carry on with even the heaviest of burdens."

So, before you return home tonight, put the burden of work down. Don't carry it home. You can pick it up tomorrow. Whatever burdens you're carrying now, let them down for a moment if you can.

Why not take a while to just simply *relax*? Put down anything that may be a burden to you right now. Don't pick it up again until after you've rested a while.

— *The Power of a Dream*

THE WEIGHT OF WATER – PART II

L ife is short. Enjoy it! Here are some great ways of dealing with the burdens of life:

Keep your words soft and sweet, just in case you have to eat them.

When in doubt, just take the next small step.

Read stuff that will make you look good if you die in the middle of it.

Drive carefully. It's not only cars that can be recalled by their maker.

If you can't be kind, at least have the decency to be vague.

If you lend someone $20 and never see that person again, it was probably worth it.

It may be that your sole purpose in life is simply to serve as a warning to others.

Never buy a car you can't push.

Never put both feet in your mouth at the same time, because then you won't have a leg to stand on.

Life is too short to waste time hating anyone.

The second mouse gets the cheese.

Your job won't take care of you when you're sick. Your friends and family will. Stay in touch.

When everything's coming your way, you're in the wrong lane.

You may be only one person in the world, but you may also be the world to one person.

Some mistakes are too much fun to only make once.

We could learn a lot from crayons . . . Some are sharp, some are pretty and some are dull. Some have weird names, and all are different colours, but they all have to live in the same box.

A truly happy person is one who can enjoy the scenery on a detour.

— *The Power of a Dream*

KNOW WHEN TO TAKE A RISK

It goes without saying that all entrepreneurs make mistakes along the way. They are risk-takers, willing to do things differently in order to develop new and better solutions. That being said, taking unnecessary risks is not a requirement for success; in fact, it can often be detrimental to a new venture. There is a time for daring and a time for caution; as an entrepreneur, you must know the difference.

In truth, successful entrepreneurs are often risk-minimizers; they take risks from necessity because it comes with the territory, but they also do everything they can to ensure the stability and success of their enterprise. In business as in life, a little common sense — and a practical plan — goes a long way. The motto of one of the minor Chinese monkey gods sums it up well, "Be cautious, be bold," the two work well hand in hand.

— *The Runway of Life*

"TAKE CALCULATED RISKS.
THAT IS QUITE DIFFERENT
FROM BEING RASH."
— General George S. Patton

A RECIPE FOR TASTY GRAPES

During a speaking tour in New Zealand, my wife Kay and I took a Quickcat ferry from Auckland Harbour to Waiheke Island. The purpose of our little daytrip was to tour a selection of vineyards that included Pinnacle Vineyard, Mudbrick Vineyard and Restaurant, Stonyridge Vineyard and Onetangi Road Vineyard.

As we toured around, we were told that although the island — which is found on the same latitude as the southern tip of Sicily — offers almost ideal conditions for growing grapes for winemaking, there is one exception: the soil on the island is very dry, clay-like and ridden with stones. Because of the lack of nutrients in this type of soil, the vines struggle to get enough nutrients, something that you would think could be a very bad thing for these winemakers. It turns out, it's not, this struggle to get nutrients results in heartier plants, which just happen to produce very tasty grapes.

Tasty grapes = tasty wine.

Sometimes in our own lives, just as with the vines of Waiheke Island, it is the things we struggle with the most that eventually produce the best results. Don't be too quick to give up on your hopes and dreams.

— Insight 2011

RECOGNIZE THE OPPORTUNITY
THAT LIES WITHIN EACH STRUGGLE.

WHO HAS SACRIFICED FOR YOU? — PART I

S everal years ago, a young married couple and their baby lived on the 12th floor of a modest downtown apartment building. As new immigrants, they were full of anticipation of the life that lay ahead in Canada. The husband had a good job with prospects for advancement and he was determined to be a good husband and father.

One winter evening, the building caught fire. Taking charge, the husband told his wife to stay in the apartment while he went for help. The fire trucks came, but their ladders couldn't reach the 12th floor. For the mother, alone in the apartment with her baby, the wait for her husband was excruciating. When he failed to return, she feared something terrible had happened and that the fire was dangerously close.

Not wanting to open the door into the smoke-filled hall, but realizing that she needed to protect herself and her baby, she took her big winter overcoat and soaked it in the bathtub, then tucked the baby close and covered them both. She huddled in a corner and waited.

The husband died in the fire. The mother and baby were saved, but while protecting the baby, the mother was severely burned. The flames had seared her face, head and hands.

After months of painful surgery, the mother was reunited with her baby and determined to do all she could to provide a safe and comfortable home. And while she would be scarred for life and often shunned by others, she would do whatever she had to do to give her daughter a good life.

Only the most menial work was available, taking in laundry from neighbours, scrubbing stairs, etc. The important thing was that she provided her daughter a clean, safe home and the child was well-fed and loved.

WHO HAS SACRIFICED FOR YOU? — PART II

The girl graduated from high school and the mother, continuing to do everything possible to ensure her success, paid her way to university. As a freshman, the girl was rushed by a sorority. The girls in charge asked if they could call at the girl's apartment at 8 p.m. to take her to the sorority house. She said no, she would meet them in the lobby.

At 7:30, wanting to surprise their new inductee, the excited sorority girls talked their way into the building, found the apartment and knocked on the door. Not expecting anyone, the girl answered and the sorority girls burst into the room.

At the kitchen sink, the girl's mother was hunched over the dishes. She turned at the sound and the sorority girls froze when they saw her scarred face.

"Who is . . . who is *she*?" asked one of the girls.

"Oh, she's nobody," said the daughter. And grabbing her coat, she hustled the visitors from the apartment.

Nobody! Can you imagine how the mother felt? The fire, the agony of healing, the years of suffering and giving and sacrificing. A nobody?

All kinds of people, whether we realize it or not, make sacrifices for us. I know many who have certainly made them for me, including my parents who came to a new country to give me a better life; my wife Kay, who worked tirelessly as a stay-at-home parent to raise our three daughters; my daughters who shared my attention with a growing business and a busy speaking career; my friends, associates, mentors and company team who have contributed to my success in so many ways. I thank them all.

— *How to Soar With the Eagles*

TODAY, THINK ABOUT THE
PEOPLE WHO HAVE MADE SACRIFICES FOR YOU.
HOW HAVE YOU THANKED THEM?

A HOLE NEW PERSPECTIVE ON ANGER

I once knew a young man who had a bad temper and was prone to taking out his anger on others. Thankfully, he also had a very wise father. Instead of lecturing the young man on his behaviour, the father gave him a bag of nails and told him that every time he lost his temper, he should hammer a nail into the back of the fence instead of acting on his anger.

The first day, the young man drove 37 nails into the fence. Over the next few weeks, as he learned to control his anger, the number of nails he hammered each day gradually dwindled. He discovered it was easier to hold his temper than to drive those nails into the fence.

After a period of time, the day came when the young man didn't lose his temper at all. He told his father about it and the father suggested that the young man now pull out one nail for each day that he was able to hold his temper. The days passed and the young man was finally able to tell his father that all the nails were gone.

The father took his son by the hand and led him to the fence. "You have done well, my son, but look at the holes in the fence," he said. "When you say things in anger, they leave a scar just like these holes. You can put a knife in a man and draw it out, but it won't matter how many times you say 'I'm sorry,' the wound is still there. A verbal wound is as bad as a physical one and just as likely to leave a lasting scar."

TO YOUR CONTINUED SUCCESS

My father Bernie Legge once told me, "Never accept success or failure — neither need be permanent."

CKNW Radio host and TV Week magazine contributor Rick Forchuk once told me: "Peter, you've worked really hard for many years to be successful — that's good, but you're still working hard to stay successful. That's even better."

Success does not guarantee continued success. You must keep working at it and growing and learning as an individual.

Eighty per cent of the professional speakers who were in the business 10 years ago are no longer in the business today. Perhaps they forgot to keep reading, studying, learning from others, improving on their craft, rehearsing and most significantly, they've forgotten how to answer the three important questions that I ask every new speaker who approaches me for advice:

1. What do you want to speak about?

2. Who will pay you for this?

3. How will they find out about you?

One of the reasons I love what I do so much is that there are always new opportunities and challenges to help me get better at what I do. When the 2010 Olympics came to Vancouver, I set my sights on getting hired to MC the opening ceremonies. Although things didn't turn out exactly as I expected, I was thrilled to be the only speaker contracted to give a motivational speech at the Olympics — I delivered my speech at the very first victory ceremony in BC Place Stadium on February 13, 2010 and it was an experience I will never forget.

WHAT CAN YOU DO TODAY TO ENSURE
YOUR CONTINUED SUCCESS
TOMORROW, AND HOW CAN YOU CHALLENGE
YOURSELF TO GET BETTER AT
YOUR CHOSEN CAREER?

PUNCTUALITY – PART I

How you do anything is how you do everything — if you have a clean car, tidy office and organized home, it reflects on your approach to business. Whether you like it or not, people will judge you by your habits. If you are late, the message it gives to others is: I'm more important than you.

Fewer than five per cent of people are punctual every single time; that's what makes them really stand out from everyone else. They are admired and respected by others. They are also considered to be more competent and valuable as a result of being punctual.

B.C. billionaire Jimmy Pattison is one such individual in both his business and his personal life. If you've been invited aboard Jimmy's boat, don't show up five minutes late, or you'll be waving to the boat from the shore. If Jimmy says the boat leaves at 7 p.m., it will. This is a lesson that more than one person I know has learned the hard way.

I read a news story from Germany about another fellow who took punctuality very seriously. The story made the news because the guy had just won $27 million in the lottery. Apparently, he was on his way to work when he stopped in at a corner store to buy his weekly lotto ticket and in checking his numbers from the previous week, the clerk informed him that he had won the jackpot.

The man's reaction to the news left the lottery operator dumbfounded.

"After he was told that he had won the jackpot, he said he didn't have time to chat because he would get into trouble if he was late to work," said the store clerk.

I think you have to admire someone who gets to work on time under those circumstances.

PUNCTUALITY – PART II

What Punctuality Says About You

1. First and foremost, punctuality shows others that you care. By keeping our commitments to others, we are acknowledging their needs and demonstrating that we value their time.

2. Punctuality shows that you are confident. It is a sign that you are ready to take on whatever task or project lies before you. On the other hand, being late can imply that you lack confidence or that you are hesitant to deal with a person or situation, possibly because you don't have the skills, knowledge or tools to create a successful outcome.

3. Punctuality shows that you are in control. Not only is it true that people want to do business with those they know, like and trust; they also want to do business with people who are in control. Individuals who always arrive on time give the impression that they manage things well and are more likely to be reliable in everything they do.

4. Punctuality shows that you hold yourself to high standards. Just like honesty and integrity, punctuality is a standard for personal excellence. Not only does it imply that you are in control of your business, it also shows that you respect yourself and others and expect a high level of performance in all things.

5. Punctuality shows that you know how to keep things on track. When you show up on time (or deliver your products and services on time), you keep your business moving forward and demonstrate that you understand that other people and events are also affected by what you do — or don't do. If you don't deliver as promised, you can negatively affect the plans of others. By showing up on time, you allow other people and things to show up on time as well.

PUNCTUALITY — PART III

"I could never have done what I have done
without the habits of punctuality,
order and diligence; without the determination
to concentrate myself on one subject
at a time." — Charles Dickens

Read about time management and incorporate good practices into your life. If you practice them diligently, personal time-management habits will become automatic to you.

Here are a few master time-management habits:

• Plan each day in advance.

• Resolve to be punctual for every appointment.

• Leave 15 minutes early for every meeting; it gives you breathing room.

• Organize your daily work by priority.

• Overcome procrastination with planning.

• Prepare thoroughly for every meeting (if it isn't worth preparing for, you are probably wasting your time by having a meeting at all).

— Make Your Life a Masterpiece

WHEN YOU IMPROVE THE QUALITY
OF YOUR TIME MANAGEMENT, YOU IMPROVE
THE QUALITY OF YOUR LIFE.

A NATURAL TALENT

The famous American painter Georgia O'Keeffe knew when she was 12 years old that she wanted to be an artist. Although as an abstract artist, she realized she was somewhat ahead of her time, noting that, "I have things in my head that are not like what anyone has taught me — shapes and ideas so near to me — so natural to my way of being and thinking that it hasn't occurred to me to put them down."

Even though she showed natural talent from a young age and took a number of painting classes, O'Keeffe initially chose to pursue a more conventional career as an art teacher rather than a painter. It wasn't until a friend showed her work to an influential gallery owner in New York, who arranged an exhibition introducing her as a major young talent, that O'Keeffe was persuaded to give up teaching and become a professional artist.

About her famously vivid paintings of flowers, O'Keeffe once said, "I found I could say things with colour and shapes that I couldn't say any other way — things I had no words for."

O'Keeffe had a long and productive career, exhibiting more than 900 works of art during her lifetime. She continued to create art until her death in 1986 at the age of 98. Her advice to another artist, Russell Vernon Hunter, in many ways sums up the sense of wonder she was able to portray through her work: "Try to paint your world as though you are the first man looking at it . . . the wind and the light and the cold . . . the dust and the vast starlit night."

— *Make Your Life a Masterpiece*

"YOU CANNOT TEACH
A MAN ANYTHING, YOU CAN
ONLY HELP HIM FIND IT
WITHIN HIMSELF." — Galileo

THE DIRECTOR OF FIRST IMPRESSIONS

T he receptionist/switchboard operator at my company has a nameplate, which reads, "Director of First Impressions." The decision to provide her with an official title came with the realization of just how important her job is to the success of everyone at Canada Wide Media.

"How so?" you might ask.

For many years, perhaps like most companies, we viewed this job as an entry-level position. We were wrong. We thought this position was simply about answering the phone and putting calls through to various departments. Then it dawned on us, the receptionist/switchboard operator is the very first point of contact with our company and the efficiency, attention to detail and pleasantness he or she displays to our customers makes all the difference.

So we searched for a mature, experienced switchboard operator. Maria wanted the job and she made such an impression on us that we couldn't help but make her our Director of First Impressions. Having the sign on Maria's desk serves two purposes: people coming in see it and know the person at the front desk is both a professional and a valued member of the team. In addition, Maria sees it every morning when she comes in and understands how important her job is and so she takes her responsibility very seriously, treating everyone with courtesy and respect and doing the utmost to provide the service they require.

By telling your employees how important they are to your success, you empower them to be the ambassadors that you need them to be for your business. It also helps to make their job more interesting and meaningful, which promotes the sense of self-respect that comes from a job well done.

— *The Power to Soar Higher*

HELP OTHERS HELP YOU
BY PUBLICLY ACKNOWLEDGING
THEIR CONTRIBUTION
TO YOUR SUCCESS.

LEAD BY EXAMPLE

I 've never met anyone who gives more than my mentor Joe Segal and that giving has, in turn, encouraged many others to give of themselves. Joe told me the story of a young man who once sent him a letter with $50 in it asking Joe if he would have lunch with him and give him some advice.

At the lunch, Joe shook the young man's hand and returned his $50. The young man explained his predicament. "Joe," he said. "I want to be successful like you, but I don't have a lot of money to invest. What should I do?"

Joe could see the young man was both serious and ambitious. He gave this advice, "If you want to make a lot of money, I would suggest that you either get into working in the stock market or real estate. You don't need capital for either of these careers; you just need the willingness for hard work, long hours and the discipline to learn the business."

The lunch ended and each man went his separate way.

Some years later, the young man showed up at the new Segal School of Business at Simon Fraser University (Joe and his family bought the old Bank of Montreal building in downtown Vancouver and donated it to the university) during the grand opening. As Joe showed him around, the young man revealed just how well the advice Joe had given him had paid off. To show his appreciation, the young man offered a $200,000 sponsorship for one of the rooms in the university. It was his way of saying thank you to Joe.

— *Make Your Life a Masterpiece*

"IF YOUR ACTIONS INSPIRE OTHERS
TO DREAM MORE, LEARN MORE, DO MORE
AND BECOME MORE, YOU ARE
A LEADER." — John Quincy Adams

NEVER HAVE LUNCH ALONE

Having a one-on-one lunch together (rather than a meeting in the office) is a great way to get to know someone. Some of the best stories in my speeches and books have come from having lunch with people who were happy to share their wisdom and experiences.

Getting together face-to-face shouldn't just be about building your contact list though. More importantly, it's an opportunity to build relationships and the best way to do that is to show an interest in other people's ideas and interests by using the time to ask questions that don't have yes or no answers (you might even want to make notes).

Need to brush up on your lunchtime etiquette? Here are a few tips:

1. Be on time. Although it's just good manners, many people think nothing of showing up late and blaming it on traffic, an important last-minute phone call or other business. Showing up late says that you don't value the other person's time as much as your own.

2. Give your full attention to the person you are dining with. If you are distracted, it gives the impression that you are uninterested. There's nothing worse than having a conversation with someone who is only half there.

3. Turn off your cellphone when you sit down. It's rude to answer your phone at the table or pick up a call and take it outside, abandoning your lunch companion.

4. Who pays? If you did the inviting, you pay (no matter what). Likewise, if they are giving you valuable advice, consider it an investment.

— The Power to Soar Higher

THE NEXT TIME YOU HAVE
AN EMPTY SPOT ON YOUR CALENDAR,
DON'T JUST GRAB A SANDWICH
AND SIT AT YOUR DESK. PICK UP THE
PHONE AND ASK SOMEONE TO LUNCH.

LEARN THE ROPES

More than 20 years ago, I made a very smart decision. I bought *BCBusiness*, a magazine that has become a cornerstone of my publishing business and also the most successful regional business magazine in Canada. Not long ago, we did a feature looking at nearly 20 of British Columbia's most successful individuals (from many walks of life) and the advice that most helped each of them get to where they are today. One of those stories is about a man I admire greatly, the Vancouver Symphony Orchestra's musical director, Bramwell Tovey. Born in England, Tovey's success isn't dependent upon a magic wand (though it might sometimes seem that way when he is up on the stage conducting), nor was he born with a silver spoon in his mouth. Yet he is most definitely living the dream that he imagined for himself as a young man just starting out on his career path in the U.K.

How did he do it? The answer comes in two parts.

First of all, he acted on some good advice from someone who had been down the path before him (the creator of the Los Angeles Opera, Peter Hemmings). The advice he received was to get out of the public eye and go work somewhere remote where he could focus on learning the repertoire of a conductor, top to bottom, front to back. Tovey did just that in 1989 when he accepted a position as artistic director of the Winnipeg Symphony. The second reason for his success is good, old-fashioned hard work. As Tovey himself says, it doesn't matter how good a musician you are; as a conductor you still have to learn the ropes.

— The Power of a Dream

WANTING TO BE A CHEF OR A DOCTOR
OR EVEN A PUBLIC SPEAKER
DOESN'T MAKE YOU ONE; YOU STILL HAVE
TO PUT IN THE HARD WORK TO
LEARN THE ROPES.

HOW MANY EXTRA MILES HAVE YOU PUT ON?

Here is an astonishing statistic from OMG Facts, an interesting website that posts weird but true facts that make you stop and think: For every pound of fat that you gain, your body has to produce seven miles of new blood vessels. Of course, most of these are tiny capillaries, but some are also mini veins and arteries called venules and arterioles. As a result, for every 10 pounds of fat gained, your heart has to pump blood through an additional 70 miles of blood vessels. From this information, it's not too difficult to see why obesity and heart disease go hand in hand. For me, this means that for no reason except my inability to control excessive food intake, over the years, my heart — the only one I've got — has had to work harder than it should. It's not only unnecessary, it's also risky.

The good news is the reverse is also true — for every pound of fat lost, your body breaks down and reabsorbs seven miles of vessels, which is great motivation for those of us who are trying to lose weight or looking for incentives to maintain a healthy weight once we get there. One pound may not look like a lot of weight lost on the outside, but pound for pound, the health benefits add up quickly. Losing weight can also reduce your risk of getting breast cancer, ovarian cancer or prostate cancer.

A small adjustment in perspective and priorities — towards a healthier, more active lifestyle — is often all it takes to start seeing positive results. Think of it as an investment in yourself.

— How to Soar With the Eagles

ARE YOUR EATING HABITS
AND LIFESTYLE HELPING OR
HURTING YOUR HEART?

30 PER CENT HERO

For most of us, when our endeavours don't turn out quite the way we expected, we become discouraged and lose all sense of perspective about our talent and potential. Although it's not that we lack either, more often it is because we are too close to the problem or too emotionally tied up with the results we are getting.

Remember this though, in the fullness of time, 70 per cent of your decisions will be wrong. I know it sounds a little grim at first blush, but it's actually a pretty good average (in baseball, if you walk up to the plate and fail to get on base 70 per cent of the time, they call you a hero). It just means that you might have to try lots of things — and risk striking out — in order to find the ones that work for you.

If you're too afraid to take your lumps, you'll never know what you could have accomplished.

If you don't believe in yourself, who else will? Through your belief in yourself, you create your world, your life and your potential.

If you don't know where your potential lies and you find yourself swinging from the fences, consider hiring a professional coach to help you out. All of the biggest sports legends have benefited from the insight that a coach can offer.

— *The Runway of Life*

EVEN OUR BIGGEST HEROES
ONLY WIN ABOUT 30 PER CENT
OF THE TIME. THE KEY
TO SUCCESS IS TO KEEP TRYING.

THE ROCKET

M aurice "Rocket" Richard's explosive 18-year career in hockey made him the most exciting player of his generation and a national hero. Fiercely competitive, a virtual demon on ice, Richard was a scoring genius. In 1944-45 he scored 50 goals in 50 games, hockey's most celebrated record for many years. He also led the league in goals five times and won the Hart Trophy. Above all, he excelled under pressure, scoring 18 playoff game-winning goals, a record that took the likes of Wayne Gretzky to break some 30 years later.

Richard passed away on May 27, 2000, and the tributes poured in; from Canada's prime minister and premiers, sportscasters, the entire hockey world and Canadians of all ages and stripes. Montreal Canadiens star Guy Lafleur related a story of how as a kid playing outdoor hockey in Montreal, every kid on the ice would be wearing their hero Richard's No. 9 jersey (on both teams). It made for a rather confusing game, but not one of them was willing to trade their jersey for another.

Of course, no team can be effective if everyone has the same talent. It's terrific to have a Rocket on your side, but you also need all of the other players — strong defensemen, guys on the wing and an impenetrable goalie — to be there as well in order to shine. We can't all be Rocket Richards, but we can still get in the game. Some of us can skate faster, some can shoot harder, some can pass better. Individually, we all count.

The brilliance of Rocket Richard inspired his team, the fans and all of the kids who wanted to wear his treasured No. 9 jersey, and his spirit continues to inspire.

— *Who Dares Wins*

USE YOUR TALENTS
TO INSPIRE THE MEMBERS
OF YOUR TEAM.

GET YOUR GOOD IDEA ON TRACK — PART I

We all have good ideas from time to time. Some of them are even brilliant ideas — ideas that if effectively executed could well change the world. I know that I've had lots of great ideas and I would guess that you have too. When it comes to great ideas, there is no shortage of creativity and genius in the world.

The problem is that somewhere between the formation of a good idea (that light-bulb moment) and the potential execution of that good idea, things sometimes go wrong. Perhaps we lose our enthusiasm because execution seems like too much work. Doubts creep in. We don't want to sweat the research. We lose confidence because we begin to fear that the end result may prove in one way or another that the idea really wasn't that great to begin with.

And then we discover that someone else not only had the same good idea, but they went all the way with it! And we're doubly upset.

Don't let good ideas die. If you believe they have merit, run with them all the way — you never know where you may end up.

Peter Armstrong was once a doorman with a good idea. Armstrong, who worked at the Hotel Vancouver, was upset with the poor quality of tours available for visitors to the city and the fact that, as a doorman, he was obliged to recommend the tours. Often, guests had to take taxis to bus terminals, stand in long lineups, search for departure gates and suffer frustrations that should never be part of a relaxing vacation.

Armstrong had a vision for a travel business that would provide visitors with a memorable vacation that included one-stop service and individualized attention and he was determined to fill that need.

GET YOUR GOOD IDEA ON TRACK – PART II

Beginning in 1990, Armstrong made his good idea happen, calling it Rocky Mountain Railtours. Today, Armstrong's company offers 45 unique Canadian vacation packages and four distinctive rail routes, all of them rich in history and natural wonders, through British Columbia and Alberta. Their world-renowned, custom-built trains travel by daylight through the wild beauty of Canada's West and, over the past 20 years, Rocky Mountaineer has grown to become the largest privately owned passenger rail service in North America (they've served over a million customers). Most importantly, the train's luxurious cars are filled with relaxed vacationers from around the world, just as Peter Armstrong dreamed would someday happen.

In 2010, Rocky Mountaineer received its fifth World Travel Award for "World's Leading Travel Experience by Train" and was acknowledged for the first time as the "World's Leading Luxury Travel Product of the Year." Rocky Mountaineer has also been recognized by *National Geographic* as one of the "World's Greatest Trips" and by the Society of American Travel Writers as "The Best Train Experience in the World." The train has even been featured on the popular reality TV show, *The Bachelorette* and included in the BBC program *50 Thing to Do Before You Die.*

Imagine, all of this from one little idea and one person's determination to make it happen.

How many great ideas are you sitting on?

Keep in mind you don't have to be an expert to get your idea on track. Once he had secured the railway rights, Peter Armstrong lost no time bringing in former railway executives and tourism experts who could provide the experience and knowledge his new venture required.

— *Who Dares Wins*

DON'T WAIT UNTIL SOMEONE ELSE
BEATS YOU TO IT. GET YOUR
IDEA ON TRACK AND MAKE IT HAPPEN!

A SHIFT IN PERSPECTIVE

Henry Ford once said, "If you think you can, you are right. If you think you can't, you are also right." In other words, if you believe the world is conspiring to make all of your dreams come true, you are right. But if you think the universe is conspiring against you, then you're right on that count too.

Belief is a powerful thing.

For many years, I have emceed the annual Variety Telethon. During that time, I have met many individuals faced with the most incredible personal obstacles. Watching them struggle, it would be easy to believe the world is a harsh, unfair place. However, a shift in perspective allows me to see all of these incredible people for what they truly are: an inspiration to those of us who have been given the gift of a much easier life. They also offer a reminder — there but for the grace of God, go I — that we shouldn't take what we have for granted. An accident or illness could change our lives in a second.

When we shift our perspective, we discover that the world is indeed conspiring to help us take action and make the most of our lives, not to waste what we have been given. Imagine if you viewed a homeless person in a different way (perhaps with love and compassion). Have you ever considered the possibility that a homeless person could very well have a divine mission to show you just how fortunate you really are?

Think about it.

— *The Power of a Dream*

TODAY, CONSIDER HOW LUCKY
YOU ARE TO HAVE THE ADVANTAGES THAT
YOU HAVE — NOW, WHAT
ARE YOU GOING TO DO ABOUT IT?

ALWAYS HAVE SOMETHING TO WORK TOWARDS

E ven if your life isn't perfect, you can always build towards a goal you're passionate about. If you aren't building towards something, you're probably stagnating and, when that happens, you can start to feel like a victim trapped by your own life. The best way to reverse this is to work towards a goal.

We can't control everything about our lives, but working towards a goal gives us something positive to focus on and lays the foundation for future success. No matter what your passion is, get out there and start doing something. As Lao Tzu said, even a journey of a thousand miles begins with a single step.

Decide what you want in life and then make a conscious choice to do what it takes to get there.

Today, choose one thing that you've always wanted to do (it might be something from your bucket list, like skydiving or climbing a mountain; it could be learning a new skill or upgrading your education; or perhaps it involves giving back to the community through volunteer work or social activism). Whatever your goal is, put it in writing and then come up with one tangible step that you can take right now to set you on your way.

Having a sense of purpose and an exciting goal to work towards makes everything you do feel more meaningful.

— 97 Tips on How to Do Business in Tough Times

TAKE THE FIRST STEP
ON A NEW JOURNEY TODAY.

JUNE

June 1

OCKHAM'S RAZOR – PART I

When I was growing up, life in London, England, was tough for my mother and father — as it was for millions of people following the war. We had no phone, no television, no central heating and very few "mod cons" as they liked to call modern conveniences. Money, careers and a future were very foreign concepts to my parents. In those difficult times, Sunday dinners were always at my grandmother's house, where one of her boarders was her brother Ernie Hammond.

Lucky for us, uncle Ernie worked as a butcher in Greenford High Street and at the end of each week he would bring home one of the unsold roasts for Sunday dinner. In those times of rationing, it was often the only meat we had all week — and I always knew that Monday night's meal would be shepherd's pie, made with the leftover meat from Sunday dinner.

It was 1953-54 and the future looked bleak. My father decided that he had had enough of scrimping and no saving. He and his family needed to emigrate somewhere to seek out a life and a country that, given enough hard work, commitment and dedication, would provide a brighter future. He thought of all the places he had visited in his younger years.

You see, when my father was 16 he ran away to sea, boarding a small freighter in Barry, South Wales. The name of the ship was *Vancouver City*. In his time as a sailor, he circumnavigated the globe seven times and visited Vancouver, B.C., four times. So it was that when my mother asked where we should go, he was quick to answer, "Of all the ports I ever visited, Vancouver was the prettiest and my very first ship was named after that city, so let's go there." And that was it . . .

OCKHAM'S RAZOR – PART II

It's funny how some of life's biggest problems can be solved by a decision that's made in a heartbeat. I'm not sure my father had heard of William of Ockham, a British-born medieval philosopher who practiced a method of problem-solving that has become known as "Ockham's Razor," but he applied the principle perfectly.

Ockham said, "The simplest and most direct resolution requiring the fewest number of steps is usually the correct solution to any problem."

As humans, we often make the mistake of overcomplicating both our problems and our goals. What Ockham realized is that the more complicated something is (even if it is a good idea), the less likely it is to ever be implemented. Therefore, if you have a problem and are torn between two different solutions that in all likelihood will be equally effective if fully implemented, by applying Ockham's Razor, you will naturally choose the solution that is less complicated.

Ockham also said, "Plurality should not be posited without necessity." Many of you might know this more commonly as the KISS principle, an acronym for "Keep It Simple Stupid."

The acronym was first coined by Kelly Johnson, a lead engineer with Lockheed who worked on the Lockheed U-2 and SR-71 Blackbird spy planes among many other aircraft.

As the story goes, Johnson once handed a team of design engineers a handful of tools with the challenge that the jet aircraft they were designing must be repairable by an average mechanic in the field under combat conditions with only those tools. Hence, the "stupid" refers to the relationship between the way things break and the resources available to fix them.

— *Make Your Life a Masterpiece*

CHALLENGE YOURSELF TO "KEEP IT SIMPLE"
AND CHOOSE THE SIMPLEST,
MOST PRACTICAL ROUTE TO SOLVING
PROBLEMS/ACHIEVING GOALS.

IT'S TIME FOR ACTION

Napoleon Hill once said, "The biggest enemy to the success of a business person is procrastination."

So, what's stopping you? It's time to stop waiting and start living.

Consider these statistics:

1. 81 per cent of people believe they have a "book" in them.

2. 700 million adults worldwide want to move to another country.

3. 85 per cent of people are less than extremely satisfied with their current jobs.

4. Six in 10 people want to lose weight.

5. People turning 50 today still have half of their adult lives ahead of them.

6. The average Canadian adult watches 1,500 hours of television a year; that works out to 25 per cent of their waking hours.

7. Mark Twain often said, "I can live for two months on a good compliment."

8. Four most important words in management: "What do you think?"

9. 80 per cent of success is showing up.

10. Banging your head against a wall uses 150 calories an hour, proving there are far better ways to spend your time and your energy.

— Insight 2011

SPEAKER/ENTERTAINER GIO LIVERA
ONCE SAID, "NO CHANGE . . . NO CHANGE."
HE WAS RIGHT, IF WE DON'T TAKE
ACTION, NOTHING EVER CHANGES.
IT'S TIME FOR ACTION!

PLAIN GOLD BAND

Till death do us part. It's a phrase of enormous finality, but if you are married, you probably included it as one of the promises you made on your wedding day. To have and to hold, in sickness and in health . . . till death do us part. Forever.

Sometimes it works.

My wife Kay and I will celebrate our 44th anniversary in 2011. I was virtually flat broke when we were married in England. Eight pounds was all I had to buy Kay's wedding ring, not a lot of money even back then. But the ring was bright, shiny and made of gold.

When the minister said: "You may put the ring on Kay's finger," it didn't slip on all that easily. But it did go on and it looked quite marvellous. We smiled at each other and knew that the ring was indeed a shining symbol of a life together, beginning that very moment.

There have been some exceptional moments in our marriage and not surprisingly, more than a few ups and downs that tested the sincerity of our promises. But till death do us part always meant exactly that for Kay and me.

Over the years, I believe that inexpensive wedding ring has become my wife's most cherished possession. It has some nicks and scratches, the kind of wear that time gives to most everything. On the surface, the lustre of the metal is less than it was on the day we were married. But the inside of the ring has grown smooth, as has our marriage. In fact, Kay says the ring fits better today than it did on our wedding day. Like our relationship, it has moulded itself into something closer, finer and more precious.

— How to Soar With the Eagles

SHARED EXPERIENCES AND
MEMORIES ARE THE REAL
GOLD IN ANY RELATIONSHIP.

SAY MY NAME

I have great admiration for people who can easily remember names. I'm not one of them; I have to really work at it. As I grow older and lose brain cells, it gets ever more difficult to remember the simplest things — let alone the names of the hundreds of people who come and go in my busy life.

I'm sure that from time to time, you've had long conversations with someone you met a week ago and who now is nothing more than a vaguely familiar face.

"So, how did it work out?"

"Er . . . as well as could be expected."

"No surprises?"

"Er . . . Not so far."

And you make an excuse and beat a nervous, frustrated retreat, racking your brain to remember who this person is.

I would never deny that it is wonderful to be called by my name. "Hello again, Mr. Legge, your table is ready." "Good morning, Mr. Legge, nice to have you with us on British Airways." Having someone use our name makes us feel important.

There are many tricks to remembering names. Some people create rhyming couplets: Lou-blue, Jean-keen, while others use repetition or associate the person's name with a certain characteristic. Clever maître d's check reservation books and credit cards to remember names. The truly desperate write things down. I think that most of the time this works very well. Nothing like a small cheat sheet as you head out into the cold, cruel world. In the end, it doesn't matter how you do it. People won't care what trick you used to remember their name, they'll simply be impressed that you did.

— *You Can If You Believe You Can*

THE WAY YOU ASSOCIATE AND REMEMBER NAMES
IS BASED ON YOUR LEARNING STYLE. TAKE THE TIME
TO DISCOVER WHAT WORKS BEST FOR YOU.

NO ONE DREAMS OF MAKING IT SMALL

While on a trip to New York, an ad in *New York Magazine* caught my attention. It simply said, "No one dreams of making it small."

My Speakers Roundtable colleague Nido Qubein says if you are going to think, think big.

In 1991, I had the unique pleasure of being on the same program as Og Mandino for a sold-out show at Vancouver's Orpheum Theatre. I was his warm-up act. One of the things he said that stuck with me is, "I am here for a purpose and that purpose is to grow into a mountain, not to shrink to a grain of sand. Henceforth, I will apply all my efforts to become the highest mountain of all and I will strain my potential until it cries for mercy."

When I bought my first magazine *TV Week* more than 35 years ago, I wanted to make it big. I invested everything I had and mortgaged my house. I risked it all. If I succeeded, the money would be repaid out of the profits of the company. If I failed, I would lose my business and my home. I couldn't fail.

As determined as I was, my competition didn't take me seriously. For the first 10 years I was in business, *TV Guide*'s head guy in Toronto would regularly call the Vancouver office and ask, "How long will this guy be around?" Each time they'd tell him, "Don't worry, it won't be long now." He kept calling. Thirty years later, they ended up going out of business and we bought their local operation.

— *The Power to Soar Higher*

No matter how big you get
or how secure your market appears
to be, never underestimate
your competition. Chances are they're
hungrier than you and they
dream big too.

THE ART OF NEGOTIATION – PART I

"In business, you don't get what you deserve. You get what you negotiate." — Chester Karrass

Whether or not it is an integral part of your job, being able to successfully negotiate with others is an important skill in life. After all, we all face situations where we must reach agreements with others and solve problems that involve people with different, and sometimes conflicting, needs. Even if we don't call it by its name, negotiation is something that takes place daily in our lives — with our spouse and children, friends, colleagues, customers — the list is virtually endless.

Although we all want to win, negotiation isn't just about getting your own way or giving in. In fact, those are the results when people fail to negotiate. If you won't, or can't, negotiate, then either you or the people around you are likely to end up feeling frustrated and resentful. And while someone may wind up with the upper hand, it will be at the cost of a good working relationship.

What successful negotiation is really about is allowing both sides to reach a good outcome, or at least one that they feel they have contributed to and can live with. For those who are new to negotiation, one of the most important factors to keep in mind is that not everyone wants the same thing out of a deal. A successful negotiator finds out what the needs of the other party are and tries to meet them without losing sight of his own goals.

Most people hesitate to negotiate because they lack confidence in their own skills. Over the next four days, we'll look at the art of negotiation and some important points to keep in mind when you enter into the negotiation process.

THE ART OF NEGOTIATION – PART II

All skilled negotiators have certain characteristics in common. First of all, they know what they want out of the deal before entering into negotiations. They are also perceptive and look for opportunities to create a win-win situation. In addition, they are good listeners (open to hearing what the other side is looking for and trying to accommodate it). They identify key issues quickly, are patient, use creativity and seek common ground. Most of all, they have empathy for others and therefore are interested in making sure that everyone's needs are considered.

Here are some steps to a successful negotiation:

Take time to prepare
This is the most important step in many negotiations. You want to be as thoroughly informed as possible about the value of items you are negotiating — both in terms of their general value and what they are worth to the other side. The party with the most information usually does better in a negotiation.

Know your bottom line
In most negotiations, there is a point beyond which you do not want to go (i.e., when you will walk away and consider other alternatives). Decide in advance (but don't disclose) what really matters to you and what doesn't matter so much. That way, you'll know where you're willing to compromise and where you're not. You should always be aware that this may change with more information and new ideas.

Choose to meet halfway
Set out to reach a win-win situation. Both sides should leave the negotiation feeling they've come away with something. When there is mutual benefit, both parties are more likely to follow through with their commitments and feel that they have an investment in the situation.

> *"The most important trip you may take in life
> is meeting people halfway."* — Henry Boyle

THE ART OF NEGOTIATION – PART III

Build respect

When the other side feels that you have respect for them, defensiveness is reduced and sharing of useful information can take place — which in turn can lead to an agreement. Alternatively, when people feel disrespected, they become more rigid and are likely to withhold important information. Always begin by saying something positive and appreciative to the person you're negotiating with. For instance, "I've noticed how hard you've been working on this deal," or "You really did a great job on that report outlining the alternatives to the proposal." It will increase the goodwill on both sides. If the other party is angry or hostile, refrain from getting drawn into a confrontation. Stay calm and remain open to communication and sooner or later they'll calm down and join you in the negotiation.

"Never cut what you can untie." — Joseph Joubert

Don't attribute your motives to other people

It is not unusual to go into a negotiation and assume that any other intelligent person is going to think and feel the same way we do. Wrong. In many cases, people are strongly influenced by emotional factors that we have no knowledge of; that is why an important part of negotiating is listening to find out what the other party really wants.

Ask questions

Before stating a position or making proposals, it is very helpful to inquire about the other side's interests and concerns. This will help you understand what is important to them and may provide new ideas for mutual benefit. As the negotiation progresses, ask clarifying questions to really understand the other side's concerns and to determine their approach — whether it be win-lose or win-win, to enable you to make more realistic proposals.

THE ART OF NEGOTIATION — PART IV

"If you come to a negotiation table
saying you have the final truth, that you know
nothing but the truth and that is final,
you will get nothing." — Harri Holkeri

Listen
And keep listening. It's vital to understand what the other party is truly saying and their point of view. Listening shows respect and good intentions in addition to letting the other party know that you are concerned about their needs as well as your own.

Employ cautious disclosure
It is fully appropriate and wise to start a negotiation without disclosing all of your information and your "bottom line." Give yourself room to maneuver. Make sure you have something to offer the other party, as well as something you want. If the other side is using a win-lose approach and you disclose too much too soon, you will lose all of your bargaining power. If the other side is using a win-win approach, then you can work together to explore all of the possible solutions as trust builds between the two parties and each discloses more information.

Make a proposal
It is a good bargaining strategy to ask for more at the start of a negotiation than you expect to receive in the final agreement. By proposing your ideal settlement, it lets the other side understand your needs and allows you to show good faith later on by revising your offer after hearing their response. It helps to make a new proposal, rather than to criticize the one the other side has offered to you. This is also a good point to try brainstorming a list of options together (without being critical of any of the options proposed) to see if an alternative agreement may emerge that no one had thought of before and which everyone can live with.

THE ART OF NEGOTIATION – PART V

*"During a negotiation, it would be wise not to take anything personally.
If you leave personalities out of it, you will be able to see opportunities
more objectively."* — Brian Koslow

Develop trust

People tend to be more generous towards those they like and trust. An attitude of friendliness and openness generally is more persuasive than one of deception and manipulation. Being honest about the information you provide and showing interest in the other side's concerns can help.

Back up your position

If necessary, let the other side know in detail how strong your point of view is — by showing them financial information, legal precedents or other strong data that supports your position. If you believe the other party's assumptions are based on false information, you will need to re-educate them in a tactful manner. Be pleasant and persistent, but not demanding.

Keep your options open

If you don't get what you want, resist the impulse to insult the other person or storm out. End the negotiation politely and with a smile. That way you can always try again later.

*"He who has learned to disagree without being disagreeable
has discovered the most valuable secret of a diplomat."*
— Robert Estabrook

Write it down

Many potentially great agreements fall apart because everyone's memory of them is different. You should write down the details so that both parties understand the exact terms — who has agreed to do what, when and where.
— *Make Your Life a Masterpiece*

DEVELOP CONFIDENCE IN YOUR SKILLS BY NEGOTIATING MORE
FREQUENTLY, BOTH IN YOUR BUSINESS AND AS A CONSUMER.

ALWAYS LEAVE THEM LAUGHING

Humour is a powerful language, the power being that it can open us up to new ways of thinking and doing — making it a valuable tool for any leader.

When my friend Carole Taylor became chair of The Vancouver Board of Trade the year before I was to serve a term as chair myself, she arrived at the AGM wearing a beautiful red suit with matching red shoes. And when it was time for her to address the members, she delivered a moving and passionate speech on her vision as chair. After the AGM, Board of Trade governor Bob Kadlec sought me out and said to me, "Pete, did you see that? Carole spoke flawlessly for 20 minutes without using a single page of notes. You've got big shoes to fill next year."

A year later, as it approached the time for me to take over as chair, I called Carole and asked her if she would do me the great favour of wearing the same red suit and shoes to my inauguration. She graciously agreed.

During my speech, I related the story of the previous year and Bob's comment to me. When I got to the point of Bob telling me I had big shoes to fill, I produced my own size 10 loafers painted red. Now I did this for two important reasons. The first was to cleverly pay tribute to the outstanding job Carole had performed as chair. The second was to make the audience laugh and get them on my side, while relieving some of the tension I felt in taking on the great responsibility of being chair of such a high-profile organization.

— *The Runway of Life*

HUMOUR IS A GREAT WAY
TO BREAK THE ICE AND BUILD
BRIDGES BETWEEN PEOPLE.

ARE YOU A BOUNCE-BACK PERSON?

In 2011, the National Oceanic and Atmospheric Administration (NOAA) announced that they expected 12 to 18 named storms in the coming hurricane season, of which six to 10 would become hurricanes and three to six would become major hurricanes.

These storms, as we have read in the news, can be devastating and sometimes, even deadly.

Halfway through 2011, the Canadian business climate was still not 100 per cent, but no matter where we are in any economic storm, we can still learn plenty from the palm tree about how to survive a storm and bounce back.

Palm trees are designed to bend, but not break, in high winds and storms. They can bend over until their top touches the ground and still not break. Even in a hurricane when you think they would break in two, the very resilient palm tree bounces back. No matter how strong the gusts or how hard the rain drives and lashes at it, it's only a matter of time before the palm tree is upright again.

Biologists say that in a hurricane, when a palm tree is bent over, its root system is actually strengthened by the stress and given new opportunities to grow.

So, learn to bend with the hard times, become stronger through adversity and grow.

Psalm 92:12 says:

"The righteous man will flourish like the palm tree."

Pretty good advice!

— Insight 2011

WHATEVER STORMS COME
YOUR WAY, TRY TO REMAIN FLEXIBLE
AND BEND WITH THE WIND.

ENTHUSIASM WILL GET YOU EVERYWHERE

The word enthusiasm comes from the Greek word *entheos*, which means "God within." In most cases, the happiest and most interesting people are those who have found the secret of maintaining their enthusiasm. What's more, everyone likes to be around people who are enthusiastic about life because that positive charge tends to jump from one person to the next and, pretty soon, everyone is charged up and feeling excited.

My dad taught me the power of enthusiasm. He used to say, "I have never met an enthusiastic failure." In my experience, there are two keys to enthusiasm. The first comes from learning and the second comes from accomplishment. Learning new things keeps our interest and enthusiasm high, it also opens us up to new opportunities as we increase our skills and expand our knowledge. The second key ties into this nicely, as the sense of accomplishment we feel when we master a new skill further buoys our enthusiasm and confidence.

Motivational guru Earl Nightingale said that the saddest days of our lives are those days in which we can find nothing to be enthusiastic about. I have to agree with him, that's why I always like to share insights and inspiring stories with as many people as possible. We all deserve to be charged up with enthusiasm every day.

The most enthusiastic people are on top of life regardless of the circumstances or situations that come their way. As the old saying goes, if life gives them lemons, they simply make lemonade.

— *Who Dares Wins*

TODAY, SHOW OFF YOUR CONFIDENT,
ENTHUSIASTIC APPROACH TO LIFE; YOU'LL BE
SURPRISED WHERE IT CAN TAKE YOU.

FIVE DOLLARS AND TWO HOURS

*"The cover-your-butt mentality of the workplace will get you only so far.
The follow-your-gut mentality of the entrepreneur has the potential
to take you anywhere you want to go or run you right out of business —
but it's a whole lot more fun, don't you think?"* — Bill Rancic

I f you were given five dollars and two hours to "make as much money as possible," what would you do? This is the task that Tina Seelig, executive director for the Stanford Technology Ventures Program, sets for her entrepreneurial classes.

Working in groups, the students are given several days to devise their plans (although they have no idea how much money they will get). Then they are given an envelope that contains their seed capital. Once they open the envelope, they have just two hours to execute their plan.

At this point, the majority of students get caught up worrying over the fact that they *only* have five dollars of capital and limited time to launch their ideas. However, the teams that consistently make the most money ignore the fact that they are given five dollars. They move forward with the ideas they brainstormed *before* they knew how much capital they were given. In many cases, they come up with ideas that require no cash at all.

The teams that make the most money are those that realize they can't be bound by limitations. An entrepreneur's world is filled with opportunities, and successful entrepreneurs learn to recognize them while ignoring anything that might hold them back.

— Insight 2011

"NOBODY TALKS ABOUT ENTREPRENEURSHIP AS SURVIVAL, BUT THAT'S EXACTLY WHAT IT IS AND WHAT NURTURES CREATIVE THINKING . . . " — Anita Roddick

LIFE IS ABOUT WORKING WITH WHAT YOU'VE GOT, NOT WHAT YOU WISH YOU HAD.

GO FISH

A few years ago, I was having dinner with a friend of mine, Tony Galasso, president of Quebecor World Canada. He was visiting Vancouver with his wife and their seven-year-old daughter, staying at the Pacific Palisades Hotel.

When you stay at the Pacific Palisades and have a child with you, the hotel staff bring a pet goldfish to the room. It's a great idea and Tony's daughter loved the fish. However, when Tony leaned over to take a closer look at his daughter's new pet, he realized it was clearly bloated and dying.

Knowing the last thing he wanted his daughter to see when they came back from dinner was a dead fish, Tony called the front desk and explained the situation. Sympathizing with his concern for his daughter's feelings, the hotel clerk instructed Tony to tell his daughter that the goldfish was pregnant before they headed out for dinner — and she would take care of the rest.

Take care of it she did. When the family returned from dinner, sitting on the table was a fishbowl exactly like the one that had been delivered earlier, except now there was both a big fish and a little fish swimming happily around inside.

The daughter was thrilled.

"Look, daddy," she exclaimed. "You were right, the fish had a baby while we were at dinner."

Tony was duly impressed and immensely grateful for the sensitivity of the clerk who went out of her way to ensure that his family had a happy memory of their visit to Vancouver. He has also, I am sure, shared this story with many friends and colleagues and that's the kind of positive publicity that any business would love.

— *The Power of Tact*

EVERY DAY BRINGS NEW OPPORTUNITIES
TO GO OUT OF OUR WAY FOR OTHERS.

IT'S IN THE STARS

"Efficiency is doing things right. Effectiveness is doing
the right things. Success is doing the right
things right, right now." — Nisandeh Neta

When we were just starting out with *TV Week* magazine, we bought all of our editorial content from the King Syndicate in New York. One day the editor came to me and said, "I've got a big problem. We go to press at noon on Thursday and the horoscope column hasn't come in. What do I do?"

As is often the case at moments like this one, the first thought that popped into my head was something that my dad always told me, "Be resourceful, be creative and do what is required." So I said to the editor, "Go into your office and write your own."

"What exactly do you mean by that?" she asked me.

"Well," I said, "it seems to me that our readers are expecting a horoscope in their issue of *TV Week* and many of them will be disappointed if they don't find one. So I am asking you to make it up. Just make sure that everyone has a good week next week."

So she did and I believe that thousands of our readers had the best week of the year even though they had no idea where it came from.

While this may be an amusing story, I think it also has a very serious point. We should be very discerning about what we allow to influence our lives if we are to create our masterpiece.

— *Make Your Life a Masterpiece*

BE RESOURCEFUL,
BE CREATIVE AND DO
WHAT IS REQUIRED.

NEVER GIVE IN

I am a huge admirer of Sir Winston Churchill. While browsing through a bookstore in New York a few years ago, I found a leather-bound first edition of *Never Give In* signed by Sir Winston's grandson. The book was number 1222 of 1225 — almost the last copy.

This precious book has the best of Winston Churchill's speeches — he was nicknamed The Bulldog for his determination, commitment and tenacity — including his immortal speech delivered on June 18, 1940, before a packed House of Commons in which Churchill wanted to quell suggestions that Britain might soon succumb to the German onslaught as France had.

Many consider this speech to be one of his finest and it certainly demonstrated Churchill's unwavering commitment to defending England come hell or high water. On the day before that speech Churchill had said, "The news from France is very bad. The gallant French people have fallen into the terrible misfortune." However, the Germans had underestimated the tenacity of the newly elected prime minister. The very next day he delivered this remarkable speech:

"The whole fury and might of the enemy must very soon be turned on us. Hitler knows that he will have to break us in this island, or lose the war. If we can stand up to him, all Europe may be freed . . . But if we fail, then the whole world . . . will sink into the abyss of a new dark age made more sinister and perhaps more prolonged by the light of perverted science. Let us therefore brace ourselves to our duty and so bear ourselves that if the British Empire and Commonwealth lasts for a thousand years, men will still say, 'This is their finest hour.'"

— *The Runway of Life*

IT IS NOT THE EASY THINGS
IN LIFE THAT REVEAL OUR CHARACTER.
NEVER GIVE IN.

LIFT UP THE ONES YOU LOVE

*"If you want to lift
yourself up, lift up someone else."*
— Booker T. Washington

Early in my career, I did a lot of gigs as a stand-up comedian. At that time, wife jokes were standard fare on the comedy circuit and so invariably, I would tell jokes about my wife in my routine. For the most part, they were the kind of one-liners that often make the rounds as "dumb blonde" jokes aimed at getting a cheap laugh. For example, "I told my wife I was going to have an affair and she asked me who would be doing the catering."

Kay never said anything to me about the content of my routine and I didn't really think anything of the jokes or relate it to the relationship I have with my wife until one day when I was asked to entertain at a Young Life retreat. Following my performance, Jack Mortensen, the director of Young Life in Calgary, took me aside and told me how offensive these jokes must be to Kay and the effect that they were likely having on her self-esteem. "Whether she says anything or not, you can be sure she is dying inside every time you speak," he said.

Right then and there, I decided I would never again make fun of Kay and that whenever I did speak about her in front of an audience, I would always lift her up and talk about how proud I am to be her husband. I am grateful to Jack Mortensen for teaching me an important lesson. It is one that I have carried through more than 40 years of marriage to a wonderful woman.

— *The Power to Soar Higher*

REMEMBER TO LIFT UP
THE PEOPLE YOU LOVE.

TEEING UP FOR LIFE

It took me a long time to get the hang of golf. For years, golfing friends and colleagues would tell me, "There's nothing more relaxing than a game of golf."

And I would tell them in response, "There's nothing more frustrating, intimidating and demeaning."

For many, golf relieves stress. That satisfying click as the club connects and the ball flies off into the stratosphere; to see the ball leap from the sand and bite the green six inches or less from the pin; to putt and watch the ball roll with seeming confidence to a rattling end in the cup — all very satisfying moments . . . unless you don't know how to make those moments happen. In which case, golf can be a hapless misadventure filled with hooks, slices, whiffs, chops, flying divots, sand in your shoes and atrocious language.

Red Poling, former CEO and chairman of the Ford Motor Company and an accomplished golfer, often said that his office game paralleled his golf game. According to Red, the three most important things in business and in golf are consistency, dependability and predictability.

"If my game is good, it's because I'm consistent in my swing. I don't need a big wide fairway," explains Red, who believes in practicing fundamentals and focusing on whatever is going to win you the game. "Everyone likes to hit a drive the farthest, but you actually use a driver less than a putter."

Finally, he stresses the importance of giving full attention to the task at hand. "As you walk up to the next shot, you're not looking at the beautiful scenery around you. You're watching the terrain, noticing the impact of the wind, looking at the green, checking the hazards and planning your next shot."

— How to Soar With the Eagles

HOW'S YOUR GAME?

THE 250 MULTIPLIER EFFECT

*"The richest people in the world
look for and build networks. Everyone else looks
for work."* — Robert Kiyosaki

The average number of people at a wedding is about 250. The average number of people at a funeral is about 250. Restaurants average about 250 seats. A box of business cards holds about 250 cards.

So if you think about it, most people know about 250 other people.

That means every time you make a good impression or cultivate a relationship with one person, you have actually expanded your influence by 250 people. If you consider that this applies to every single person you meet, the multiplier effect for increasing your network is exponential.

Think about this the next time you find yourself sitting or standing next to a stranger with a few minutes to spare (whether it is in a business setting, at your child's soccer practice, standing in line at the supermarket or at a social function). Rather than checking email on your phone or staring at the wall in an uncomfortable silence, strike up a conversation and get to know something about them, then, before you leave, make sure you give them one of your business cards. You never know who they might know or when someone might need what you have to offer (and every one of those people also has a network of 250 people).

MAKE A POINT TO INTRODUCE
YOURSELF TO AT LEAST ONE NEW PERSON
EVERY DAY AND SEE THE POSITIVE
EFFECT IT HAS ON BOTH YOUR NETWORK AND
YOUR BUSINESS PROSPECTS.

CRITICISM – PART I

Respect and ridicule don't go together. Offering criticism should be an act of respect: communication with the intention of helping someone do better work, or understand their work better. If you find yourself making remarks that are snide or sarcastic, the intention of being helpful is unlikely to be served. Although it is entirely possible to offer criticism, commentary and advice without it becoming a negative interaction, it is something that requires a great deal of diplomacy so as not to damage relationships.

There's no doubt that criticism is easy to give but hard to take. Remember this the next time that you plan to dish some out and think about whether the goal you wish to accomplish couldn't be achieved just as easily by focusing on the positive.

Here is a story on the subject that you might enjoy.

A wise old gentleman retired and bought a modest home near a junior high school. He spent the first few weeks of his retirement in peace and contentment . . . and then a new school year began. The very next afternoon three young boys, full of youthful after-school enthusiasm, came down his street beating merrily on every trash can they encountered. The crashing percussion continued day after day until finally the elderly man decided it was time to take some action.

The next afternoon, he walked out to meet the young percussionists as they banged their way down the street. Stopping them, he said, "You kids are a lot of fun. I like to see you express your exuberance like that; I used to do the same thing when I was your age. Will you do me a favour? I'll give you each a dollar if you'll promise to come around every day and do your thing."

CRITICISM – PART II

The kids were elated by the prospect of getting money to beat on the garbage cans and continued to do a bang-up job. However, after a few more days, the old-timer greeted the kids again, but this time he had a sad smile on his face. "The recession's really putting a big dent in my income," he told them. "From now on, I'll only be able to pay you 50 cents to beat on the cans." The noisemakers were obviously displeased, but they accepted his offer and continued their afternoon ruckus.

A few days later, the wily retiree approached them yet again as they drummed their way down the street. "Look," he said. "I haven't received my Social Security cheque yet, so I'm not going to be able to give you more than 25 cents from now on. Will that be okay?"

"A lousy quarter?" the drum leader exclaimed. "If you think we're going to waste our time beating these cans around for a quarter, you're nuts! No way, mister. We quit!"

From then on, the old man enjoyed his retirement in peace.

In my personal experience of more than 35 years in business, when you criticize, people build up resistance and resentment. On the other hand, when you encourage people and build them up, you could literally ask them to perform the impossible and they will rise to the challenge and do all that they can not to let you down.

— *Make Your Life a Masterpiece*

"ANY FOOL CAN CRITICIZE, CONDEMN AND COMPLAIN BUT IT TAKES CHARACTER AND SELF-CONTROL TO BE UNDERSTANDING AND FORGIVING." — Dale Carnegie

WHEN WE JUDGE OR CRITICIZE ANOTHER PERSON, IT SAYS NOTHING ABOUT THAT PERSON; IT MERELY SAYS SOMETHING ABOUT OUR OWN NEED TO BE CRITICAL.

DON'T KNOW NOTHIN 'BOUT HISTORY

We all need a laugh now and then. Here are some answers given by sixth-graders on their history tests.

1. Ancient Egypt was inhabited by mummies and they all wrote in hydraulics. They lived in the Sarah Dessert. The climate of the Sarah is such that the inhabitants have to live elsewhere.

2. Solomom had three hundred wives and 700 porcupines.

3. Socrates was a famous Greek teacher who went around giving people advice. They killed him. Socrates died from an overdose of wedlock. After his death, his career suffered a dramatic decline.

5. In the Olympic Games, Greeks ran races, jumped, hurled biscuits and threw the java.

6. Joan of Arc was burnt to a steak and was canonized by Bernard Shaw.

7. Gutenberg invented removable type and the Bible. Another important invention was the circulation of blood. Sir Francis Drake circumsized the world with a 100-foot clipper.

8. The greatest writer of the Renaissance was William Shakespeare. He was born in the year 1564, supposedly on his birthday. He never made much money and is famous only for his plays. He wrote tragedies, comedies and hysterectomies, all in Islamic pentameter.

8. Writing in the same time as Shakespeare was Miguel Cervantes. He wrote Donkey Hote. The next great author was John Milton. Milton wrote *Paradise Lost*. Then his wife died and he wrote *Paradise Regained*.

9. Johann Bach wrote a great many musical compositions and had a large number of children. In between he practiced on an old spinster which he kept up in his attic. Bach died from 1750 to the present. Bach was the most famous composer in the world and so was Handel. Handel was half German, half Italian and half English. He was very large.

— *Make Your Life a Masterpiece*

USE THE DIFFICULTY

When legendary actor Michael Caine was asked what fatherly advice he had for his children, he relayed the story of a direction he had been given by a theatre producer early in his career. The situation in question took place when Caine was rehearsing with other actors and found himself waiting behind a door for his cue to come onstage during a scene in which a couple were having an argument.

As the scene progressed, the actors started throwing furniture around and a chair became lodged in front of the door. When Caine was cued, he found that he couldn't open the door to make his entrance.

"I can't get in!" he shouted, breaking character. "The chair's in the way."

Without hesitation, the producer turned to Caine and told him, "Use the difficulty."

Confused, Caine asked the producer just what he meant.

"Well," the producer explained, "If it's a drama, pick the chair up and smash it. If it's a comedy, fall over it."

Caine said the point was not lost on him and the idea stuck in his mind.

"I taught it to my children," he revealed. "That with any situation in life that's negative, there is something positive you can do with it."

What obstacles and difficulties do you face as you work to accomplish your goals? Do you have negative self-talk that keeps you from moving forward? Ask yourself, is there a way to use the difficulties I am currently facing?

— Make Your Life a Masterpiece

IN THE SAME WAY THAT A ROCK CLIMBER
USES AN OUTCROPPING OR LEDGE
THAT APPEARS IN THEIR PATH TO GET A FOOTHOLD
TO PROPEL THEM ONWARD AND UPWARD,
WE MUST LOOK FOR WAYS TO USE THE DIFFICULTIES
THAT ARISE IN OUR PATH TO ACHIEVE OUR GOALS.

A SIMPLE LIFE – PART I

How do you measure success?

T he answer to that question is different for everyone, or at least I believe it should be. Many people mistakenly measure success according to their income, even though they are not truly happy or satisfied by what they do to earn that income.

Others take a different approach, like the fisherman in the following story:

A businessman was at the pier of a small coastal Mexican village when a small boat docked. Inside the boat were several large yellowfin tuna. The businessman complimented the fisherman on the quality of his fish and asked how long it took to catch them.

"Only a little while," he replied.

So the businessman asked why he didn't stay out longer and catch more fish. The fisherman said he had enough to support his family's needs. The businessman then asked, "But what do you do with the rest of your time?"

"I sleep late, play with my children, take a siesta with my wife Maria, stroll into the village each evening where I sip wine and play guitar with my amigos; I have a full and busy life."

The businessman scoffed, "I'm a Harvard MBA, I could help you. You should spend more time fishing so you can buy a bigger boat and then several boats; eventually you would have a fleet of fishing boats. Instead of selling your catch to a middleman, you would sell directly to the processor and eventually open your own cannery. You would control the product, processing and distribution. You would need to leave this small village and move to Mexico City, then L.A. and eventually New York to run your expanding enterprise."

"But señor, how long will it take?" the fisherman asked.

"Fifteen to 20 years."

"But what then?"

A SIMPLE LIFE – PART II

The businessman laughed, "That's the best part! When the time is right you would sell your company and make millions."

"Millions, señor? Then what?"

"Then you would retire. Move to a small coastal fishing village where you would sleep late, play with the kids, enjoy spending time with your wife, stroll to the village in the evenings where you could sip wine and play your guitar with your friends."

The fisherman, still smiling, looked up and said, "Isn't that what I'm doing right now?"

What does success mean to you?

How do you define happiness?

Do you have a way to measure success in your life?

Whether we want a simple, uncomplicated existence like the fisherman, or to have all the trappings of wealth and power like the businessman, each of us must choose for ourselves how we define and measure success and what kind of life we want to live. However, once you've made that decision, don't waste any time. There's a danger in waiting to live the life that you really want to live. So much can happen along the way.

— Insight 2011

LIVE THE LIFE YOU WANT,
NOT THE ONE THAT OTHERS THINK
YOU SHOULD BE LIVING.

BE THE CHANGE

I remember reading some comments by a young entrepreneur in Toronto some time ago. He was talking about how our success in life is determined more by what we choose to focus our energy on each day than it is by being the first, the best or the brightest. He offered Terry Fox as an example, saying, "A one-legged kid with cancer runs halfway across Canada while millions complain that there's nothing on TV tonight."

Terry Fox died on June 28, 1981 at the age of 22. His life wasn't very long. He was an average young man from an average Canadian family who decided to do something with the time that he had. Today, people all over the world know his name and run each year in honour of his Marathon of Hope to raise money for cancer research.

In our individual lives, we should feel great empowerment in the knowledge that our choices determine what is to be or not. And yet, too often we would rather that someone else initiate, take the risk, do the groundwork and pave the way for us to follow at a comfortable distance. If Terry had waited, all too soon his time would have run out, none of us would now know his name and millions of people with cancer would not have benefited from the research that his Marathon of Hope continues to fund. He is a great reminder that we need to live our lives from the inside out.

— *The Runway of Life*

TODAY, REMEMBER MAHATMA GANDHI'S
POWERFUL WORDS,
"BE THE CHANGE YOU WANT
TO SEE IN THE WORLD."

THE 10,000-HOUR RULE

In 2010, I spoke to undergrads at the Sauder School of Business at UBC. Prior to the event, many students asked what I was planning to speak about. I responded, "What do you want me to speak about?" To a person, they said, "We want to know the secrets of success — the shortcuts to get to the top."

I mentioned this in my opening and then I asked, "What do you think it's going to take to graduate?"

"Be prepared for a lot of missed sleep for studying," I told them. "Lost weekends when you'd rather be out with friends, tons of reading, cramming for papers — and a lot of sacrifices. In other words, it's going to take a lot of hard work."

There are no real secrets to success. In Malcolm Gladwell's book, *Outliers*, he looks at a study done by psychologist K. Anders Ericsson at Berlin's Academy of Music. Ericsson divided the school's violinists into three groups: the stars, the "good" performers and those who were unlikely to play professionally. Each student was asked how much they had practiced since they started playing. By the age of 20, the elite performers had totaled 10,000 hours of practice (most putting in more than 30 hours a week). In contrast, the good students had put in 8,000 hours and the last group had practiced 4,000 hours. Ericsson determined that people at the very top don't just work harder, or even much harder than everyone else, they work much, much, much harder and this is true even for prodigies like Mozart.

Neurologist Daniel Levitin agrees, saying 10,000 hours of practice is required to achieve the level of mastery associated with being a world-class expert in anything: basketball playing, public speaking, computer programming. There are no shortcuts to success.

— Insight 2011

BE WILLING TO PUT
IN THE EFFORT REQUIRED
TO SUCCEED.

ENCOURAGEMENT

*"You need to be aware of what others are doing,
applaud their efforts, acknowledge their
successes and encourage them in their pursuits. When we
all help one another, everybody wins."* — Jim Stovall

In his booklet, simply titled *Tact*, Sir John Lubbock shares the story of the retired head of a well-known company and his experience on his first day of work:

He started as a very young fellow of 16 and on the first day he was set to work sewing buttons on sample cards. The day was hot and sultry. The work of pushing the needle through the stiff cards hurt his fingers. He was to receive $3 a week and by noon he had planned exactly what he was going to do about the half-dollar he was to earn for the first day's work. He wasn't coming back for it. He was through with the job.

But then something happened.

During the afternoon one of the members of the firm came to him and said, "You are sewing those buttons on very nicely, but you aren't doing it in the best way and you're hurting your fingers. Let me show you how to do it."

The result was that instead of quitting his job, the young man went home and, flushed with pleasure, told his mother how a member of the firm had complimented him and then had shown him a better way to do his work. His enthusiasm to learn responded to this first sign of encouragement and in later years he became one of the strongest forces in the development of a great business.

If you want someone to perform better than they are, try using encouragement rather than criticism.

— The Power of Tact

JULY

TWO GLASSES OF RED WINE – PART I

M y good friend and mentor Joe Segal, president of Kingswood Capital Corporation, has always dreamed big and during a career that has spanned nearly seven decades, he's made his dreams come true (if you'd like to know more about Joe's story, pick up my book *The Runway of Life*, which was inspired by Joe's personal philosophy of life). In addition to his willingness to share his time and wisdom with me, the thing that I have always most admired about Joe is that he's a man who has definitely got his priorities straight, as illustrated by the following story, which he shared with me one day over lunch.

A professor stood before his philosophy class with a number of items in front of him. When the class began, wordlessly, he picked up a very large and empty mayonnaise jar and proceeded to fill it with golf balls.

He then asked the students if the jar was full. They agreed that it was.

The professor then picked up a box of pebbles and poured them into the jar. He shook the jar lightly. The pebbles rolled into the open areas between the golf balls. He asked the students again if the jar was full. They agreed it was.

Next, the professor picked up a box of sand and poured it into the jar.

Of course, the sand filled up everything else. He asked once more if the jar was full. The students responded with a unanimous "Yes."

The professor then produced two glasses of red wine from under the table and poured the entire contents into the jar, effectively filling the empty spaces between the grains of sand. The students laughed.

TWO GLASSES OF RED WINE — PART II

"Now," said the professor as the laughter subsided, "I want you to recognize that this jar represents your life. The golf balls are the important things: your family, your children, your health, your friends and your favourite passions; things that if everything else was lost and only they remained, your life would still be full.

"The pebbles are the other things that matter, like your job, your house and your car. The sand is everything else; the small stuff.

"If you put the sand into the jar first," he continued, "There is no room for the pebbles or the golf balls. The same goes for life. If you spend all your time and energy on the small stuff, you will never have room for the things that are important to you.

"Pay attention to the things that are critical to your happiness. Play with your children. Take time to get medical checkups. Take your partner out to dinner. Play another 18 holes of golf. Do one more run down the ski slope. There will always be time to clean the house and fix the faucet. Take care of the golf balls first; the things that really matter. Set your priorities. The rest is just sand."

One of the students then raised her hand and inquired what the wine represented.

The professor smiled. "I'm glad you asked. It just goes to show you that no matter how full your life may seem, there's always room for a couple of glasses of wine with a friend."

— *The Power of a Dream*

EACH OF US NEEDS TO FIGURE OUT
WHAT IS MOST IMPORTANT TO US AND MAKE SURE
THAT WE MAKE SPACE IN OUR LIFE
FOR THAT BEFORE WE FILL IT UP WITH
OTHER, LESS SIGNIFICANT, THINGS.

NOBODY LIKES A WHINER

I f you want to go far in life, to make friends and influence people, here's an important piece of advice: Don't whine.

People don't like whiners. Of course, that doesn't mean that you can't say anything negative or provide constructive criticism when it is needed; just be aware of the difference between that and whining.

Whining is when you continually say negative things about something without any interest or commitment to make what it is you're whining about better. Whining isn't just annoying, it's also debilitating. The more you whine, the more depressed you get and the more helpless you feel about the situation. What's worse is that when you whine, it affects everyone around you. That's why people avoid whiners.

But not whining isn't just about winning friends and influencing people; it's about your own personal happiness. Whining makes you more aware of everything that is wrong in your life without taking into account all that is right. Whining gives away your power to make positive changes. Who wants to do that?

When you make a commitment to make changes rather than complaining about them, you take back control of the situation and your emotions. You also make it easier for others to help you with your problems. For example, instead of whining, "I hate my boss!" turn it around and ask for advice, "How do I deal with a difficult boss?" Suddenly, you've turned pointless self-misery into a conversation focused on finding solutions.

— Insight 2011

DON'T COMPLAIN
UNLESS YOU'RE WILLING
TO MAKE A CHANGE.

IT'S BIGGER THAN YOU AND ME

O ne of the great paradoxes of life is that we are put here in separate compartments and yet we are always part of something much greater than ourselves, something that we affect and something that affects us. Whatever we do or don't do has an impact on the lives of others — that's just the way it is. Therefore, we have a certain responsibility to each other.

Often in our busy lives it can be easy to overlook the fact that we are part of something greater than ourselves — a community, humankind, inhabitants of Planet Earth. Because of our tendency to forget this, we might make decisions in our lives that don't reflect that responsibility. Too many times, we focus just on the immediate gain to ourselves without worrying about the long-term consequences. Other times, we may shy away from serving the greater good because it seems like "hard work." The challenge we all face is to expand our minds beyond the distinction between ourselves and others, so we are aware of how our choices and actions can impact a greater cause.

Happily, contributing to the greater good isn't all about self-sacrifice. For example, if you plant a tree in your community, it will shade and protect you as well as your neighbours. When you serve the greater community, you also serve your greater good. When you know that what you do can serve a greater cause, you are aware of your power and ability to influence and create positive change in the world.

— Insight 2011

COLLECTIVELY, WE CAN DO
GREAT THINGS. EMBRACE YOUR
INTERDEPENDENCY.

IS IT AN OBSTACLE OR AN OPPORTUNITY?

The Royal Palace in Tehran in Iran contains what is undoubtedly one of the most beautiful mosaic masterpieces in the world. The interior walls and ceiling sparkle with multifaceted reflections as if encrusted with thousands upon thousands of diamonds. However, this vision of beauty is not quite as it was intended to be.

When the palace was first designed, the architect in charge specified that huge sheets of mirrors should hang on the walls. Unfortunately, when the first shipment of mirrors arrived from Paris, the builders found that the glass has been shattered in transit. The contractor in charge promptly threw the mirrors into the trash and sadly informed the architect of the problem.

To the surprise of the builders, the architect did not despair at this news. Instead, he ordered that all of the broken pieces be gathered together and brought to him. The architect then proceeded to smash the glass into even smaller pieces before ordering that the pieces be glued onto the walls, creating a mosaic of shimmering pieces of glass.

Obviously, the architect had the eye of an artist to be able to take something broken and turn it into a beautiful masterpiece. However, there is another lesson to be gleaned from the story and it is this: If we simply choose to see it from a different angle, what looks like an obstacle can in fact be a glorious opportunity.

— *Make Your Life a Masterpiece*

OBSTACLES ARE A FACT OF LIFE, WE
ALL ENCOUNTER THEM. WHAT'S
IMPORTANT IS HOW WE DEAL WITH THEM.
WHEN YOU'RE PRESENTED WITH
AN OBSTACLE, STEP BACK FOR A MOMENT
AND TRY TO SEE HOW YOU
CAN TURN IT TO YOUR ADVANTAGE,
THEN, ONCE YOU'VE DECIDED ON A STRATEGY,
STAY FOCUSED UNTIL YOU GET AROUND IT.

TENACITY

When I asked my good friend and mentor Joe Segal what one characteristic is a sure-fire indicator that someone will turn out to be a successful person, he was quick to answer.

"Tenacity!" he exclaimed, "the ability to pick yourself up, regroup and keep going when you encounter obstacles on your runway of life." According to Joe, failure is a fact of life and a great learning opportunity.

"The secret to success, the thing that many people never figure out," Joe told me, "is that we all fail many times before we succeed. I've always believed experience is the best teacher. I say, show me a person who is a failure and I will show you someone who gave up while success still lay before them. Then show me a person who is a success and I will show you someone with many failures behind him. Failure is an event, not a person."

Joe concluded that while having a special talent or ability is no doubt a great advantage, unless it is developed and applied, it is no guarantee of success. Likewise, acquiring specialized knowledge or training can also contribute to your success; however, it is only valuable to the extent that you are prepared to apply it.

In the end, some of the most successful people in the world, including Joe himself — those who have excelled beyond what most of us could even imagine — are not the most talented or even the most educated. They are the individuals who are able to stand committed to one goal or purpose, come hell or high water.

— *The Runway of Life*

WHAT ARE YOU PREPARED
TO COMMIT YOURSELF TO,
COME HELL OR HIGH WATER?

THE EXTRA MILE

In the last 35 years, I have had the very real privilege of meeting all kinds of successful people. Get close to success and it sometimes rubs off! Some have been the presidents and CEOs of large prosperous companies, others have been stars in show business, entrepreneurs, self-made billionaires, inspired motivational speakers, sports celebrities and others who attract enthusiastic crowds wherever they go.

Invariably, conversation with these people gets around to the all-important question, "What is the single most important thing a person can do to ensure success?" The answer I have received time and time again is, "If you want to set yourself apart from the crowd, always go the extra mile. Do more than is expected of you and do it with a positive attitude."

Napoleon Hill spent much of his life studying the most successful entrepreneurs in American history and concluded that success followed predictable and distinct patterns of behaviour, one of the most important being the willingness to do more than you are paid for without expecting something in return. In his books, he wrote extensively on the benefits of going the extra mile. Here are just a few.

Going the extra mile:
• Develops the important quality of personal initiative;
• Demonstrates personal integrity and makes others more confident in our abilities;
• Tends to develop a keen, alert imagination because it is a habit that inspires one to continuously seek new and better ways of being of service to others;
• Leads to the development of a positive, pleasing mental attitude, which is essential for enduring success.

— *How to Soar With the Eagles*

IF YOU WANT TO GET NOTICED, TRY
DOING MORE AND GIVING MORE THAN IS
EXPECTED. GO THE EXTRA MILE.

IT'S OKAY TO DAYDREAM

S pend some time every day thinking about what you want from life. Unfortunately, most people think about what they don't want, but where's the fun in that? Remember when you were young, lying on your back in the grass watching the clouds go by, daydreaming about all the things you would do when you grew up. Remember too, how those daydreams filled you with a sense of anticipation and optimism. When did you stop doing that?

Remember that you have the creative power to accomplish the deepest desires of your heart. And what's more, you can never be truly happy as long as you deny your innermost dreams. So take the time to think deeply on what you want in your life. Be bold and imaginative.

Whatever you give attention to is what you get in your life. When you focus on something, not only are you voicing your support or approval of it, you are also making room in your life for more of it. So if you choose to spend your time focusing on what is positive and constructive, that's what you'll get.

— *The Runway of Life*

"DON'T BE AFRAID OF THE SPACE
BETWEEN YOUR DREAMS AND REALITY.
IF YOU CAN DREAM IT, YOU CAN
MAKE IT SO." — Belva Davis

FIVE MOST IMPORTANT PEOPLE

B enjamin Franklin once said, "If you lie down with dogs, you will wake up with fleas."

The five people we spend the most time with have a significant influence on our lives. They also have a powerful effect on the path we select for ourselves (whether it is geared towards success or failure) and our attitudes toward the future. Lord Chesterfield remarked that we are more than 50 per cent of who and what we are by the models we choose — so it is critical that we be careful in choosing whom we follow and whom we allow to influence our life.

It is said that even our income will be reflected as an average of the five people we spend the most time with. That is just one way we are influenced.

Of course, it doesn't mean we turn our back on our friends, but it does mean that we add significant and successful people to our lives; people who will encourage us to go after our dreams, have a positive effect on our character and cause us to become a person of significance, therefore making the path we seek to success more apparent.

— The Runway of Life

TAKE SOME TIME TODAY
TO CONSIDER HOW THE PEOPLE
IN YOUR LIFE ARE
INFLUENCING YOU.

TAKING ON GOLIATH – PART I

E very year, our flagship magazine hosts the BCBusiness Top 100 luncheon, which has been motivating and inspiring B.C.'s business leaders for more than 20 years. This year was a real coup for the magazine as we managed to convince B.C. billionaire Jimmy Pattison to participate in a special question-and-answer session with me, instead of delivering our usual keynote address. What you might not know about Jimmy is that at one time, he actually owned *BCBusiness* and I bought it from him. Here's how it happened.

There are plenty of legends about Jimmy Pattison, real and imagined (many of them built around his practical, yet unorthodox business practices), but if there is one thing that he is famous for it is making deals, which would explain how he has built a personal fortune of nearly $6 billion. At one time, that included getting into the publishing business, which of course, is also the business I am in.

At the time, I was looking to acquire one or more well-known business magazines in Vancouver to add to the solid stable of publications we already owned, but with no luck.

Then Jimmy moved in and successfully acquired one of the publications we had been chasing — along with three similar publications in Western Canada.

In the months that followed, we watched them closely and learned that perhaps all was not well in the new division of Jimmy's publishing enterprise. So I phoned, suggesting that a sale might make things more comfortable for the Pattison Group and was offered a price of $2.5 million.

I knew immediately that the figure was high, but I was wise enough to say that if all things checked out in the due-diligence report, I could accept the price.

TAKING ON GOLIATH – PART II

After a decent interval and being very much aware of Jimmy's reputation as a killer deal-maker, I called back with a counter-offer of $1 million, payable over time, interest free. If I may use poetic license here, they laughed in my face. But I sensed that all was not lost and 10 days later they called again saying that an alternative offer had fallen through and they were again interested.

With incredible support from my executive assistant Karen Foss and bravado that somehow won the day, we purchased four magazines for $800,000, to be paid over four years, interest free. Jimmy was off an uncomfortable hook and we acquired a magazine that we knew could become an important asset in our portfolio.

Observers looked at the deal (which got a lot of press) as a kind of David and Goliath thing and, all things considered, I was very proud that we had been able to pull it off. What I learned from the experience of going toe-to-toe with Jimmy Pattison is that the fear and trembling we feel in life is often quite unjustified. In our case, Jimmy wanted to unload something that was unfamiliar to him, we wanted it, and somewhere in the middle was a price that was comfortable for both of us. His imagined reputation had absolutely nothing to do with it.

The uncertainty that comes when we think about meeting bankers, going to the dentist and all of the other things we often dread, has mostly nothing to do with reality, so don't let it slow you down.

— How to Soar With the Eagles

DON'T THINK ABOUT THE POTHOLES
ON THE ROAD TO SUCCESS
(YOU'LL FIND A WAY AROUND THEM).
FOCUS INSTEAD ON WHAT'S
AT THE END OF THE ROAD.

WHY YOU SHOULD LAUGH IN THE FACE OF ADVERSITY

*"The human race has only
one really effective weapon and that
is laughter."* — Mark Twain

Laughter can help relieve tension in even the heaviest of matters. For example, during the Cuban missile crisis in the 1960s, American and Soviet negotiators found themselves deadlocked. They sat together in silence until someone suggested that each person should tell a humorous story. When it was his turn, one of the Russians offered a riddle: "What is the difference between capitalism and communism?" he asked. The answer, "In capitalism, man exploits man. In communism, it's the other way around." The tactic worked and the mood lightened, the talks continued.

I believe that not only can you laugh at adversity, but it is necessary to do so if you are to deal with setbacks without defeat. When you do find humour in trying times, one of the first and most important things you experience is that you see your difficulties in a new way — you suddenly have a new perspective on them. As a result of this new vantage point, you may also see new ways to deal with problems.

— *The Runway of Life*

LAUGHTER IS THE SHOCK
ABSORBER THAT EASES THE
BLOWS OF LIFE.

LEADING WITH KINDNESS

A company, feeling that it was time for a shake-up, hired a new CEO. This new boss was determined to rid the company of all slackers. On a tour of the facilities, the CEO noticed a guy leaning on a wall, so he walked up to the guy and asked him, "And how much money do you make a week?"

A little surprised, the young fellow looked at him and replied, "I make $300 a week, why?"

The CEO then handed the guy $1,200 in cash and screamed, "Here's four weeks' pay, now get out and don't come back!"

As the young man made a beeline for the door, one of the workers, with a sheepish grin on his face, remarked, "You sure made his day. He's the pizza delivery guy from Dominos."

Aggressive tactics like those used by the CEO in the story above cost companies dearly because they intimidate everyone, even the most hardworking, dedicated employees. You don't have to be a jerk to be a strong leader and being a kind, compassionate person doesn't make you a wimp.

In their book, *Leading With Kindness*, authors William F. Baker and Michael O'Malley, PhD, explain that being genuinely kind is to clearly communicate expectations and goals, push colleagues to improve and excel and mentor employees to take on difficult tasks and challenge their abilities. In listing the hallmarks of successful leaders, the authors include: compassion, integrity, gratitude, authenticity, humility and the importance of maintaining credibility with employees and clients.

— *The Power to Soar Higher*

PEOPLE WILL FORGET WHAT YOU SAID.
THEY WILL FORGET WHAT YOU DID.
BUT THEY WILL NEVER FORGET HOW YOU MADE
THEM FEEL. BE KIND, LEARN TO LISTEN AND
BE SENSITIVE TO THE NEEDS AND EXPECTATIONS
OF THE PEOPLE YOU LEAD.

NOT A CARE IN THE WORLD

A couple of years ago I was listening to a radio interview while sitting in the back of a limo en route from Toronto's Lester B. Pearson airport to a speaking engagement at Niagara on the Lake. At one point in the conversation, the interviewer asked the caller, "What is the difference between ignorance and apathy?" The caller responded, "I don't know and I don't care."

Although I realize the caller was going for a laugh with his comment, it got me thinking about the destructive power of the words, "I don't care."

"I don't care" is a dead-end road, it leaves us with nowhere to turn.

As Eleanor Roosevelt said, "So much attention is paid to the aggressive sins, such as violence and cruelty and greed with all their tragic effect, that too little attention is paid to the passive sins, such as apathy and laziness, which in the long run can have a more devastating effect."

If we are genuinely intent on living a worthwhile life, we cannot say, "I don't care" and do nothing. We must look for the things that we do care about and pursue these with passion.

— *The Runway of Life*

"THE OPPOSITE OF LOVE IS NOT HATE,
IT'S INDIFFERENCE. THE OPPOSITE
OF ART IS NOT UGLINESS, IT'S INDIFFERENCE.
THE OPPOSITE OF FAITH IS NOT
HERESY, IT'S INDIFFERENCE. AND THE
OPPOSITE OF LIFE IS NOT DEATH,
IT'S INDIFFERENCE. " — Eli Wiesel

WICKED – PART I

*"Within you right now is the power
to do things you never dreamed possible. This power
becomes available to you just as soon
as you can change your beliefs."* — Max Maltz

I took two of my daughters to see the play *Wicked*. A musical, *Wicked* is like the prequel to *The Wizard of Oz* and tells the story of how Glinda the Good and the Wicked Witch of the West were once friends, in the time before Dorothy came to Oz.

In the play, the Wicked Witch of the West has supernatural abilities that any human would love to have. Given her powers, what struck me as odd is that halfway through the play, she says to Glinda, "I have limitations." From where I was sitting, it didn't look to me as if she had any limitations, but afterwards I got to thinking that although other people might not be able to see them, we all have limitations — even if they are simply the ones that we have put on ourselves.

Limitations aren't real; they are something that the mind conjures to deal with fear. In reality you have no limitations. You can do anything if you make up your mind to do it because determination always finds a way around obstacles. Do you remember Henry Ford's words? "If you think you can, or if you think you can't, you're right." It all depends on what you believe about yourself.

When you have self-limiting beliefs, it is like stepping on the brakes in your car and expecting the car to move forward. More often than not, our limitations come from a distorted perspective of the world around us.

WICKED — PART II

We look at other people and we see all that they have, then we look at ourselves and only see what we don't have or we carry on into adulthood with negative programming that we picked up in our earlier years when we experienced criticism, embarrassment or failure.

Fortunately, you can rid yourself of self-limiting beliefs, but to do so you have to identify what they are. Often, these thoughts and beliefs lurk in the background without us being consciously aware of them. Talking with a friend or colleague or consulting with a coach or mentor could provide you with more objective feedback as to which beliefs are getting in the way of your success.

Once you have identified them, these limiting beliefs must be challenged every time they come up in your mind. One way to do this is to consciously replace your thoughts about limitations with mental or verbal affirmations such as, "I can accomplish anything I set my mind to," or "there are no limitations to what I can achieve."

Attacking these self-limiting thoughts and replacing them with positive ones is like pulling the weeds from your garden so that you can plant fruits and vegetables that will provide you with food. As Jim Rohn advises, "You cannot take the mild approach to the weeds in your mental garden. You have got to hate weeds enough to kill them. Weeds are not something you handle; weeds are something you devastate."

— *The Power to Soar Higher*

NEVER UNDERESTIMATE THE POWER
OF YOUR OWN THOUGHTS TO DETERMINE
THE DIRECTION OF YOUR LIFE. CHOOSE
TO NURTURE ONLY THOSE THAT ENHANCE
YOUR PERCEPTION OF WHAT IS POSSIBLE
AND HELP YOU ACHIEVE YOUR GOALS.

ONLY FOR TODAY

P ope John XXIII offered these 10 tips on how to live a better life, day to day:

Only for today:

1. I will seek to live today positively without wishing to solve the problems of my life all at once.

2. I will not raise my voice; I will be courteous in my behaviour; I will not criticize anyone; I will not claim to improve or to discipline anyone except myself.

3. I will be happy in the certainty that I was created to be happy, not only in the other world but also in this one.

4. I will adapt to circumstances, without requiring all circumstances to be adapted to my own wishes.

5. I will devote 10 minutes of my time to some good reading, remembering that just as food is necessary to the life of the body, so good reading is necessary to the life of the soul.

6. I will do one good deed and not tell anyone about it.

7. I will do at least one thing I do not like doing; and if my feelings are hurt, I will make sure that no one notices.

8. I will make a plan for myself: I may not follow it to the letter, but I will make it. And I will be on guard against two evils: hastiness and indecision.

9. I will firmly believe, despite appearances, that the good Providence of God cares for me as no one else who exists in this world.

10. I will have no fears. In particular, I will not be afraid to enjoy what is beautiful and to believe in goodness. Indeed, for 12 hours I can certainly do what might cause me consternation were I to believe I had to do it all my life.

UP, WHAT DOES IT REALLY MEAN?

M y fellow Speakers Roundtable member Ty Boyd from North Carolina sent me this bit of wisdom. It cracked me up.

UP. In the English language, this little two-letter word has more meanings than any other. It's easy enough to understand UP when it is referring to the direction (meaning toward the sky) or going UP in the elevator, but when we awaken in the morning, why do we wake UP? And when we are mad, why does everyone want us to lighten UP?

At a meeting, why does a topic come UP? Why do we speak UP and why are the officers UP for election?

We call UP our friends, brighten UP a room, polish UP the silver, warm UP the leftovers and clean UP the kitchen. We lock UP the house and fix UP the old car.

Some people also stir UP trouble, line UP for tickets, work UP an appetite and think UP excuses.

Sometimes UP is just plain confusing. A drain must be opened UP because it is stopped UP. We seem to be pretty mixed UP about UP!

To understand the proper uses of UP, look UP the word UP in the dictionary. It takes UP almost a quarter of the page and can add UP to about 30 definitions. If you are UP to it, you might try building UP a list of the many ways UP is used. If you don't give UP, you may wind UP with a hundred or more.

One could go on and on, but I'll wrap it UP for now because my time is UP!

Oh, one more thing. What is the first thing you do in the morning and the last thing you do at night?

U

P

— Insight 2011

REMEMBER TO KEEP YOUR CHIN
"UP" AND ENJOY YOUR DAY.

READ, REREAD AND APPLY

Many people will read an enlightening book or attend a motivating seminar that inflates them with confidence and direction only to have the excitement and glow wear off after a few days because they don't follow through. That is why it is so important to read, reread and apply.

Think of it this way, ideas are the tools you will use to build the life you dream about. Once you have acquired some good tools, make a commitment to yourself to use them regularly. With application comes a deeper sense of understanding that will lead you to success.

Of course, using knowledge is not just the purpose of your learning; it is the very basis of the learning process. In his book, *How to Study*, Arthur Kornhauser, an associate professor of business psychology at the University of Chicago, wrote, "Knowledge is acquired only through thinking and doing . . . Learning is an active process. Use your knowledge by thinking, talking and writing about the things you are learning."

Next to not following through, one of the biggest mistakes people make in regards to reading is to put a book down when they come to an idea they don't agree with. No one says that each situation will apply to you or that you have to agree with the author at every turn.

Many of the best articles and books about success have been written for a sales or business audience. That doesn't mean that just because you are not involved in running a business you should ignore them. Simply be willing to explore other ways of thinking and then take what you can use from each book.

— *The Runway of Life*

"THE MORE THAT YOU READ,
THE MORE THINGS YOU'LL KNOW.
THE MORE THAT YOU LEARN,
THE MORE PLACES YOU'LL GO."
— Dr. Seuss

SEAL IT WITH A KISS

When was the last time you wrote a love letter to your spouse or significant other? A letter that was important enough for them to tuck it away in a special place and keep it forever. You know, the old-fashioned kind of letter that oozes adoration and is full of hearts and flowers.

Life goes by so fast these days that most of us just don't have the time to communicate in the ways that people once did. Letters, who writes letters? A card is about the best most of us can do.

Okay, so if you don't write letters, let me ask you this, when was the last time you talked to your significant other in a supportive, loving way and told them how much you appreciate all that they bring to your life? Words that they could tie up with an imaginary ribbon and keep in their heart.

You did it when you were first smitten with them, remember?

"I don't really know how to say it right, but you're the prettiest girl I've ever met, sitting there in the moonlight, swinging your legs and smiling. I've never felt this way about anyone before."

Pure poetry.

And then somewhere along the way, the words dried up.

"Seen my phone?"

"What's for dinner?"

Before long, the moonlight and the warm, soft words are just a distant memory. But they don't have to be. I think it's fun now and then to drop a note to your partner, to say something nice in a letter and send it in the mail. Even if it is just a few words to express your love, the way you did before.

And don't forget to seal it with a kiss.

— *You Can If You Believe You Can*

THE PRICE OF SUCCESS

My speaking career and annual engagements total about 100 occasions per year. The invitations I receive to address groups range from industry associations to credit unions, real estate organizations, investment groups, hotels, car dealerships, provincial governments, charities and conventions of all kinds; in total, a very wide range of audiences.

The majority of my speeches centre on topics revolving around leadership and business success, and every speech is very heavy on motivation and inspiration with plenty of personal anecdotes and stories from my own experience and life in general.

Following almost every speech, these are the three most common responses I receive from the men and women I speak to:

• How do you make it look so easy?

• I wish my children could have heard that talk.

• I want to be a speaker just like you . . . I want to travel first class, ride in a limo, stay in five-star hotels, get standing ovations from audiences and be paid big bucks!

To those people who want to live my life, my rejoinder is always the same, "That's great! Now tell me, what are you prepared to do in order for that to happen?"

Not surprisingly, very few people have an answer. No doubt they dream of being in "the business," that is, the business of being a well-paid public speaker. However, what they often fail to realize is that the speaking business is just that, a business, and the people who succeed are those who are willing to work hard, sacrifice and give it their all. It's exactly the same in any other business.

— *Make Your Life a Masterpiece*

THE PRICE OF SUCCESS IS A WILLINGNESS
AND DEDICATION TO BECOME THE BEST IN YOUR FIELD,
TO BECOME A MASTER OF YOUR CRAFT.

TURN IT AROUND

We all have little annoyances to deal with every day. But how we choose to respond to the little things that happen can actually have a significant impact on how the bigger things turn out.

Let me tell you a story about a pharmacy that decided to turn an inconvenience into an advantage. As it happened, this particular pharmacy's telephone number was very similar to the number of a nearby movie theatre. As you can expect, they got a lot of wrong numbers, mostly from people calling to ask what time the movie started.

For a long time, the pharmacy employees simply told callers they had the wrong number, until one day somebody came up with the idea to turn this minor but frequent annoyance into a win-win opportunity.

From then on, whenever someone called to ask about a movie, the pharmacy employee would say, "I'm sorry. This is the Walgreen's store just down the street from the movie theatre. But I have the schedule right here. What movie were you interested in?"

Once they had answered the caller's question, the pharmacy employee would then say, "When you finish the movie, you might consider coming over here. We have a great sale going on right now. I hope you enjoy your movie."

Instead of being irritated by 50 wrong-number calls each day, this store turned it into 50 promotions per day. They provided a small extra by giving out the movie schedule, but they got a fair amount of business in return.

— *Make Your Life a Masterpiece*

THINK ABOUT WAYS THAT
YOU CAN "TURN IT AROUND" TO MAKE
THE SMALL ANNOYANCES
IN YOUR LIFE WORK FOR YOU.

WHAT WE'RE NOT

In his book *Authentic Happiness*, Dr. Martin Seligman notes, "You cannot be anything you want to be — but you can be a lot more of who you already are."

Too many of us try too hard to be something that we're not, or worse yet, we devote more time to fixing our shortcomings than to developing our strengths. Sometimes we do it to please others, sometimes we do it because we think it will lead to wealth, fame or success. More often, it ends in depression, failure and disappointment.

Each of us is valuable because of the special talents that have been given to us, so why focus on what we're not?

A little over 10 years ago, the Gallup Organization (the global researcher company famous for the Gallup poll) developed a tool called the Strengths Finder to help people discover and develop their natural talents. Drawing on more than 40 years of research, they discovered the following basic truths about human achievement and success:

> A life spent focusing on improving our weaknesses leads to dissatisfaction and mediocrity.

> Spending time doing what we love and are best at is what drives success.

> We cannot be great at everything, so we need to acknowledge our limitations, build on our strengths and get on with life.

> Every day should be spent focusing on developing what we believe to be our true gifts.

> When choosing who to work with (on projects or in business) opposing strengths can lead to the strongest partnerships.

WHAT WOULD TRUMP DO? — PART I

A speaking associate of mine, Harvey McKay, who is with the National Speakers Association, has often said that it's the people you *don't* fire who cause you the biggest problems — not the ones you do.

Vancouver business executive Jake Kerr agrees and notes that it is an issue for many business owners. Kerr held a retreat in Whistler with 10 similar-minded business leaders. One of the projects they undertook during the retreat was to each take time alone to make a list of five elements that they believed they could have done better to be more successful in business.

When they returned to share their five points, the group found that while they had a wide cross-section of other concerns, the common element that each of them shared was, "I wish I had fired certain people sooner."

They're not alone. A majority of business owners admit they're scared to fire employees — even the incompetent ones or those who, through their obnoxious behaviour and constant bullying, often cause good employees to quit. This is despite the fact that human resources studies show one of the biggest costs in both time and money to organizations is the management of poor performance (i.e., keeping employees who are a drag on productivity).

How do you find the courage to say, "You're fired"? Let's face it, we're not all Donald Trump. In a national survey in the U.S., 61 per cent of small-business owners said they find it hard to fire an employee no matter how bad they are. But firing an employee shouldn't be an emotional decision. Rather, it should be based on a documented record of poor performance or inappropriate behaviour.

In addition to doing regular performance reviews with employees and keeping detailed records, all companies need to have a formal termination process in place. Here are three more important reasons why you should act quickly to get rid of problem employees:

1. Toxic people damage your organization.
2. The longer you allow them to stay, the more damage they do.
3. When you don't do anything about bad employees, people begin to doubt your leadership.

WHAT WOULD TRUMP DO? – PART II

F ollowing are some do's and don'ts from experts on how to handle firing an employee.

DO:

- Get right to the point. Avoid a long build-up to soften the blow; it will only confuse the point.
- Detail clearly why the employee is being terminated and the effective date.
- Focus your discussion on performance-related issues.
- Let your employee respond if they have something to say.
- Inform the employee of any rights or entitlements they may have coming.
- Cover all areas of security including computer passwords and access to company property/data.
- End on a positive note. Thank the employee for their contributions and wish them luck in the future.
- Document the termination conference.

DON'T:

- Don't give an employee false hope and say you'll help them find a new job.
- Don't get defensive or pass the buck by saying the firing was not your idea.
- Don't assess blame or make apologies. Simply say the company's needs don't match their skills.
- Give honest answers, but don't debate.
- Don't use words like "dishonest" or "incompetent."
- Don't discuss the termination with anyone other than the employee and those directly involved.

— *The Power to Soar Higher*

IT'S THE PEOPLE YOU DON'T FIRE WHO
CAUSE YOU THE BIGGEST PROBLEMS.

WASTE NOT, WANT NOT

I f I were to ask any one of you reading this book, "Do you want to waste your life?" I would be surprised if anyone said, "Yes."

How about a decade? Nope.

How about a year? Nope again.

What about a month or even a week? Still no.

But how about a day?

Well, a day, big deal! Most people wouldn't think twice about wasting a day. They think they have so many left that it's no big deal.

Well, a day quickly becomes a week. A week becomes a month, then a year. Before we know it, a decade has passed and soon we realize that we have more life behind us than before us — and we still haven't learned the value of a day and its importance to our entire life.

The truth is most of us waste at least a little bit of every day without even thinking about it. We waste it by procrastinating, we waste it by doing work we aren't really passionate about, we waste it fighting with loved ones over things that aren't really important or wrestling with our conscience rather than taking care of the things that are really important to us.

— The Runway of Life

SO, HOW MUCH TIME ARE YOU
WILLING TO WASTE? HOW MUCH CAN YOU
REALLY AFFORD TO WASTE?

STOW YOUR BAGGAGE

A t the airline check-in at London's Heathrow airport, a man walks up to the counter with three bags. He puts them down and says to the young woman behind the counter, "I'd like you to send this one to Los Angeles, that one to Hong Kong and the last one to Durban."

The young woman's face shows signs of confusion before her training takes over and she says, "I'm afraid we can't do that, sir."

"Why not?" demands the man. "You did the last time I flew with you."

We've all got baggage from our past experiences. The problem is that too many people let that baggage (preconceived ideas or issues related to negative experiences from the past) weigh them down and keep them from enjoying whatever is happening in the present moment.

If it won't fit into a carry-on, stow your baggage, or better yet, jettison it — you'll feel a lot better and so will everyone who comes into contact with you.

— Insight 2011

TODAY, CHOOSE TO STOW YOUR BAGGAGE
AND FACE ALL OF THE EXPERIENCES THAT COME
YOUR WAY WITH A FRESH OUTLOOK.

IT'S YOUR CALL – PART I

*"People who are funny and smart and
return phone calls get much better press than people who are
just funny and smart."* — Howard Simons

Some tools of success are simpler than others. Although the tool that I am going to focus on today is one of the simplest, it is also one of the most effective in building your credibility with others. It is the art of returning phone calls (and emails, letters, replies to invitations, or proposals) in a timely manner.

"What is a reasonable amount of time?" you ask. I would suggest 24 hours.

Steve Halliday, managing director at Rosewood Hotels & Resorts, has a similar habit that he shared with me during a conversation on customer service. He calls it his First-Ring Rule and I believe it is one that sets him apart from many other top-level executives. It is his practice of picking up and answering the telephone on the first ring whenever possible. It may not be rocket science, but it is very, very effective. "Anyone who wants to make customers feel more valued should try practicing this rule," advises Steve.

Because we spend so much of our time communicating over the phone, here are eight more strategies for making the most of your communications:

1. When you answer the phone, greet callers with energy and enthusiasm. Given that the first few words out of your mouth will set the tone for the conversation, make sure that the image you are projecting is positive and professional.

2. Ask for the caller's name if he or she doesn't offer it. Use their name during the first few moments of your conversation, then one or two more times during the call (just don't overdo it) and end by thanking the caller by name (it adds a personal touch that gives you a connection with the caller).

IT'S YOUR CALL – PART II

3. Take brief notes during your telephone conversation if you will need the information for future reference. People are impressed when you can recall important details later on; likewise, they can feel harassed if they need to recall the same details time after time in following up with you.

4. Sit up tall, smile and use gestures when you are speaking. Callers can hear the smile in your voice and they can also hear your slouch. Practicing good posture helps you breathe better and stay alert during the conversation.

5. To build rapport with a caller, match the pace of your speech with theirs. If you are hearing long silences, it probably means you are speaking too quickly. Use pauses effectively to slow down so the caller can follow what you're saying.

6. Use professional but conversational vocabulary and grammar. Avoid using industry jargon unless you are sure the caller shares your knowledge of it and definitely stay away from swearing or slang.

7. Before you put someone on hold or transfer their call, ask permission from the caller. Small courtesies like this help to build rapport and enhance your image.

8. End the call with sincere thanks and appreciation for the caller's time. Be positive and courteous, especially if the caller discussed a problem or complaint. Focus on positive results.

— Make Your Life a Masterpiece

"THE BATHTUB WAS INVENTED IN 1850 AND THE TELEPHONE IN 1875. IN OTHER WORDS, IF YOU HAD BEEN LIVING IN 1850, YOU COULD HAVE SAT IN THE BATHTUB FOR 25 YEARS WITHOUT HAVING TO ANSWER THE PHONE." — Bill Dewitt

COULD FAILURE BE GOOD FOR YOU?

M ost of us view failure as a bad thing — but is it really?
Albert Einstein was clearly a brilliant man whose work contributed much to the advancement of science and our understanding of physics. But if you think that geniuses get it right every time, you'd be wrong. Einstein made plenty of mistakes, famous ones even, but that never stopped him from continuing to develop new theories and ideas about the universe.

In his book titled *Einstein's Mistakes: The Human Failings of a Genius*, author Hans Ohanian talks about how scientists have identified serious flaws in four of the five papers that established Einstein's reputation in theoretical physics in 1905. Ohanian also points out Einstein's repeated failure to provide a valid proof for his most famous equation, $E = mc^2$, and talks about how, despite his repeated mistakes and in some cases, because of them, time after time Einstein came to correct conclusions and achieved theoretical breakthroughs that eluded other scientists — which goes a long way to explain why he remains an iconic scientist and household name so many decades after his death.

Imagine if Einstein had believed that his genius meant that he wasn't allowed to make mistakes, or worse, if he allowed his failures to stop him from continuing forward with the development of his theories. Real life comes with ups and downs because it's all about experimenting to find what works and we learn valuable lessons from each one of our mistakes. There is no successful experimentation without failure.

— *How to Soar With the Eagles*

LIKE EINSTEIN, WE SHOULD ALLOW
OUR FAILURES TO ACT AS THE STEPPING STONES
THAT EVENTUALLY LEAD US TO WHAT
WE ARE LOOKING FOR.

FIVE TIPS TO MAKE LIFE MORE ENJOYABLE

We could all use a little more time for the things we enjoy. One way to get it is by implementing a few simple routines to make everyday tasks easier to manage. Here are five ideas to help:

1. Clean a little bit each day. Whether it's cleaning between the sofa cushions while watching a movie, giving the shower a quick wipe or tidying the kitchen counters, a little cleaning here and there cuts down on the time you'll spend later. Chores are also less daunting when you don't have to face them all at once.

2. Sort paper clutter the day before your work week begins. Bills, receipts, newspapers, notes, etc. Put systems in place to avoid paper build-up: a filing system for receipts and bills, a recycling box for papers and magazines and a message centre for notes and appointments.

3. Organize monthly. We all function better when we don't have to spend time searching for things that aren't where they should be. Bring some order to your life at least once a month. Start by organizing your wallet or handbag, clearing the clutter at home or organizing your workspace.

4. Unwind daily. Keep stress under control by re-energizing yourself every day. Walk for 20 minutes in the morning, read for half an hour at lunch or enjoy a hot bath and a cup of cocoa before bed. Need inspiration? Print out some meaningful quotes and display them where you'll see them every day.

5. Make time for the people and activities you love. Get in touch with old friends, go on an adventure with your family, revisit a sport you enjoyed in the past or nurture a new passion; having something to look forward to makes every day more enjoyable.

AUGUST

AIM FOR THE STARS

"Success is not final, failure is not fatal:
it is the courage to continue that counts."
— Winston Churchill

I've heard it said that great companies are not built by individuals who rely on somebody else to take care of them. They are built by men and women who rely on themselves, who dare to shape their own lives, who have enough confidence in themselves to take the necessary risks.

When my mentor Joe Segal left Vegreville, Alberta, as a young man with nothing more than his good name to come to Vancouver to seek his fortune, friends said, "It's so big, you can't succeed." But Joe saw it differently. "It's so big, I can't miss," he told them. And he was right. Joe went on to build his own empire.

The world is in need of more leaders like Joe. Countries need leaders. Businesses need leaders. Communities need leaders.

Joe has often said to me that one of life's problems is not that we aim too high and fail. It is that we aim too low and succeed. Henry David Thoreau said, "In the long run, men hit only what they aim at. Therefore, though they should fail immediately, they had better aim at something high."

— *The Runway of Life*

DO YOU HAVE YOUR SIGHTS
AIMED HIGH ENOUGH?

ACTING OUT

When Albert Einstein was making the rounds of the speakers' circuit, he usually found himself longing to get back to his laboratory work. One night, en route to yet another rubber-chicken dinner, Einstein mentioned to his chauffeur (a man who somewhat resembled Einstein in looks and manner) that he was tired of speech-making.

"I have an idea, boss," his chauffeur said. "I've heard you give this speech so many times. I'll bet I could give it for you."

Einstein laughed loudly and said, "Why not? Let's do it!"

When they arrived at the dinner, Einstein donned the chauffeur's cap and jacket and sat in the back of the room. The chauffeur gave a beautiful rendition of Einstein's speech and even answered a few questions expertly.

Then a supremely pompous professor asked an extremely esoteric question about anti-matter formation, digressing here and there to let everyone in the audience know that he was nobody's fool.

Without missing a beat, the chauffeur fixed the professor with a steely stare and said, "Sir, the answer to that question is so simple that I will let my chauffeur, who is sitting in the back, answer it for me."

Why are certain people so difficult to deal with? Although some are intentionally disruptive, many others can appear to be difficult simply because we don't understand what motivates them to behave the way they do. Is it simply a matter of not having learned proper communication and social skills? Surprisingly, more often than not, the answer is yes. Because these people don't perceive their behaviour as being anything out of the norm, they continue on, oblivious to the fact that their actions are having a negative impact on those around them.

— *The Power of Tact*

UNDERSTANDING WHAT MOTIVATES
PEOPLE CAN MAKE IT EASIER TO DEAL
WITH THEIR BEHAVIOUR.

ALWAYS BUILD ON COMMON GROUND

In July 2002, Vancouver was shortlisted to bid for the 2010 Olympic Games. The Vancouver Board of Trade was a strong supporter of the bid. However, during the bid process, concerns arose that hosting the Olympics would divert significant resources away from serious and urgent community concerns, all for the benefit of the business community.

During the Community Leadership Summit later that fall, the Board thought it was important to provide a forum to discuss those concerns and look for solutions that would involve people from all corners of the community. Following the summit and a very open exchange of ideas, even more people were motivated to come forward with proposals addressing issues such as poverty, homelessness, property crime and drug addiction.

Perhaps the most important lesson I learned from this experience is that when you find yourself with an opposing view, keep in mind that people don't want you to carry on about what you *disagree* on, they want to hear what you can agree to. This is especially true when negotiating with grassroots organizations where people have invested a lot of personal effort and passion into a specific issue. Although you may have very different objectives, remember, you have a shared goal — to solve the problem — and that is the common ground upon which you can begin to build.

Something else I learned is that decisions made behind closed doors rarely work. You need to bring people along with you as you work through a problem or challenge. If you're going to have them buy into the solution, you'd better ask them how they'd solve the problem. Asking people for help also communicates that you understand the part they play in your success, giving them an incentive to make the solution work.

— The Runway of Life

BOOST YOUR ENTHUSIASM

*"Years may wrinkle the skin, but
to give up enthusiasm wrinkles the soul."*
— Samuel Ullman

I know people who are so uninspired about life that the first thing they do when they get up in the morning is start making plans about going to bed that night.

Where's the enthusiasm?

It can be tough to get out of bed some days, but if we never do anything differently from one day to the next, how can we expect different results?

If you're finding yourself stuck and want a little boost to get going again, try these ideas:

Get some fresh air. Give your body and mind an oxygen boost by taking a walk in the park. Every cell in your body needs oxygen to survive, so it only makes sense that fresh air will make you feel more energetic.

Take off your gravity boots. The problems of the world can weigh you down if you let them. Sometimes you just need to turn off and tune out the bad news and listen to something positive instead.

Stop complaining about what you don't have. Stop focusing on what is lacking in your life. Instead focus on what you do have. Be grateful and say thank you to those around you.

Find your balance. Eat good food, listen to music you enjoy, make time for play, spend time in nature and with people you love, take care of yourself. Look for things that boost your energy and integrate them into your daily life.

Ralph Waldo Emerson said it best: Enthusiasm is one of the most powerful engines of success. When you do a thing, do it with all your heart, mind and soul.

BE ACTIVE, BE ENERGETIC, HAVE FAITH IN YOURSELF AND YOU WILL FIND THAT YOUR LEVEL OF ENTHUSIASM NATURALLY SOARS.

DITCH IT AND DRIVE ON

I f you dislike something enough to spend the time and energy to criticize it, make a point to push it out of your life to ensure that it will not continue to take up future time and energy.

Why go to the trouble of pushing it out of your life forever? Because, while positive emotions give you energy, negative emotions create leaks that let your energy seep out and disappear. I'm sure you've experienced this for yourself; when you are excited and happy and interacting with people in a positive way, you are filled with energy and enthusiasm. Yet, when you are angry, depressed or negative for any reason, you feel tired, frustrated and, eventually, burned out.

We all need as much energy as we can muster to focus on the things that are important to us, so why would we want to waste any of that energy or give it away?

— *The Runway of Life*

WHATEVER YOU CRITICIZE,
DITCH IT AND
GET ON WITH YOUR LIFE.

FOCUS ON OPPORTUNITIES

With all of the shifts in the global economy in recent years, we've all learned that our lives and the lifestyle we've become accustomed to can change quickly. In an instant, the possessions and financial security we have worked hard to acquire can disappear, leaving us feeling exposed and vulnerable.

That's why it is always important to actively seek out new ideas, new opportunities, new resources and new connections. This may require that you push your boundaries and force yourself out of your comfort zone, but when you do, you'll soon find that change is not nearly as scary as you imagined and you may even discover that you're happy to be out of that old familiar rut you'd made for yourself.

After that, who knows where those new ideas and opportunities may take you? The important thing is to explore as many options as possible. Having a multitude of options means never feeling like your back is to the wall or that you need to compromise your ethics and standards just to make ends meet.

— 97 Tips on How to Do Business in Tough Times

SEEK OUT AT LEAST ONE
OPPORTUNITY TODAY TO INTRODUCE
YOURSELF TO A NEW
EXPERIENCE OR SOME NEW PEOPLE
AND SEE WHAT NEW DOORS
OPEN TO YOU.

A MIRACLE MOMENT IN HISTORY – PART I

*"When you come to the edge of all
the light you have, and must take a step into
the darkness of the unknown, believe that
one of two things will happen to you; either there will be
something solid for you to stand on, or you will be
taught how to fly."* — Patrick Overton

Vancouver's Empire Stadium was torn down in the spring of 1993, something that often happens to old stadiums. With it went a lot of rubble and even more memories.

The new Empire Field, built for the 2010-11 CFL football season, opened on June 20, 2010 on the very same site.

My father was in that old stadium on a hot August 7th in 1954, when history was made. Along with some 30,000-plus spectators, Dad witnessed the race between England's Roger Bannister and Australian runner John Landy. For the first time in history, two athletes ran a mile in less than four minutes in the same race. Everest had been conquered the year before and now another "impossible" barrier had come down, another dream of mankind would go into the record books.

Coming into Vancouver for the then British Empire Games, both Bannister and Landy were already sub-four-minute milers. Bannister was the world's first, at 3:59.4 in England. Six weeks later in Turku, Finland, Landy did it in 3:58.0.

The world was waiting for a battle of the champions in Vancouver. Who would win? Could Landy beat Bannister?

For many months, Bannister had trained hard in England, setting his sights on a mile in less than four minutes. Regularly, his long-time Oxford friend Chris Chataway paced him, offering him not just challenge, but the inspirational words that might help him change the record books forever.

A MIRACLE MOMENT IN HISTORY — PART II

Despite the "first-person-under-four-minutes" fame that followed his assault on the clock in England, Bannister arrived in Vancouver full of doubt. After attaining the impossible, he needed a miracle. To beat Landy must have seemed like a goal beyond comprehension — not helped by many on the sidelines who said he could never do it. It would be interesting to know how many of Bannister's family, friends, coaches and athletic peers really believed the race would be his. Four times round the track in less than four minutes — and beat Landy doing it! The tallest of orders.

For many years, a life-size statue of the record-breaking race's most compelling moment stood outside Empire Stadium. It showed Landy in the lead during the last 150 yards. The drama and the irony was that he was looking over his left shoulder as he ran, the precise moment when Bannister streaked by him on his right and went on to victory. Bannister's time was 3:58.8 and Landy's was 3:59.6. They called it the Miracle Mile.

I have often wondered how Roger Bannister — now Sir Roger, and a teacher at Oxford — kept his dream alive when so many must have fed his mind with the distinct possibility of failure. What an enormous ability to focus on one magnificent goal.

It's vital for all of us to persist for our dreams. I'm not talking about instant results that can be measured with yardsticks, but Big Dreams. In this instant world, where we all want results *right now*, too many people give up too soon, walking away from their dreams without ever realizing that if you just stick with it, records can indeed be broken.

— *The Power of a Dream*

WITH PERSISTENCE, WE CAN ALL
HAVE OUR "MIRACLES."

THE MAN WHO BUILT LEONARDO'S HORSE
– PART I

"What we need are more people
who specialize in the
impossible." — Theodore Roethke

Leonardo da Vinci was perhaps one of the most successful people in the history of the world, known for a diverse range of accomplishments, not the least among them masterpieces of art like the Mona Lisa, anatomical studies of the human body and designs for inventions such as parachutes and flying machines. However, there were some projects that da Vinci never finished and the fact that he didn't was something that troubled him for the remainder of his life. On his deathbed in 1519, Leonardo expressed two regrets about his life — that he was never able to fly and that he never finished his "horse."

The project was a commission for his patron, Ludovico Sforza, the Duke of Milan. *Il Cavallo* was to be a magnificent 24-foot-tall bronze statue of a horse, the largest equine statue ever built. Leonardo began the project by constructing a full-scale clay model of his idyllic stallion in a vineyard. Unfortunately for him, the French army invaded Milan. As a result, the Duke ordered that the bronze set aside for the statue be used to make a cannon and Leonardo's monumental clay cast of the horse was destroyed by the archers of the French army, who used it for target practice.

Leonardo fled Milan, the Duke fell and the French captured the city. Although Leonardo died nearly 500 years ago, his dream of *Il Cavallo* did not. In 1977, United Airlines pilot and amateur Renaissance scholar Charles Dent read about the intriguing story of Leonardo and his horse in an issue of *National Geographic* magazine. Filled with great enthusiasm and inspiration, Dent's instantaneous response to the story was, "Let's give Leonardo his horse."

THE MAN WHO BUILT LEONARDO'S HORSE
— PART II

Realizing that this was no small undertaking, Dent sold his own art collection to support the project and then created a non-profit organization to continue raising funds. He also brought together a group of sculptors, friends, relatives, horse lovers and hundreds of enthusiasts who, after hearing the story, contributed time, effort and financial resources to help make Leonardo's dream come true.

Coincidentally, like Leonardo, Charles Dent did not live to see his "crazy, romantic scheme" come to life. He died on Christmas Day in 1994, but by then the momentum behind the $6-million project to reconstruct the horse from Leonardo's sketches had gained so much momentum that it was unstoppable.

It is ironic that after Dent's death, his will (which was essentially a bequest to *Il Cavallo*) provided the substantial sum that took the model to the foundry in Beacon, New York, where it was to be enlarged to a colossal scale and cast in bronze.

On September 10, 1999, more than 500 years after the Duke of Milan and Leonardo had envisioned it, the completed 24-foot sculpture was unveiled to more than 1,000 spectators in Milan. It was presented as a gift to the people of Italy from the American people as a thank you for the treasures of the Renaissance and also as a tribute to the marriage of scientific thinking and artistic creativity — two of Leonardo's greatest passions.

Some people look at a challenge and ask, "Why bother?" Others, when faced with exactly the same circumstances, ask, "Why not?"

Which are you?

— Make Your Life a Masterpiece

"WE ALL HAVE DREAMS. BUT IN ORDER TO MAKE
DREAMS COME INTO REALITY, IT TAKES
AN AWFUL LOT OF DETERMINATION, DEDICATION,
SELF-DISCIPLINE AND EFFORT." — Jesse Owens

IT'S NOT JUST YOUR SHOES
THAT NEED TO SHINE

I can't emphasize enough how important attitude is, it really is everything in life. Research shows: 15 per cent of your success in life can be attributed to your technical skills. The other 85 per cent of your success is the result of your people skills and your ability to get along with others — to be real, to be you. Eighty-five per cent is a lot. I once heard, "Be who you is, cause if you ain't who you is, then you is who you ain't."

It costs to have a negative attitude. Attitude is a choice. If you've read *The Power to Soar Higher,* you've heard the story of Shed. I met Shed on a trip to St. Louis, Missouri, where I was giving a speech. He shines shoes for a living and as I was having my shoes shined, I asked him, "S-H-E-D, is that your real name or a nickname?"

"No," he said. "My name is Shed, my mama named me Shed . . . that's my name!"

I noticed he had a stethoscope around his neck. I said, "What's that for?"

"I is the doctor of shoes," he said. "I ain't lost a patient in 37 years. In fact, some people call me the saviour of soles."

And then I noticed a sign on his shoe-shine stand that said, "Shoe Shine: $2, Shoe Shine: $6."

"What's the difference?" I asked.

He said, "If you've got a good attitude, I charges you $2, but if you got a bad attitude, I charges you $6, cuz it costs to have a bad attitude."

— *The Power of a Dream*

IT PAYS TO HAVE A GOOD ATTITUDE.
WHEN YOU'RE POSITIVE AND PLEASANT,
PEOPLE NATURALLY WANT TO
HELP YOU, SO LET YOUR ATTITUDE
SHINE THROUGH.

MORE AND LESS

L ife is too short to perfect your weaknesses or struggle to make something work when your instincts tell you it won't. It's a funny thing that so many people have been brainwashed to believe endless struggle is a good thing. Instead of just working hard, wouldn't it be more fun to work smart?

Usually, I find we have opportunities to be more effective and productive right under our noses that we aren't recognizing or taking advantage of. Just as technology companies invest in research and development, so should you. A simple assessment of where you are spending your time and where your results are coming from will help determine what is working.

After that, it's all about doing more of what works and less of what doesn't. So, the next time you find yourself stuck, take a moment to look at what is working and see if you can do more of that. Also, when you discover something that works for you, don't be afraid to run with it and possibly distill it down to a formula that can be used in other areas of your life.

It's also important to take time on a regular basis to assess what isn't working in both your business and life. This is no time for ego; if you're too proud to admit you're wrong, you'll fail by continuing to pour your efforts into things that aren't working rather than moving on to new things that might be more successful.

While there is pain associated with admitting something didn't work, feeling shame and assigning blame are not very productive — they take up precious time and energy. The point here is to eliminate what isn't working and move on.

— *The Runway of Life*

REGULARLY ASSESS WHAT
IS AND ISN'T WORKING; THEN MAKE
NECESSARY ADJUSTMENTS.

OPEN WITH YOUR BEST MATERIAL

American comic Louis C.K. has a unique approach for developing his comedy act: "I take my closing bit and open with it. Because then I have to follow my strongest bit."

That's good advice for anyone who wants to take their performance to a higher level. If you're making a presentation to a client, start with your best ideas; if you're interviewing for a job, zero in on your biggest strengths and highlight them; if you're in a debate, open with your strongest argument.

By putting your best material out there first, you set high expectations on the part of your audience for the rest of your presentation and therefore challenge yourself to make sure everything that follows lives up to your strong opening. If the rest of your material doesn't measure up, you'll need to bump it up a couple of notches and rework it until it does.

Honing your material takes time, practice and patience. Stand-up comics spend years paying their dues on the circuit and figuring out what works with different audiences, and so do speakers.

If you're not sure about your material, try it out on a few people ahead of time and get their reaction, then rework and revise as necessary until you know it's the best it can be.

— Insight 2011

SEE IT BIG, KEEP IT SIMPLE

I met Larry Larsen, a dynamic speaker, at a speakers' convention years ago. At that time, he gave me a copy of his book, *The Winner Within*, which is about developing a big-picture mindset.

As he explained to me, he got the idea for his trademark phrase, "See it big, keep it simple," from a freckle-faced kid standing on a street corner trying to sell his puppy.

The kid was dirty, the puppy was dirty and his tiny sign read: "Puppy for Sale — 15 cents."

Larry stopped to see if he could help the poor kid.

"Son, if you want to sell your puppy, take him inside, clean him up, brush him until he shines, put a red ribbon round his neck, get a bigger sign and increase your price."

The boy said thanks and disappeared.

Early the next morning, Larry saw a complete transformation. The same corner with a clean boy and a shiny puppy with a big red bow and a huge sign that read: "Puppy for Sale — $10,000."

'Wow,' Larry thought. 'This kid is definitely seeing it big now, but is he keeping it simple?'

He didn't have time to stop, but he came back two hours later. To his surprise, the sign way lying on its side with SOLD painted all over it in red.

'That's impossible,' thought Larry. 'There's no way that kid sold his dog for $10,000.' He went up to the boy's house and knocked. The kid came to the door with a grin.

"Son, did you really sell your puppy for $10,000?"

"Yep, mister, sure did."

"How on earth did you do it?" asked Larry.

"Simple," said the budding young entrepreneur, "I traded him for two $5,000 cats!"

— *You Can If You Believe You Can*

HOW CAN YOU SEE IT BIG AND KEEP IT SIMPLE TODAY?

TELL YOUR OWN STORIES

During the early years of my speaking career, my presentations were made up too often of the borrowed, begged and stolen material of others. There's no doubt at all that it was wonderful material, but I've since learned that my own stories are not only easier to tell, but they are also more rewarding for my audiences. People are fascinated to hear about personal agony, ecstasy, struggles and accomplishments, how the hardships were overcome and the triumphs celebrated. What they often say to me after a presentation is, "If you can do it, I can do it."

Despite all of the perks that come with being an international speaker, I'd have to say that inspiring others may just be the best part of my job; it's certainly the most rewarding part. Especially when people contact me years later and tell me how a certain story helped them to achieve a dream or to deal with a particularly difficult time in their life.

We all have stories to share and even if you aren't comfortable in a public speaking environment there are many other ways to share the insights you have gained from your own life experiences — by talking with colleagues, mentoring others, submitting a story about one of your experiences to a magazine or other publication, writing a blog, or maybe even talking to your own children or grandchildren.

— You Can If You Believe You Can

TODAY, SPEAK UP AND SHARE
YOUR WISDOM WITH OTHERS. YOU
NEVER KNOW HOW YOU MIGHT
MAKE A DIFFERENCE.

INTEGRITY

W hen I originally wrote this Insight, I was sitting in the New York Marriott Marquis Hotel following a 90-minute speech to the top book and magazine publishers in the U.S. With the TV on in my room, I watched as the political life of then-New York governor Eliot Spitzer crumbled before my eyes. He'd been accused of meeting with a prostitute in a Washington hotel.

Speaking to the question of why public figures such as Spitzer continue to get involved in situations that they know will most likely lead to scandal and humiliation, Rabbi Brad Hirschfeld explains that it's about being bigger than the normal rules. The same ego that leads a person to imagine they are equipped to be CEO of a major corporation, a sports superstar or president of the United States, can also lead to illusions of grandeur that make them believe they'll never get caught when they step outside the boundaries.

Governor Spitzer later resigned from his position, ending what New York state assemblyman John McEneny called, "one of the most promising careers I've seen in a generation."

It takes 20 years to build a reputation and just five minutes to lose it. When it does happen, it's usually the result of one or more of the following: ego, greed, booze, drugs or illicit sex.

History books, newspapers and magazines are filled with people who damaged their good name and reputation because they thought the rules didn't apply to them. Quite mistakenly, they probably believed that they alone controlled their fate or that their achievements entitled them to break the rules. At some point in the past, it may have even been true, but in today's digital world no one's behaviour is beyond scrutiny.

— *The Power to Soar Higher*

H OW WILL WHAT YOU SAY
AND DO TODAY AFFECT YOUR
REPUTATION?

ALWAYS GIVE YOUR BEST

George Halas, Hall of Fame coach for the Chicago Bears, once said, "Nobody who ever gave his best regretted it."

Talk-show queen Oprah Winfrey was right when she said, "Do your best and people will notice."

People do notice how much effort we expend, even though they may never mention it. And there is no doubt in my mind that it influences their opinion about our reliability and performance.

How do we know when we're doing our best?

If we're honest, most of us know when we've given our very best effort to the task at hand and when we've just done what was expected but nothing more.

When Henry Kissinger was Secretary of State for the United States, an aide presented him with a report. Without looking at the contents, Kissinger asked, "Is this the best you can do?" The aide responded that he could do better. A few days later, the aide resubmitted the report. Kissinger inquired again, "Is this the best you can do?" The aide once again answered that he could do better. This interaction went on several more times, until finally the aide responded, "Yes, it is the best I can do." To which Kissinger replied, "Now I'll read it."

Next time you feel yourself slacking off or just making a half-hearted attempt at something, try the Kissinger test and ask yourself, "Is this the best I can do?" If it's not, you know what you need to do.

THE LITTLE THINGS

In 2003, when I became chair of the Vancouver Board of Trade, the very first event I was scheduled to host was a luncheon with guest speaker Darren Entwistle, president and CEO of Telus.

We had a sellout crowd of 750 at the Bayshore Hotel in downtown Vancouver and as chair, I was very excited. I arrived early just as Darren was finishing his rehearsal. I introduced myself as he was making notes with a very handsome-looking pen. I happened to mention to Darren that I thought it was a great-looking pen and to my surprise he offered to give it to me as a gift after the speech.

The luncheon was a great success and as I was thanking him for his presentation, I looked on with some disappointment as Darren casually put the pen back in his pocket. Obviously, he had forgotten that he had offered it to me and I didn't have the jam to say, "Hey Darren, you promised me that pen."

In the days that followed, I didn't see Darren as I carried on with a busy schedule, so I was quite surprised when a package arrived with the following handwritten note inside:

> *Peter,*
>
> *Here is the pen I promised you. Use it well and thank you for a great luncheon.*
>
> *Sincerely,*
> *Darren*

He had included a nice fleece vest with his company's logo on it as well. I still have both. Although it may have seemed like nothing more than a small gesture on Darren's part, it meant a lot to me. As you go about your business, remember the little things. They can count for a lot.

— *Make Your Life a Masterpiece*

"OUR DEEDS STILL TRAVEL WITH US FROM AFAR.
AND WHAT WE HAVE BEEN MAKES US
WHAT WE ARE." — George Eliot

TURN ERRORS INTO ADVANTAGES

Back in 1985, my mentor Ray Addington asked me to help promote the British Pavilion at Expo 86 in Vancouver. I jumped at the opportunity. The biggest part of the job was to find corporate sponsors. To do this, we put together a promotional package and a group of us went to London, England, to solicit British companies.

We had a variety of sponsorship levels available, each one named after a district of London. As I recall, they included Mayfair (the most expensive), Piccadilly and Leicester Square among others. Each level was priced based on the district for which it was named (kind of like the game Monopoly) and featured a list of benefits for the sponsor.

On the plane, the group had a meeting to review our sales pitch and in looking over the brochures, we discovered — to our collective horror — that the word Piccadilly had been misspelled. By this point in time, there was absolutely no way we could have the brochures reprinted in time for the presentation and we could hardly reschedule everything to a later date. Therefore, we did the only thing we could do; we came up with a scheme to turn our error into an advantage.

Here's how it worked.

Through the British trade association, we invited numerous big companies to come to a presentation where I was to be the MC. We started off the program by playing a video about Expo 86 to introduce the transportation theme of the fair. Then, as we prepared to hand out the brochures with the spelling mistake, we announced that we had purposely misspelled one of the place names and the first person to find it would win a prize.

— *Make Your Life a Masterpiece*

WHERE SOME SEE ERRORS,
OTHERS SEE OPPORTUNITIES.

THE LOWDOWN ON LUCK

We all know people who just seem to have a magic touch and really excel at what they do. In my company, Canada Wide Media, one such super salesperson's success was often attributed to luck by other members of the team, so one day I asked him about it.

"Not so," he told me. "I get up two hours earlier than the other salespeople and I work two hours longer than my colleagues. What I'm really doing is giving luck the opportunity to find me."

In my own career, I have found that the harder I work, the luckier I get. What is often referred to as luck is really just hard work and perseverance viewed through the eyes of those who aren't willing to put in the same effort. In truth, the only place that luck comes before work is in the dictionary.

— *Who Dares Wins*

MAKE IT EASY FOR LUCK
TO FIND YOU BY PUTTING YOUR
BEST EFFORT INTO EVERYTHING
YOU DO.

August 21

HAPPINESS IS YOUR OWN HOTDOG STAND
– PART I

Perhaps we are all entrepreneurs at heart, with dreams of being our own boss, calling the shots and ultimately being the architect of a hugely successful enterprise. However, while nearly every entrepreneur has visions of grandeur, the reality is that most businesses start out as small family operations. My first business was no different. In fact, my first entrepreneurial venture was a concession stand at the Pacific National Exhibition, Vancouver's annual summer fair.

At the time, I had a full-time job at *The Columbian Newspaper* in New Westminster but I wanted to buy a second car for my wife and this seemed like a good opportunity to do that. So, for a modest amount I purchased "Bunny's Foot Long Hotdogs" from a business associate and became the proud owner of my first venture. And that's when the problems started, problems I hadn't even imagined when I handed over the money. For example, I had no idea who would run this little venture from morning to night for 17 days, and what about contract negotiations with the fair and suppliers?

We eventually decided that my wife would run the stand, but how was she going to get to work? You guessed it, we had to go out and buy the car before we'd sold even one hotdog and the kicker was that we had to pay cash since we hadn't built up our credit yet. In the end, my mom and dad worked alongside my wife from 10 a.m. to midnight every day and because we couldn't afford a babysitter, Kay brought our daughter Samantha too. I think Samantha must have eaten our profits. When the 17 days were over, we barely broke even because it rained every day of the fair.

HAPPINESS IS YOUR OWN HOTDOG STAND
— PART II

What I learned from that summer selling hotdogs in the rain is that we shouldn't be afraid to try a new venture because the only way we are going to develop the skills to run a business is by actually doing it. Just like everything else in life, we learn by doing.

Of course, it is inevitable that we will make mistakes, but hopefully we will learn from those mistakes and they will make us stronger and wiser. As you can tell from this story, I wasn't born with business smarts; just like everyone else, I had to develop them from life experience. As Brian Tracy says, "If you can learn to drive a car — one of the most difficult things to master — you can learn any business skill." What I did have was the guts to try something new, to seek out an opportunity and take a chance.

Along the way, I discovered that the beauty of starting small is that you can learn skills as you go along and test your ideas and theories in a somewhat controlled, safe environment. Because I had a full-time job to go back to, I knew that hotdog stand wasn't going to make or break my future. I wasn't risking the mortgage money or the security of my family. At the same time, I wasn't willing to simply stick it out at my day job and wait for the years to pass until I could finally afford that second car.

I learned a great deal that summer; primarily that entrepreneurism isn't about the "perfect opportunity." It is about passion, challenge, creativity and seizing the opportunities that do come along.

— *The Runway of Life*

A SIMPLE THOUGHT FOR TODAY:
NOTHING VENTURED, NOTHING GAINED.

OPPORTUNITYISNOWHERE!

Be honest now, how did you read that headline? Opportunity is nowhere, or opportunity is now here? If you know me at all, you know that the second version is the one I like.

But far more important than deciphering titles is the ability, the "response-ability" we all have to recognize opportunities in life. Opportunities abound. Recognizing them is not a matter of any particular genius or even luck. It's a matter of studying your surroundings and doing something creative with what you see.

When you see opportunity, don't let it pass, do something about it.

When Michael Jordan realized that he had been left off the university basketball team because he did not meet the height requirement, rather than give up he intensified his training routine to ensure that it would be impossible for anyone to ignore his talent. Jordan went on to become the most famous player in NBA history, winning six NBA titles, five MVP awards and two Olympic gold medals.

J.K. Rowling was a single mother living on welfare when she got the idea for her first novel. She created Harry Potter and became the first writer to become a billionaire.

Oprah Winfrey faced numerous career setbacks including being fired from her first job because she was unfit for TV. Undeterred, she landed a job as a talk-show host and found her true calling. The rest, as they say, is history.

Now you're probably saying, "Yeah, Peter, pick out the best and make me feel bad. We're not all Jordans, Rowlings and Winfreys."

How right you are, but none of these three came from a privileged background. And how many times have you said to yourself, "I could have done that"?

Opportunity is always NOW HERE, but it's up to you to take action.

— *How to Soar With the Eagles*

TAKING RESPONSIBILITY

Perhaps one of the hardest lessons we all have to learn is that we are ultimately responsible for the choices we make and therefore responsible for the eventual success or failure of all of our endeavours. This of course, reminds me of a story.

I was on a 30th-wedding anniversary cruise from Istanbul to Rome with my wife Kay, aboard P&O's *Pacific Princess*. Our first port of call was Athens and in addition to the Parthenon, Kay and I were excited to visit Mars Hill where Paul from the New Testament stood centuries ago and welcomed the people to Athens.

Scheduled to leave Athens for our next port of call at 6 p.m., we got back and dressed for dinner, but were surprised when the ship did not disembark. As we sat down to eat at 7 p.m., we were still in Athens. At 9 p.m., I said to Kay, "I'll bet there's some sort of problem." At about 9:15, the captain informed us that we did in fact have a serious problem.

Two chefs from the ship had been caught smuggling drugs and were being detained. In fact, because of the seriousness of the offence, Greek officials had arrested the entire ship, including the crew and 650 passengers. We were subsequently stuck in Athens for six days, after which, P&O cancelled the entire cruise, paid for passengers to return home and refunded the entire cost of the trip.

As for the chefs, I think they offer a valuable lesson about responsibility for all of us. Our life is a blank canvas and we are the painters. We can choose to paint a masterpiece — or we can choose to spend the next 25 years in a jail in Greece.

— *Make Your Life a Masterpiece*

"RESPONSIBILITY IS THE PRICE OF
GREATNESS." — Winston Churchill

THE CHOICE IS YOURS – PART I

John is the kind of guy you love to hate. He is always in a good mood and always has something positive to say. When someone asks him how he's doing, he replies, "If I were any better, I'd be twins!"

He's also a natural motivator. If an employee were having a bad day, John would always be there telling them how to look on the positive side of the situation. His positive outlook on life really made me curious, so one day I went up and asked him about it.

"I don't get it!" I said. "You can't be so positive all of the time. How do you do it?"

"Each morning I wake up and say to myself, you have two choices today," he explained. "You can choose to be in a good mood or you can choose to be in a bad mood. I choose to be in a good mood. Each time something bad happens, you can choose to be a victim or you can choose to learn from it. I choose to learn from it. Every time someone comes to you complaining about life or someone who irritates them, you can choose to accept their complaining or you can point out the positive side of life. I choose the positive side of life."

"Yeah, right," I protested. "It's not that easy."

"Yes, it is," he insisted. "When you cut away all the junk, life is all about choices. You choose how you react to situations. You choose how other people's behaviour affects you. You choose to be in a good mood or a bad mood. The bottom line: it's your choice how you live your life."

THE CHOICE IS YOURS — PART II

Several years after that conversation, I heard that John had a serious accident, falling 60 feet from a communications tower. After 18 hours of surgery and weeks of intensive care, he was released from the hospital with rods in his back.

I saw him six months later.

When I asked how he was, he replied, "If I were any better, I'd be twins. Wanna see my scars?"

I declined to see his wounds, but asked what went through his mind during the accident.

"The first thing was the well-being of my soon-to-be-born daughter," he replied. "Then, as I lay on the ground, I remembered that I had two choices: I could choose to live or to die. I chose to live."

"Weren't you scared?" I asked.

"The paramedics were great," he said. "They kept telling me I was going to be fine. But when they wheeled me into the ER and I saw the expression on the faces of the doctors and nurses, I got really scared."

"What did you do?" I asked.

"Well, there was a big burly nurse shouting questions at me. She asked if I was allergic to anything. 'Yes,' I replied. The doctors and nurses all stopped working to listen. I took a deep breath and yelled, 'Gravity!'"

"Over their laughter, I told them, 'I'm choosing to live. Operate on me as if I am alive.'"

He did live, thanks to the skill of his doctors and his amazing attitude.

Attitude really is everything and I agree with John, how we respond to what happens on any given day is always a choice.

— *The Power to Soar Higher*

TODAY, CHOOSE TO MAKE THE MOST OF WHAT IS
HAPPENING IN THIS MOMENT, RATHER THAN
WORRY ABOUT WHAT ALREADY HAS OR COULD HAPPEN . . . .
OTHERWISE, GRAVITY IS SURE TO GET YOU DOWN.

ALVIN'S LAWS

As you may know, Alvin Law and I co-hosted the annual Variety Telethon together for years. Alvin is a remarkable man. He was a thalidomide baby and as a result was born with no arms. He has written a best-selling book called *Alvin's Laws of Life: 5 Steps to Successfully Overcome Anything*.

Based on his considerable accomplishments — he is a talented musician, playing trombone, drums and piano; holds an honours degree in Broadcasting and Communications; is a Certified Speaking Professional (CSP); has won an Emmy Award and raises millions of dollars for charity — Alvin is well qualified to offer advice on how to achieve your dreams. Here are the principles that underlie Alvin's Laws:

Attitude is more than just being positive — it's a way of looking at life. Attitude defines who we are and what we become.

Learning is the greatest gift we give ourselves. It is also the greatest equalizer on earth. In learning, we must ask questions — that's good because people need to listen more and talk less. To listen is to learn, and to learn is to grow.

Value your life and spirit. Too many people live another "V" — victim. It's true, bad things happen to good people, but there is no answer to the question, "Why me?" Everyone has value — finding it, that's the trick.

Imagination is the key that unlocks our potential. It is not owned by the young, but they are best at using it. It defines the difference between obstacles and possibilities. Imagination leads to dreams — dreams make life worth living.

Never give up! Easy to say, hard to do. The biggest enemy we will ever encounter is the one we face in the mirror. Yet mirrors do not reflect who we truly are — our lives do.

— *The Power of a Dream*

WHAT YOU GIVE IS WHAT YOU GET BACK

There are some physical laws and some laws of life that, no matter what happens, never change.

One of them is the law of gravity. I won't go into why it does what it does because I don't know. All I do know is that if you trip, chances are you'll fall and if you jump from the top of a tall building, you won't fly like Superman. Instead, you will begin to plummet at a rate of 32 feet per second and continue to fall ever faster until you hit the ground. At which point, other laws of physics come into play, causing horrible things to happen to your body. Please don't try it, just trust me. The law of gravity works the same for all of us, young or old, rich or poor, tall or short, male or female, when it comes to jumping off buildings, we all travel at the same rate.

Another great principle of life is that what we reap in life is directly related to what we have sown. Send out anger, you get it back. Serve up misery and misery will soon find you. Smile and some will look the other way because they think you're crazy, but most will smile back and share in the sense of goodwill.

Give of yourself and the bounty that comes back will astound you.

Zig Ziglar says you can get everything you want or need in life if you just help enough people get what they want and need. You keep giving, you keep getting. It's a simple but powerful law.

— *You Can If You Believe You Can*

ONLY SEND OUT INTO
THE WORLD TODAY
THAT WHICH YOU HOPE TO
RECEIVE IN RETURN.

August 29

YOU GOTTA SHOW UP

In May 2011, Canadians went to the polls yet again. In the last federal election in 2008, only 58 per cent of eligible voters cast a ballot. I suspect the poor turnout was the result of two things, the first being voter fatigue (four elections in seven years with similar results). The second reason is more troubling; it is the belief many people hold that they alone don't have the power to make a difference in the world. To those people I say, you are mistaken. In 2008, Liberal member of parliament Ujjal Dosanjh won his seat by just 22 votes. Imagine if those people hadn't shown up because they didn't believe they could make a difference.

Some years ago, an Eastern Airlines jet crashed shortly after takeoff from National Airport in Washington, D.C. and plunged into the icy Potomac River.

That morning, Aaron Williams was driving to an early shift at work and came across the horrific crash scene. Without hesitation, he dove into the water and pulled out one passenger, then another, then a third and a fourth. He plunged in a fifth time, but never resurfaced. Most likely, he was overcome by the cold. The miracle is that four people lived because of what Aaron Williams did that day. So, where would you place him and his individual effort in the scheme of things? I can only imagine how grateful those four people are that he showed up that day.

Do you have to die to make a difference? Absolutely not. It can happen at the edge of a frozen river, it can also happen the moment you put down this book, but to make it happen, first you've got to show up.

— *You Can If You Believe You Can*

WHAT DO YOU NEED
TO SHOW UP FOR TODAY?

UNLOCK YOUR POTENTIAL

While cruising in the Mediterranean, my wife Kay and I took a day trip to the city of Florence. Our first visit of the day was to the Galleria dell'Accademia where we got a first-hand look at the 13-and-a-half-foot sculpture of David by Michelangelo. It took him three years to finish this colossus.

As you walk towards "The David" you are reminded that Michelangelo worked on 45 sculptures in his lifetime and only completed 14 of them (if each took three years, that would be 42 years of work). *David* and *Moses* are probably the most famous finished works. There are also several unfinished statues including *The Prisoners, Atlantis, The Young Slave* and *The Awakening Slave*. These are the unfinished works and unfulfilled potential of a true genius.

It's been said that the average person only develops between one and two per cent of his or her potential over a lifetime. For others it may be as high as 10 per cent. I imagine if you were to use 25 per cent, you would be called a genius like Michelangelo.

Given these estimates, what's truly astonishing is the amount of potential we will never use. Yet it doesn't take much to start using more of our potential. As we look around our workplace, our community and even our home life, we can clearly see our own "blocks of stone" that, as yet, have not been developed to unlock our hidden potential.

How best to start?

Seek out mentors and other motivated people who will help you stretch outside of your comfort zone and reach new heights.

— *The Power to Soar Higher*

LIKE MICHELANGELO, YOU MAY
NOT BE ABLE TO FINISH EVERYTHING
YOU START. HOWEVER, BY STRETCHING
YOUR POTENTIAL, YOU MAY JUST
DISCOVER YOUR OWN GENIUS.

YOU NEVER KNOW

His name was Fleming and he was a poor Scottish farmer. One day, while trying to eke out a living for his family, he heard a cry for help from a nearby bog. He dropped his tools and ran. There, mired to his waist in mud, was a terrified boy, screaming and struggling to free himself. Farmer Fleming saved the boy from what could have been a slow and terrifying death.

The next day a fancy carriage pulled up to the Scotsman's farm and an elegantly dressed nobleman stepped out and introduced himself as the father of the boy the farmer had saved.

"I want to repay you," said the nobleman. "You saved my son's life."

"No, I can't accept payment for what I did," the farmer replied just as his own son came to the door.

"Is that your son?" the nobleman asked.

"Yes," said the farmer.

"I'll make you a deal. Let me take him and give him a good education. If the boy is anything like his father, he'll grow to be a man you can be proud of."

And that is what he did. In time, the farmer's son graduated from St. Mary's Hospital Medical School in London and went on to become Sir Alexander Fleming, the discoverer of penicillin.

Years afterward, the nobleman's son was stricken with pneumonia and penicillin saved his life.

The name of the nobleman? Lord Randolph Churchill. His son? Winston Churchill.

Someone once said that what goes around comes around.

— *Who Dares Wins*

MAKE AN EFFORT TO HELP OUT
WHERE YOU CAN. SMALL
ACTS OF KINDNESS ARE APPRECIATED
AND OFTEN REWARDED.

SEPTEMBER

TIME

I have to admit, I find the term "time management" to be a little strange. You can't actually manage time because it exists independently of anything we choose to do. The same holds true for all of the other things we attempt to do to time: wasting time, marking time, saving time, spending time, killing time . . . I think that last is probably the worst one. Why would you want to kill time?

As we get older, I think most of us wish that we had more time, particularly for all the things we thought we'd have time for later. Suddenly, we find ourselves running out of time. If only we could borrow some time from the younger generation who are busy wishing that time would go faster, especially near the end of the school day or those last few days leading up to Christmas or the summer break.

In truth, we can only manage ourselves and how we choose to use the time that we have, which means that we inevitably have to make some hard choices. As much as possible, I think we should choose to spend our time deliberately and use it wisely rather than wasting it or killing it, because more than anything else, time is precious.

— Insight 2011

"WE SAY WE WASTE TIME,
BUT THAT IS IMPOSSIBLE. WE WASTE
OURSELVES." — Alice Bloch

NO MISTAKE SHOULD EVER GO TO WASTE

*"I have learned throughout my life
as a composer chiefly through my mistakes and
pursuits of false assumptions, not by my
exposure to founts of wisdom and
knowledge."* — Igor Stravinsky

F ear of making mistakes is one of the biggest obstacles to having an interesting and fulfilling life. If you aren't making any mistakes, chances are you're not trying very hard at whatever you are doing. Successful people make lots of errors and they learn valuable lessons as a result. The expectation that things need to go perfectly is unrealistic and extremely limiting. Not only are mistakes a wonderful source of insight that we can use to make progress towards fulfilling our dreams, at times they are absolutely necessary to make us stop and pay attention. Sometimes we have to hit that brick wall to realize that we need to try a different tack and discover other alternatives.

So next time you make a mistake, don't beat yourself up. Instead, be thankful for the insight you've been given and ask yourself, "How can I apply what I've learned?" No mistake should ever go to waste.

— The Power of a Dream

"FAILURE IS, IN A SENSE,
THE HIGHWAY TO SUCCESS . . ."
— John Keats

NEVER KNOW WHEN TO QUIT

Football coach George Allen often said, "People of mediocre ability sometimes achieve outstanding success because they don't know when to quit. Most men succeed because they are determined to." He also said, "Each of us has been put on this earth with the ability to do something well. We cheat ourselves and the world if we don't use that ability as best we can."

Allen himself lived for coaching. During 12 years in the National Football League he never had a losing season and although he never won a Super Bowl ring, of all the coaches in the Pro Football Hall of Fame, only Vince Lombardi had a higher career winning percentage. But Allen's success wasn't because he had a flashy style or exciting plays. In fact, it was just the opposite. Allen was often criticized for his unexciting offence and for trading away his draft choices in favour of seasoned veteran players, year after year.

So how did he do it? A lot of football people believed the reason Allen was able to take his team to the playoffs again and again was because he'd managed to convince his players that they were better than they ever thought they'd be. Allen was absolutely committed to discipline, conditioning and an extraordinary attention to detail. "Winning," he explained, "is the science of being totally prepared."

You can't ever lose if you simply refuse to quit.

— *The Runway of Life*

TAKE A MOMENT RIGHT NOW
AND ASK YOURSELF THIS QUESTION,
"WHAT GREAT THING WOULD
I ATTEMPT TO DO IF I KNEW I COULD
NOT FAIL?" BECAUSE THE TRUTH
IS, YOU REALLY CAN'T FAIL.
YOU CAN ONLY FAIL TO TRY.

SEIZE YOUR OPPORTUNITIES – PART I

"Then indecision brings its own delays,
and days are lost lamenting o'er lost days. Are you in earnest?
Seize this very minute. What you can do,
or dream you can, begin it; boldness has genius,
power and magic in it."

As Johann Wolfgang von Goethe so eloquently put it in the above quote, the secret of success in life is to be ready for opportunity when it comes and to seize it.

As a teenager in New Westminster, B.C., I attended Lester Pearson High School. It was there that I emceed a few pep rallies, performed at assemblies and really caught the show business bug. If you've ever seen TV shows like *Happy Days*, you'll know that high school in the late '50s, early '60s, was a blast. However, as is inevitable, life became a little more serious once we graduated; as young adults, we had to get jobs and begin fending for ourselves.

With the showbiz bug still in my system and fancying myself as an up-and-coming comedian, I watched every comic on TV, studying their technique and material. Watching *The Ed Sullivan Show*, a Sunday-night ritual, I dreamed of the day when it would be me in front of the cameras making everyone laugh.

After a few years of performing, an opportunity came my way to entertain at the Marine Drive Golf and Country Club in Vancouver. In the audience was John Usher, the booking manager for the P&O Shipping Line. He liked what he saw and offered me a position onboard the *SS Oriana*, sailing from Vancouver to Southampton, England. I jumped at the opportunity and after a teary farewell from my parents, set sail for my first big solo adventure.

SEIZE YOUR OPPORTUNITIES – PART II

My very first night on the ship, I met an enchanting young lady. Kay Tanner, who had grown up in England, had spent the previous year living in Seattle with her family while her father worked in the U.S. Now, she was returning to England to see the fiancé she had left behind and discover if there were still any sparks between them. I learned about Kay's engagement three of four days into the trip and realized I would have to work fast if I wanted to have any chance of changing her mind.

On the dock in Jamaica — the last port of call before the transatlantic crossing that would take us to Lisbon, Cherbourg and then Southampton — I took fate into my own hands, asking Kay to write her fiancé and advise him that he needn't meet her at the dock when we landed.

"What are you going to do about it?" she asked me.

"I would like to marry you," I told her.

Luckily for me, she said yes. We have now been married 44 years and counting. Looking back, I wasn't at all sure where my future would lead me, but I knew that if I didn't act on the opportunity, Kay would have promptly sailed out of my life as quickly as she had sailed into it and I wasn't willing to let that happen.

— Make Your Life a Masterpiece

"YOU'LL SELDOM EXPERIENCE REGRET FOR
ANYTHING YOU'VE DONE. IT IS WHAT YOU HAVEN'T DONE
THAT WILL TORMENT YOU. THE MESSAGE,
THEREFORE, IS CLEAR. DO IT! DEVELOP AN APPRECIATION
FOR THE PRESENT MOMENT. SEIZE EVERY SECOND
OF YOUR LIFE AND SAVOUR IT. VALUE YOUR PRESENT
MOMENTS. USING THEM UP IN ANY SELF-DEFEATING
WAY MEANS YOU'VE LOST THEM FOREVER."
— Wayne Dyer

EVERYONE NEEDS A DREAM

As you have discovered, this book is full of ideas and stories about people who are pursuing their own dreams — dreams that come in all shapes and sizes. My purpose in sharing these stories is to demonstrate that every one of us has the potential to fulfill our dreams, but it takes action and commitment to get there. It is my hope that you will find inspiration from the many people in this book, people like my friend and business associate, Mel Zajac. In two separate tragic accidents, Mel lost both of his sons.

Following a period of grieving, he decided to channel his energy and love for his sons into something healthy to help other kids. He had a dream to create an amazing place where children with disabilities or serious health concerns could go to have fun and feel like normal kids for a change. To fulfill his dream, together with his wife, he established the Mel Jr. and Marty Zajac Foundation and the Zajac Ranch for Children in Maple Ridge, B.C. It's difficult to gauge the impact that Mel's dream has had on kids who attend the ranch's programs each summer, but it is obvious that it has helped hundreds of kids with disabilities to do things that otherwise seemed impossible. In 2007, Mel Zajac was awarded the Order of Canada for his philanthropy and he continues to live his dream.

— The Power of a Dream

EVERYONE NEEDS A DREAM, WHETHER
IT IS TO BRING NEW PURPOSE
TO THEIR LIFE OR SIMPLY A REASON
TO JUMP OUT OF BED
IN THE MORNING.

AN OLD FARMER'S ADVICE

We can always learn from other people. Here are some words of wisdom that we can apply to our business and personal lives.

Life is simpler when you plow around the stump.
Words that soak into your ears are whispered . . . not yelled.
Meanness don't just happen overnight.
Forgive your enemies; it messes up their heads.
Do not corner something that you know is meaner than you.
It don't take a very big person to carry a grudge.
You cannot unsay a cruel word.
Every path has a few puddles.
When you wallow with pigs, expect to get dirty.
The best sermons are lived, not preached.
Most of the stuff people worry about ain't never gonna happen anyway.
Don't judge folks by their relatives.
Remember that silence is sometimes the best answer.
Live a good and honourable life, then when you get older and think back, you'll enjoy it a second time.
Don't interfere with something that ain't bothering you none.
If you find yourself in a hole, the first thing to do is stop digging.
The biggest troublemaker you'll probably ever have to deal with watches you from the mirror every morning.
Always drink upstream from the herd.
Good judgment comes from experience, and a lotta that comes from bad judgment.
Letting the cat outta the bag is a whole lot easier than putting it back in.
If you get to thinkin' you're a person of some influence, try ordering somebody else's dog around.
Live simply, love generously, care deeply, speak kindly and leave the rest to God.

— Insight 2011

September 8

GOOD OLD-FASHIONED PRIDE

I recall a story that billionaire Jimmy Pattison told me one time about how he had an annual "pride" convention for his employees where upon opening the first meeting of the day, he proceeded to pair people up. Once everyone had a partner, he gave them a mop and pail and assigned them to clean each other's rooms.

When everyone was done, Jimmy had the hotel staff inspect each room and grade it based on their professional opinion. The purpose of the exercise was to emphasize the importance of service and humility in business and to send home the message that no one in the organization is above any task.

As Robin Sharma writes in his book, *The Greatness Guide*, "There is no such thing as an unimportant day. Each one of us is called to greatness. Each one of us can have a significant impact on the world around us — if we so choose. But for this power that resides internally to grow, we need to use it."

The point here is that we should take pride in everything we do and be willing to do any job we expect others to do. As a leader, nothing should be beneath you, so set the example you want others to follow. As General George S. Patton is famous for saying, "Give direction, not directions."

Here are some suggestions to help you build pride in your business:

- Provide sufficient training for all new employees, new tasks and new programs.
- Share information and encourage feedback.
- Allocate sufficient resources to accomplish goals.
- Offer coaching and give employees authority to make decisions.
- Reward performance with incentive/promotions.

— *The Power to Soar Higher*

"THE SMALLEST TASK,
WELL DONE, BECOMES A MIRACLE OF
ACHIEVEMENT." — Og Mandino

NEVER TOO LATE

When Kay and I were first married, we didn't have a lot of money; nevertheless, we agreed that Kay would be an at-home mom to our children. As a result, she spent the first 15 years of our marriage attending to the needs of our three daughters, Samantha, Rebecca and Amanda. It was an investment of her time that pays wonderful dividends today. We have three spectacular and accomplished daughters, each one pursuing her own dreams.

Kay had a dream too. Even before the children, Kay dreamed of becoming a marriage counsellor and helping others. That dream didn't change throughout the years — if anything it became stronger. So as the girls matured into young women and didn't need Kay nearly so much, her thoughts returned once again to pursuing her dream.

Realizing that she would need to return to university to complete both a BA and a Masters degree to reach her goal, Kay worried she had left it too long. "It's going to take almost six years and I'll be nearly 50 when I graduate," she said to me one evening.

"Whether you do it or not, in six years you will be 50," I responded. "Why not go for it?"

Kay decided to follow her heart. After completing her BA, she enrolled in the Masters of Counselling program at Trinity Western University and today she works part time at a clinic in Langley, B.C. She's been doing it for 12 or 13 years now and she absolutely loves it. Her mission, she says, is to bring people together and there is no doubt in my mind that by having the courage to pursue her own dream, she has enriched the lives of others.

— *The Power to Soar Higher*

IT'S NEVER TOO LATE
TO PURSUE YOUR DREAM.

IT'S *YOU* WHO CHANGES THINGS

I often share the following statistic with my audiences during speaking engagements. Eighty per cent of the things we see and think about in any given day are negative. Our media is negative, we all too often view our fellow human beings negatively (think about the last time you were in traffic), we're negative about our jobs, the price of gas, our politicians and even our country in general.

If we subscribe to the idea that we become what we think about most of the time, we could easily end up being an extremely negative bunch. Yet there is no reason to be that way when there is such opportunity within each of us to be the most passionately positive people on the planet. And if we look at events taking place in many other parts of the world today, we have a lot to be positive about and much to be thankful for.

Despite whatever economic hiccups we may encounter or whether we have to endure one election after another, the incredible truth is that we enjoy tremendous personal liberty and the kind of democratic freedom that people in other countries are willing to die for. Of course, with such freedom and power comes responsibility. The most important responsibility being that we actively participate in the democratic process (at the very least, by voting whenever we are eligible to do so) and to be willing to stand up and take action when necessary to protect the freedoms we enjoy.

— *You Can If You Believe You Can*

IT'S YOU WHO CAN CHANGE
THINGS. COUNTERACT NEGATIVITY BY
TAKING POSITIVE ACTION TO
CHANGE WHATEVER IT IS THAT YOU
DON'T LIKE IN YOUR WORLD.

REFLECTIONS FROM GROUND ZERO

My wife Kay and I were in New York a few days before the second anniversary of 9/11. It was a glorious and brilliant sunny Friday morning. As we looked upon Ground Zero, a fenced-in area where the World Trade Center's twin towers had once stood, I couldn't help but think of where I was on that fateful day and how it made me feel about the world I live in.

Those who committed the horrific acts on September 11, 2001, wanted to disrupt the western world and our way of life. So even though I am thankful to live in Canada, I also realize that because New York is considered to be the centre of the western world — particularly the financial centre — this tragedy was really devastating for all of us. The personal tragedy that resulted will be felt for many years to come, as thousands of families and friends continue to grieve for their loved ones.

On the day we were at the World Trade Center site, a New York CBS reporter was taping that day's noon news and we struck up a conversation. She told me her husband had worked in one of the towers but was late for work on the day of the attacks. She shed a tear as she jumped into her van but turned to me and said, "I'll have to be gentle with him this week." As I turned to say goodbye I noticed a sign hanging from a nearby building. It read: *"The human spirit is not measured by the size of the act, but by the size of the heart."*

— The Runway of Life

ASK YOURSELF THIS, IF TOMORROW
I AM NO LONGER HERE, WHAT
WILL I WISH I HAD DONE DIFFERENTLY
THIS DAY, WHILE I STILL HAD
THE CHANCE?

BULEMBU

There is a little village in Swaziland, Africa, called Bulembu. In 2001, the U.K. mining company that had built and operated Bulembu for more than 60 years closed its doors and walked away. With no jobs for the inhabitants, the town was soon abandoned. Located in a country that continues to be ravaged by the AIDS pandemic, the result was an orphan crisis for the village of Bulembu (which has more than 2,000 AIDS orphans).

Enter Volker Wagner, a B.C. man whose dream after visiting Bulembu in 2004, was to buy the town and apply his mind, body, soul and spirit to restoring the lives and the heart of this little community — a pretty big dream to be sure.

In 2006, Wagner, together with a team of entrepreneurs and social developers, purchased the abandoned town with a clear vision — to restore Bulembu to a vibrant, self-sustaining community by the year 2020. This vision for sustainability includes providing total care for more than 1,000 orphaned, vulnerable children, developing innovative business enterprises and fostering the development of a new generation of emerging leaders.

Since 2009, the fundraising campaign *Voices for Bulembu* has raised over $2.4 million for Bulembu's rejuvenation by hosting concerts in Canada with well-known performers such as The Canadian Tenors. I attended one of their 2010 concerts at the Mission Hill Winery in Kelowna and was absolutely blown away by the passion all of these people have to make a difference in the world. The money they have raised, together with funding from partners in other countries, is being used to build important infrastructure for the village, including a new primary school.

— Insight 2010

THE BIGGER YOUR DREAM IS, THE MORE
HELP YOU WILL NEED TO MAKE IT COME TRUE.
SEEK OUT AND COLLABORATE WITH
PEOPLE WHO SHARE YOUR PASSION AND VISION.

WHAT'S IN A NAME?

How important is a name? Your name is everything; it's the link between all of the successes of your past and your future potential. If you want to be successful, you will spend your lifetime developing, enhancing and protecting your name.

In the speaking business, our name is our calling card. Most of our engagements and referrals are based on our name and the reputation we have built up and, while it is a fact that most of us will never be celebrity speakers, we still need to be the best journeymen speakers that we can be. When asked to give advice to other speakers, I almost always say, "Concentrate on developing your skills to be a great speaker. Be passionate, exciting and on topic and your future will be just fine." Actually, I believe that message is relevant no matter what profession you are in. Whatever you decide to focus on, it should be something you believe in, something you can be accomplished at and something you are willing to commit yourself to for long-term results.

Associate your name with quality and remember the very best referrals come from people who have been impressed with your performance in the past.

Here are a couple more tips to keep in mind:

Always deliver more than you promised, even if it means going out of your way or taking a short-term loss on a project that you have already committed to.

Be generous with your knowledge and expertise. Mentor newcomers or hold a workshop or seminar with newcomers in your industry. When you are helpful and kind, people remember your name.

— *The Runway of Life*

SPEND TIME DEVELOPING YOUR
CHARACTER BECAUSE THAT IS WHAT
YOUR NAME STANDS FOR.

FOCUS ON THE TOP LINE

W hen you think about it, there's something innately negative about "the bottom line" and in business, we never know if the bottom line is going to be a nice surprise or monumental bad news.

Money comes in and money goes out and what's left at the end of the month or year is the bottom line. To tell the truth, it doesn't sound very inspiring or appealing. Have you ever thought of just turning the whole thing around and choosing to work for the top line instead?

It's easy enough to do. At the beginning of the month (or year), say to yourself that what's left over is no longer going to be good enough. Then, set a realistic goal and work to meet it. Unlike bottom-line thinking, which is defensive, top-line is focused on growth, improvement, engagement and advancement, all positive elements that motivate and uplift, exactly what we all need with the current level of economic turmoil in our lives.

As former Apple CEO Steve Jobs once advised, "Manage your top line, which is your business strategy, your people, the talent that you have and your products; do all that stuff right and the bottom line will follow."

— *How to Soar With the Eagles*

WHY WAIT FOR THE SURPRISE
AT THE BOTTOM WHEN YOU CAN
SHOOT FOR THE TOP?

A WINNER'S ATTITUDE – STEP 1

I've learned a great deal over the years from my friend Nido Qubein. In his book, *How to Get Anything You Want*, Nido talks about how we need to have a winner's attitude in order to achieve our goals, and he allowed me to share this idea in my book, *Who Dares Wins*. Over the next three days, I'd like to share them with you too.

Nido writes: There are three basic steps to developing a winner's attitude. They are simple to say and easy to understand, but they require more effort than anything you have ever tried.

Step 1 — Make a strong and permanent commitment to invest your life and talents only in those pursuits that deserve your best efforts.

If it's worth doing at all, it's worth doing to the best of your ability. If it's not worth the best you can do, it's not worthy of the winner's time.

No matter how inspirational, nobody can really motivate another person, it's something that each of us must do for ourselves. Alcoholics Anonymous is a perfect example of this principle. It's an organization that has been highly successful at helping people overcome a severe habit. Yet, any member of AA will tell you that he or she can do nothing to help an alcoholic — until that person is totally committed to the goal of sobriety.

Only when you are totally committed to an overriding purpose will you put forth the effort required to battle discouragement, bounce back from failure, overcome handicaps and meet fear head on.

— *Who Dares Wins*

ONLY COMMIT TO GOALS
THAT ARE WORTHY
OF YOUR BEST EFFORTS.

A WINNER'S ATTITUDE – STEP 2

When asked the secret of his success, writer Charles Dickens said, "Whatever I have tried to do in life, I have tried with my heart to do well."

Step 2 — Make a strong and irrevocable commitment to give all that you have and all that you are to achieve your goals.

What's the difference between winners and losers? Losers do what is required of them or even less; but winners always do more than is required — and they do it with enthusiasm. Losers are always looking for an easy way out. But winners, having committed themselves to work only toward their chosen goals, roll up their sleeves and take on challenges as they come.

The great philosopher Elbert Hubbard once said, "Folks who never do more than they get paid to do, never get paid any more than they do."

Much has been said about escaping from reality with drugs like LSD and methamphetamines. However, a far more dangerous escape vehicle is much more common than these drugs. It is SFN, or something-for-nothing. For many people, its temptation is almost irresistible and it is frighteningly habit-forming, destroying self-reliance and self-respect.

Winners accept the fact that problems are only opportunities in disguise. Edmund Burke declared:

"The battle of life is in most cases fought uphill and to win it without a struggle is almost like winning it without honour. If there were no difficulties, there would be no success; if there were nothing to struggle for, there would be nothing to be achieved. Difficulties may intimidate the weak, but they act only as a wholesome stimulus to men of resolution and valour."

— *Who Dares Wins*

YOU MAY HAVE THE LOFTIEST GOALS,
THE HIGHEST IDEALS AND THE
NOBLEST DREAMS, BUT REMEMBER, NOTHING
WORKS UNLESS YOU DO.

A WINNER'S ATTITUDE – STEP 3

"So live — decently, fearlessly, joyfully . . ."
— Adlai Stevenson

Step 3 — Make a strong commitment to reach your full potential as a human being.

Consider who you are! You were born for greatness, because you were born from greatness. Consider for a moment some of the unique capabilities you possess as a human being: the ability to create; the ability to love; the ability to make ethical and moral judgments. And then there is the ability to reason. Of all the creatures on earth, only humans have such an enormous capacity to reason, to store massive amounts of knowledge, to develop wisdom, to evaluate. Yet scientists tell us that even geniuses like Socrates, Da Vinci and Einstein, never used all of the mental capacities they possessed.

We also have the unique ability to pass knowledge to the next generation. Animals have to start from scratch with only what they have inherited through their genes, yet humans have the ability to transmit great amounts of knowledge from one generation to the next. Aren't you happy you don't have to reinvent the wheel, rediscover fire or develop a language? It is humbling to realize that most of the comforts and conveniences we enjoy today are possible only because of the strivings and creativity of those who have gone before us. It is equally humbling to realize that what we do today will affect the lives of people for centuries to come. Therefore, we have a great responsibility to do all we can to use the potential that has been given us and to leave the world a better place for future generations.

— *Who Dares Wins*

OUR THOUGHTS AND IMAGINATION
ARE THE ONLY REAL
LIMITS TO OUR POSSIBILITIES.

PUT YOUR BRAIN TO WORK WHILE YOU SLEEP

Although it's been proven that we do in fact use all areas of our brain, not just 10 per cent as has been quoted in popular literature for decades, what is still true is that when it comes to harnessing the immense power of our brain to solve problems, most of us only use a fraction of its potential.

While we have both a conscious and subconscious, we are generally more aware of the conscious mind because we spend most of our waking time there. When we sleep, it is the subconscious mind that becomes active. The fact that we think, reason and compute with our conscious mind would seem to make it superior to whatever the subconscious mind does and until recently, the vast powers of the subconscious remained fairly untapped. As science continues to explore its depths, we learn more about its capacity as the quiet dynamo behind the conscious mind.

Here is a simple way to harness more of the potential of your subconscious mind.

Each night before you go to bed, write a few pressing questions in a notebook and then go to sleep. Research shows that much of the insight you experience happens while you're focused on not focusing. You read that right. For the brain to do its magic, it needs to be untethered from biases and judgment and negative self-talk. That freedom happens while you sleep. If you continue to do this on a regular basis, you'll train your brain to make the connections to find the answers for you. It worked for Thomas Edison (who registered a total of 1,093 patents in his lifetime); it can work for you.

— *Insight 2011*

TONIGHT, BEFORE
YOU GO TO SLEEP, PUT YOUR
BRAIN TO WORK.

THE HOW OF "WOW"

A while back, when my friend and fellow speaker Brian Tracy had just released a new book, *The Art of Closing Sales*, I decided to put on a one-week sales course for the team at Canada Wide Media. I bought a copy of the book for each of the guys and every morning for five days we sat down to talk about one chapter.

Working through the book together, the week was very productive. To show my appreciation for their hard work, I prepared a graduation certificate for each member of the sales team. But I also wanted to add a "wow" factor to the experience to make it truly memorable, so I got in touch with my good friend Brian Tracy and I asked him if he would phone our boardroom at exactly 8:30 a.m. on the Friday.

When the call from Brian came in right on cue, my sales guys were suitably impressed and, as Brian did a 10-minute motivational message live on the phone, I could see that they were hanging on his every word. It was exactly what was needed to get them pumped up and ready to put what they had learned into action and I knew it would be something they would remember for a long time. I could also tell by the looks on their faces at the end of the call that they were thinking, "Wow, how the hell did he get Brian Tracy to phone at exactly 8:30 while he was handing out those certificates?"

— *The Power to Soar Higher*

WHAT CAN YOU DO
TO PRODUCE A "WOW" FACTOR
FOR THE PEOPLE THAT
YOU INFLUENCE AND MOTIVATE?
LOOK FOR OPPORTUNITIES TO MAKE
EXPERIENCES MEMORABLE.

September 20

EVERYDAY DIPLOMACY

*"Manners are a sensitive awareness of the feelings
of others. If you have that awareness, you
have good manners, no matter what fork you use."* — Emily Post

Manners are a small but significant way of showing those people we come into contact with that we recognize the importance of their needs and wishes in addition to our own. "Please" and "Thank you" are the cornerstones of common courtesy, yet amazingly, many people no longer find it necessary to acknowledge the helpfulness of others — particularly strangers — with these two little phrases.

Think about your own behaviour. How often do you show gratitude to others for: holding the door open for you; serving you in a store or restaurant; handling your complaint about a product or service; or giving you the right-of-way on the road?

It's such a small thing and yet when we do remember our manners, we are often immediately rewarded for our good behaviour with a smile or other friendly gesture. No matter where you go or what you do, you cannot underestimate the positive power of treating everyone you meet with kindness and respect. In fact, whether you speak more than one language or not, you can get along almost anywhere in the world by simply knowing how to say "please" and "thank you" in the local language.

— The Power of Tact

"YOU CAN GET THROUGH LIFE WITH BAD MANNERS,
BUT IT'S EASIER WITH GOOD MANNERS." — Lillian Gish

WHAT CAN YOU DO TO UP
YOUR COURTESY QUOTIENT AND BECOME
AN EVERYDAY DIPLOMAT?

September 21

NEVER LEAVE A COMPLAINT UNANSWERED

Many large companies simply ignore complaints received by email in the hope that the problem will go away. In our highly connected world, that can be a fatal mistake. Imagine if you had a problem, how it would feel to be ignored in this way. Some customers are deciding to take matters into their own hands, like Dave Carroll, the guy who wrote the song, "United Breaks Guitars," and posted it on YouTube. Prior to writing and posting his song, which, incidentally, got over 10 million views, he tried for 18 months to communicate his problem to the company without success.

I can only guess that the people at United Airlines regret not dealing with the complaint before it got to that point. An article in the U.K.'s *London Sunday Times* reported that the company's stock plunged 10 per cent within four days of the song's debut, costing United an estimated $180 million, which, incidentally, could have bought Carroll 51,000 replacement guitars. Most companies couldn't survive what happened to United.

How well do you deal with customer complaints?

Rather than thinking about it as a negative, approach every complaint as an opportunity to satisfy a customer who has already invested in the relationship by giving you their business. If you take the time to listen, they will tell you what they need and how best to serve those needs. It is much easier to keep an existing customer happy than it is to find a new customer.

— *The Power to Soar Higher*

IT'S NOT ALWAYS EASY
TO FACE UP TO CRITICISM, BUT WITHOUT
YOUR CUSTOMERS YOU WOULDN'T
BE IN BUSINESS AT ALL. VIEW EVERY COMPLAINT
AS AN OPPORTUNITY TO STRENGTHEN
YOUR RELATIONSHIP WITH THE CUSTOMER
AND GROW YOUR BUSINESS.

DEVELOP A PLEASING PERSONALITY — PART I

It's a fact of life that up to 20 per cent of people will not like you. In some cases, you may be able to do something about this and in others not. As an individual, the kind of personality you develop can be your greatest asset or your biggest liability for it determines more than just how others see you, it also greatly affects the way you experience life. Therefore, it is essential that you develop a pleasing personality — for yourself and others.

Here are some factors that make up a pleasing personality:
- positive mental attitude
- tolerance
- kindness
- sense of fair play
- sincerity
- friendly disposition
- a sense of humour
- enthusiasm
- patience
- control of temper and emotions

Very often, how we choose to interact with someone the first time sets the tone for how the relationship develops, as demonstrated in the following story about a city man who bought a farm.

On the first day at his new farm, the city fellow went out to look at the fence and as he walked, the neighbouring farmer appeared and said to him, "That fence is a full foot over on my side."

"No problem," said the new owner. "We will set the fence two feet over on my side."

"Oh, but that's more than I claim," stammered the surprised farmer.

"No worries, I would much rather have peace with my neighbour than two feet of earth," said the man.

"But I couldn't let you do that," replied the farmer. "The fence will stay right where it is."

— *Make Your Life a Masterpiece*

DEVELOP A PLEASING PERSONALITY – PART II

*"Don't flatter yourself that friendship authorizes
you to say disagreeable things to your intimates. The nearer
you come in relation with a person, the more necessary
do tact and courtesy become."* — Oliver Wendell Holmes

The best way to sell yourself to others is to sell the others to yourself. Check your attitude against this list of obstacles to a pleasing personality: interrupting others; sarcasm; vanity; being a poor listener; insincere flattery; finding fault; challenging others without good cause; giving unsolicited advice; complaining; maintaining an attitude of superiority; envy of others' success.

Although the way you treat others affects the way that they treat you, the way another person treats you shouldn't determine how you treat them in return. Therefore, respond to what appears to you to be rude behaviour with the utmost kindness. You can't know what has gone on in that person's life that day, but you can probably assume that things have not gone well — and whatever the cause of the rudeness, you don't need to accentuate the problem. Perhaps a kind word or a gentle, understanding smile may be just what they need to remind them that everyone is not against them. Even if it doesn't work, you can walk away knowing that you didn't add fuel to the fire.

William James once said, "The deepest principle in human nature is the craving to be appreciated." And probably the most important rule in the world is, "Do unto others as you would have them do unto you." If you have difficulty practicing this rule in your own life, imagine a sign hanging around every person's neck that only you can read, and it says, "Make me feel important."

— Make Your Life a Masterpiece

WE ALL HAVE THE ABILITY TO MAKE OURSELVES
MORE PLEASING TO OTHERS.

DEVELOP A PLEASING PERSONALITY — PART III

Here are some ideas on ways to develop a pleasing personality:
The greatest way to make a positive first impression is to demonstrate immediately that the other person, not you, is the centre of action and conversation. Try to keep all of the attention for yourself and you'll miss opportunities for friendships, jobs, love relationships, networking and sales. Take a genuine interest in others and people will be drawn to the warmth of your personality.

How we speak speaks volumes about us. Listeners judge our intelligence, education, cultural sophistication and even leadership ability by what we say and how we say it. Therefore, make sure you speak clearly, enunciate properly and use language that is appropriate to the situation.

Be careful what you say about others. An offhand comment might be repeated and you'll soon be in the midst of a controversy. Don't waste your energy on gossip and remember that whatever you say about someone else is going to be interpreted by the person hearing it.

Remember who you are. Most of us more or less live up — or down — to our stereotypes. Compared to most of the world, North Americans are abrupt and action-oriented, we'd rather skip the small talk and get right to business. This can be interpreted as rudeness by other cultures. Self-awareness can help us adjust our behaviour and attend to the sensitivities of those we want to interact with.

Employ humour, but proceed with care. Although a quip or two might serve as an ice-breaker, be thoughtful about the kinds of witty remarks you make or the jokes you tell. Make sure they are appropriate to the audience to ensure you don't give offence.

— *Make Your Life a Masterpiece*

PERSONALITY HAS THE POWER
TO OPEN MANY DOORS.

September 25

AN OPTIMISTIC TAKE ON ATTITUDE

Pastor Chuck Swindoll has made famous his affirmation on attitudes. "The longer I live, the more I realize the impact of attitude on life. Attitude for me is more important than facts, it is more important than the past, than education, than money, than circumstances, than failures, than successes, than what other people think or say or do. It is more important than appearance, giftedness or skill. It will make or break a company, a church, a home. The remarkable thing is we have a choice every day regarding the attitude we will embrace for the day. We cannot change our past; we cannot change the fact that people will respond in a certain way. We cannot change the inevitable. The only thing we can do is play the only string we have, and that is our attitude. I am convinced that life is 10 per cent what happens to me and 90 per cent how I react to it. And so it is with you. We are all in charge of our attitudes!"

Your attitude is a little thing that makes a big difference. The dictionary defines it as "one's feelings or mood toward things and people." Well, if our life is dealing with people virtually every day, then we must believe noted University of Pennsylvania psychologist Martin Seligman, who says, "Individuals who are optimistic and have a positive attitude are more successful than similarly talented pessimists."

— *The Runway of Life*

IT'S NOT THAT OPTIMISM SOLVES ALL
OF LIFE'S PROBLEMS; IT IS JUST
THAT IT CAN SOMETIMES MAKE THE
DIFFERENCE BETWEEN COPING
AND COLLAPSING. — Lucy MacDonald

CHANGE YOUR MENTAL FILTER

What were the first thoughts you had when you woke up this morning? Were you just happy to be alive and excited about the opportunity of a new day, or did your mind immediately fill up with thoughts of all the things you need to do and worry about how you will deal with a whole list of problems and concerns?

Looking at life through a pessimistic lens is a habit that many of us have and it can be difficult to break. Left unattended, chronic negative thinking can begin to darken our perception of the world in general and cast a cloud over all of our experiences and interactions. We look for difficulties and, no surprise, we find them everywhere, meaning the glass is always half-empty.

But it doesn't take much to begin to change that mental filter by allowing positive thoughts to sift in as well. Starting right now, begin a little experiment with yourself whereby you try to find at least one good thing in every circumstance. For example, a long wait at the doctor's office is a great opportunity to chat with your spouse or child; a stressful time at work provides you with the chance to realize the inner strength you possess; even the current economic climate can have a positive effect if we challenge ourselves to live within our means and see just how much value we can get out of the money we do have.

— Insight 2011

PRACTICE LOOKING FOR
THE POSITIVE IN SITUATIONS AND
YOU WILL FIND IT.

THOSE WHO DARE TO READ, WIN

R esearch has shown that many university students never crack open a hardcover book after they graduate. Ninety per cent of the population never read non-fiction books at all. The other 10 per cent read about one book a year on a topic of personal interest or something to do with their career.

Interesting statistics.

The first business book I ever read was written by one of North America's most successful insurance salesmen, Elmer G. Leterman. The book was titled, *How Showmanship Sells* and as a young radio advertising salesman, this motivational book was an invaluable tool for me. Not only did its practical advice provide me with sound knowledge to pump my career, Leterman also shared one of the greatest secrets of success — seek out successful people and learn from them.

Author and speaker Brian Tracy has spent 35 years studying the laws of success. He asked the question, "Why do some people succeed and some don't?" Tracy discovered that there was a consistent and predictable pattern that seemed to accompany all business success. Not surprisingly, it included a commitment to reading, the study of other successful people and the application of their successful attributes.

Abraham Lincoln said, "I shall study and prepare myself and one day my chance will come." And it surely did. Preparation is an important step on the road to success and reading is an excellent way to gain access to great ideas and expand your knowledge and understanding on any subject. Even if you don't think you can read a book a week like I do, challenge yourself to read at least one book a month. You will be surprised at the positive impact it has on your life.

— *Who Dares Wins*

TODAY, FIND A BOOK
WRITTEN BY SOMEONE YOU ADMIRE
AND START READING.

CHARACTER IS DESTINY – PART I

It has been said that, "Every man has a character, but few are of character." Character is developed by living your principles. Over 2,500 years ago, a Chinese philosopher said, "Character is destiny." In an era when there is glory in narcissism and greed, does this still apply? There is no higher praise than . . . he is a man of character.

Tong Louie was such a man. He lived his life wanting to be known as an ordinary, hard-working fellow and although hard work was the very essence of who he was, during his lifetime Tong demonstrated in a multitude of ways that he was, in fact, quite extraordinary.

According to his biographer, by the time he died at the age of 84, "Tong Louie was one of the leading industrialists in Western Canada, one of its most active philanthropists and a patriarch of one of its pioneering social groups."

As the second of 11 children born to Chinese immigrants, Tong learned early in life the values that would lead to his success. In 1934, his father, Hok Yat Louie (the H.Y. in H.Y. Louie Co. Ltd.) wrote three letters to his sons while he was in Hong Kong and his sons were in Vancouver. His letters were simple truths that at the time were intended as guiding rules for the fledgling family business.

In his first letter he wrote:
"When pursuing prosperity, you must follow the laws of heaven. Don't be afraid to be kind and charitable . . . ill deeds should be avoided."

In his second letter he told his sons to preserve their own reputations:
"Be earnest, be fair and loyal in your dealings with customers."

And in his third letter he instructed his sons on one precious lesson:
"Develop your own character as well as your working skills."

CHARACTER IS DESTINY – PART II

For more than 60 years, Hok Yat's words have been a constant in the Louie family's success. Incredibly simple, completely understandable advice that came from a father who cared not just about business, but about the importance of family, respect, community and living and working together.

Tong Louie built his life, career and character on those simple truths. In recognition of the extraordinary contributions he made to his community, he was awarded the Order of B.C., the Order of Canada, the Knight of the Golden Pencil, the Astra Award and the Variety Club's Golden Heart Award.

Many of us are concerned about our reputation, but how many put as much emphasis on developing our character?

The circumstances amid which you live determine your reputation; the truth you believe determines your character.

Reputation is what you are supposed to be; character is what you are.

Reputation is the photograph; character is the face.

Reputation comes over one from without; character grows up from within.

Your reputation is made in a moment; your character is built over a lifetime.

Reputation makes you rich or makes you poor; character makes you happy or makes you miserable.

Reputation is what men say about you on your tombstone; character is what the angels say about you before the throne of God.

— *The Runway of Life*

GOOD CHARACTER IS MORE TO BE PRAISED THAN OUTSTANDING TALENT. MOST TALENTS ARE TO SOME EXTENT A GIFT. GOOD CHARACTER, BY CONTRAST, IS NOT GIVEN TO US. WE HAVE TO BUILD IT PIECE BY PIECE BY THOUGHT, CHOICE, COURAGE AND DETERMINATION." — John Luther

BELIEVE IN YOURSELF

Unfortunately, there are a great many people in this world who never realize their true worth — and worthiness of success. It is very likely that no artist suffered more to bring his masterpieces into the world than Vincent van Gogh, whose struggle with mental anguish and bouts of depression are the things of which legends are wrought. And yet, few artists have ever lived so intensely or left behind such a glorious legacy of their talent.

It has been noted that van Gogh created all of his more than 900 paintings within a 10-year period (he took his own life at the still-young age of 37) using a technique that grew more and more impassioned in its brushstroke, intense use of colour and movement of form and line.

Despite the fact that he lacked confidence in himself and sold just one painting during his lifetime, van Gogh's work is much coveted by collectors and museums — three of his paintings, *Sunflowers, Irises* and most recently *Portrait of Dr. Paul Gachet* (which went to a Japanese buyer in 1990 for $82.5 million), have, at different times, set record prices at auction.

We all have moments of doubt in our life; it is how we handle those moments that determines our success. Understand and appreciate what you have achieved. Reflect. Think of the risks you have taken and the obstacles you have overcome. Think about the difficult times and then look at where you are right now and how far you've come. This is no time to stop believing in yourself. Embrace your talents and know that you can accomplish great things.

— Make Your Life a Masterpiece

"To accomplish great things,
we must not only act, but also dream;
not only plan, but also
believe." — Anatole France

OCTOBER

AUTOGRAPH YOUR WORK WITH EXCELLENCE

A few years ago, I was speaking at the Westin Hotel in downtown Calgary at a business conference. Following my presentation, the next speaker was the legendary NHL Hall of Famer, Lanny McDonald. You might remember him for his famous overgrown moustache. He played 16 years in the NHL from 1973 until 1989 including time with the Toronto Maple Leafs and Colorado Rockies. He finished his career with the Calgary Flames.

A highlight of McDonald's career came in the 1982-83 season when his goal-scoring record rivaled that of Wayne Gretzky. At the end of the season, Gretzky finished with 71 goals and McDonald with 66.

The 1988-89 season was a banner year for McDonald; he won the King Clancy Memorial Trophy, the "Bud" Man of the Year Award, scored his 1,000th point on March 7, scored his 500th goal on March 21, and won the Stanley Cup with the Flames. After giving his all to the game that he loved for 16 years, at the end of the 1989 playoff season, McDonald retired.

Inducted into the Hockey Hall of Fame in 1992, McDonald has dedicated much of his time to helping and inspiring others through his work with Special Olympics and as a popular speaker.

As a boy growing up on a farm near Hanna, Alberta, McDonald's hero was his father, who taught him the value of hard work and honesty, two principles that exemplified his career in the NHL.

On the evening in Calgary when I shared the speaker's podium with McDonald, he closed his inspirational presentation with this message: "Every job is a self-portrait of the person who did it, so autograph your work with excellence."

— Insight 2011

ARE YOU LEAVING THE MARK
OF EXCELLENCE
ON ALL THAT YOU DO?

KEEP YOUR PASSION GOING

Some people are passionate for 30 seconds, some people are passionate for 30 minutes, some people are passionate for 30 days, but to be really successful, you need to be passionate for 30 years. Live your passion and don't be concerned if some people mistake that passion for luck. There's absolutely no way you can be "just lucky" for 30 years.

In my own life, I've received every professional speaking award — about 20 in total — you can receive in Canada. Now, maybe I lucked out with the first two, others I had to work damn hard for, studying, reading and practicing. I presented hundreds of free speeches to hone my craft, in addition to working with voice coaches and spending considerable hours developing my materials, all with great passion and enthusiasm. That's why I know in my heart that nobody could ever say I was "just lucky." Luck is really the result of hard work and a commitment — with passion — to your dreams and visions.

Obviously, it is difficult to be passionate about every single thing you do. That's why it's essential that you are truly passionate about your primary purpose. For instance, I am absolutely passionate about speaking, but I don't like flying. The paradox is that in order to do what I am passionate about, I also have to do the very thing that I don't like.

I have decided that I am willing to put aside my fear in order to obtain my goal.

— The Runway of Life

"THERE IS NO PASSION TO BE FOUND
PLAYING SMALL — IN SETTLING
FOR A LIFE THAT IS LESS THAN THE
ONE YOU ARE CAPABLE OF LIVING."
— Nelson Mandela

LEADERSHIP IS INFLUENCE

North American leadership expert John Maxwell, author of more than 40 books on the subject, once said, "The true measure of leadership is influence — nothing more, nothing less. True leadership cannot be awarded, appointed or assigned. It comes only from influence — and that cannot be mandated, it must be granted."

What makes people want to follow a leader? The answer lies in the character and qualities of the individual. Aristotle once said, "The ultimate aim of human life and activity is development of character."

The most important goal you could hope to accomplish in the course of your life is to become an exceptional person in every respect; a leader. Developing your personality and character will earn the respect, esteem and affection of the important people in your world.

Over the years, I have had the opportunity to meet many great leaders. I also make it a habit to study, read about and listen to good leaders and understand how they affect their own organizations. Here are a few of their insights:

"An effective leader is someone who is determined and convinced, someone who builds teams that excel, listens to them and encourages them to make things happen." — Rémi Marcoux, founder, Transcontinental Inc.

"At the end of the day it is a belief in your own convictions and selling that belief to others that ultimately leads to leadership." — Clive Beddoe, founder and chairman, WestJet Airlines

"As a leader, you have a profound opportunity as a result of your vision, perseverance and character. You can touch a life and make the world a better place." — Brad McRae, author, *The Seven Strategies of Master Leaders.*

— *Insight 2011*

THINK OF THE LEADERS THAT
YOU ADMIRE. HOW CAN THEIR EXAMPLE
HELP YOU IN DEVELOPING
YOUR OWN LEADERSHIP SKILLS?

October 4

PASSION DO'S AND DON'TS — PART I

*"Passion is energy. Feel the power
that comes from focusing on what
excites you."* — Oprah Winfrey

We all need a little help to keep us motivated and moving in the right direction. Here are five things you should definitely do to keep yourself excited about life and just a few cautionary don'ts.

Let's start with the don'ts. First of all, you absolutely don't need to quit your current job or career to rush off and find your passion. In fact, such a drastic move is more likely to bring you unnecessary stress than it is to result in your finding your true passion.

Secondly, for heaven's sake, don't let anyone tell you that you are too old, too entrenched in your career or expecting too much because you want to be passionate about the life you are living.

Finally, don't worry about whether or not your passion is practical in terms of "career potential." The truth is that for most of us, once we find something that we are truly passionate about, we will find a way to make it a part of our life whether or not that includes making it our "work."

Now, if you're ready, here are some suggestions for finding, or rediscovering, your own passion.

Start off simple
This is the best approach with anything in life. In this case, start by simply doing something for yourself. Try joining a group that participates in an activity that interests you, or sign up to learn something new, perhaps by taking an art course or history class (or anything else that captures your interest) at the local community college. This is a great way to meet others who are passionate about the things that interest you.

PASSION DO'S AND DON'TS – PART II

If you're not sure what you're looking for, check out college and university brochures and continuing-education flyers or browse through a listing of community organizations to see what catches your interest.

It's the journey, not the destination

Many people lose their passion in pursuit of goals because they forget to take some time to enjoy the journey. It's like getting in your car and driving non-stop from Seattle to New York. Sure, it's an accomplishment to arrive at your destination, but think of all the great people, places and experiences you missed along the way by rushing to get there.

One way to make sure you enjoy the milestones along the way is to take time each day to reflect on and share — with family, friends and co-workers — both the successes and the memorable moments you had that day, however small they may be. This is also a great way to acknowledge the contribution of others and to recharge everyone's passion for a shared goal or project.

Oh, the people you'll meet

Take time to connect with the people you meet as you travel along your runway of life. As any writer will tell you, everybody has a story; you just have to take the time to find out what it is. The payoff here is that the best ideas you will ever have are going to result from talking — and listening — to other people.

Change your point of view

You know the old saw, "If you always do what you've always done, you'll always get what you have always gotten." Well, I am here to tell you that it's still true. That's why it's important to make change a regular part of your life, even in small ways.

PASSION DO'S AND DON'TS – PART III

W hy not try some of these suggestions: drive to work via a different route, buy your groceries at a store you've never been to, talk to strangers, go to the local visitors bureau and take a guided tour of your own city and see things from a different perspective. Change is a great catalyst. Not only does it break up the routine and make everyday life more interesting, it also opens us up to new opportunities, new experiences, new ideas and new people.

New mountains to climb
As your passion moves you onward and upward, keep in mind that it is not uncommon to lose some of your momentum as you check goals off of your list. Losing your momentum isn't the same as losing your passion; more often, it is the result of having reached a plateau.

So, what do you do? The same thing that any experienced mountain climber would do. Take a bit of time to catch your breath, admire the view and reflect on what worked and what didn't on your way up.

After that, you need to refocus your efforts on the peaks ahead and make sure that the goals you have set are challenging enough to keep feeding your passion. If they are not, set your sights on new mountains. Personally, I've never met a climber who was ready to stop after just one mountain.

—The Runway of Life

"THERE IS NO GREATNESS
WITHOUT A PASSION TO BE GREAT,
WHETHER IT'S THE ASPIRATION
OF AN ATHLETE OR AN ARTIST, A SCIENTIST,
A PARENT, OR A BUSINESSPERSON."
— Anthony Robbins

DON'T LEAVE YOUR DREAMS UP IN THE AIR

Sometimes it takes a traumatic event like being fired from a job to wake us up to opportunity or make us realize that we've somehow wandered off down a path that isn't taking us where we want to go.

There's a scene in the movie *Up in the Air* where the main character, Ryan Bingham, is doing an exit interview with one of the employees he has just fired. That's what he does, he fires people for a living. When corporations need to downsize quickly but don't have the courage to drop the axe themselves, he flies in and breaks the news to the people being let go.

In the scene, Bingham is talking to Bob, who is in his fifties: "Your resume says you minored in French Culinary Arts. Most students work the fryer at KFC. You bussed tables at Il Picatorre to support yourself. Then you got out of college and started working here [he was being fired from an office job in a big company where he had clearly worked for decades]. How much did they pay you to give up on your dreams?"

"Twenty-seven thousand a year," replies Bob.

"At what point were you going to stop and go back to what made you happy?" asks Bingham. "I see guys who work at the same company for their entire life, guys exactly like you. They clock in, they clock out and they never have a moment of happiness. You have an opportunity . . . this is a rebirth. If not for you, do it for your children."

— *The Power of a Dream*

IF YOU'RE NOT DOING IT
ALREADY, WHAT WILL IT TAKE TO
MAKE YOU TAKE THAT
FIRST STEP AND GO AFTER WHAT
TRULY MAKES YOU HAPPY?

TO ALL MY RETIRED FRIENDS

The secret of life:
Before middle age — do not fear.
After middle age — do not regret.

E njoy your life while you can, don't put anything off. You never know how long you will have the health, mobility and vitality to see and do all the things you've always said you would.

When there is an opportunity, get together with old classmates, colleagues and friends. This is no time to procrastinate, such opportunities become more rare as time goes by. Sharing fond memories is one of life's simple pleasures.

Today is the rainy day you saved for. When it's time to spend, just spend and enjoy. Treat yourself well as you're getting old.

Whatever you feel like eating, eat! The most important thing is to enjoy your food and be happy. Just remember, foods that are good for health, eat often and more and foods that are not so good for health, eat less often, but don't deprive yourself.

Treat sickness with optimism. Rich or poor, we all go through birth, aging, sickness and death. There are no exceptions. So, don't be afraid or worried when you are sick. Let the doctors handle your body, let God and nature handle your life, but be in charge of your own moods. Optimism is a tonic.

Don't worry about the next generation, our kids will learn their own lessons and make their own fortunes, just as we did.

Look after four old treasures:
1. Your old body — health is wealth.
2. Your retirement funds — you've earned them.
3. Your spouse or companion — one of you will go first.
4. Your old friends — they'll be gone soon enough.

Things you must do every day: Smile and laugh!

— Insight 2011

START WITH YOURSELF

Westminster Abbey has more than 1,000 years of history and has hosted no fewer than 15 royal weddings including: King Henry I in 1100, King Richard II in 1382, King George VI in 1923, Princess Elizabeth (now Queen Elizabeth II) in 1947 and, of course, Prince William and Kate Middleton in April 2011.

However, Westminster Abbey is better known for its burials than marriages. Some pretty famous people are buried at the Abbey including: Oliver Cromwell, 1658; Sir Isaac Newton, 1727; Samuel Johnson, 1784; Charles Dickens, 1870; Charles Darwin, 1882; Rudyard Kipling, 1936; Sir Laurence Olivier, 1989.

I have visited Westminster Abbey a few times and I always learn something new when I go.

The following words were written on the tomb of an Anglican bishop (1100 AD) in the crypts of Westminster Abbey:

"When I was young and free and my imagination had no limits, I dreamed of changing the world. As I grew older and wiser, I discovered the world would not change, so I shortened my sights somewhat and decided to change only my country.

But it, too, seemed immovable.

As I grew into my twilight years, in one desperate attempt, I settled for changing only my family, those closest to me, but alas, they would have none of it.

And now as I lie on my deathbed, I suddenly realize if I had only changed myself first, then by example I would have changed my family. From their inspiration and encouragement, I would then have been able to better my country and, who knows, I may have even changed the world."

— *Insight 2011*

THE GREATEST POWER WE POSSESS IS THE POWER
TO MAKE OUR OWN LIFE A SHINING EXAMPLE FOR OTHERS IN THE
HOPE THAT WE MIGHT INSPIRE THEM TO DO THE SAME.

THE MAGIC OF FIRSTS — PART I

Linda Edgecombe is an incredibly energetic speaker, author and humorist from Kelowna, B.C., who engages her audiences with thought-provoking questions like, "When was the last time you did something for the first time?"

It's a question that made me stop and take stock of all the firsts in my life: my first business, the first time I held each of my baby daughters, my first time on stage, the first time I spoke at the House of Commons, or the first time I flew from London to New York in less than four hours at 55,000 feet and twice the speed of sound on the British Airways Concorde. Now there was a first time that will never come again. Brian Trubshaw, Concorde's first pilot, said, "It is not unreasonable to look upon Concorde as a miracle." As we all know, miracles don't happen every day, but when they do, we need to be brave enough to stand up and seize hold of them.

There is a kind of magic in firsts, it is the stuff of legends. You'll notice that people rarely tell stories about the second time they went bungee jumping. That's why we must take advantage of the unique opportunities that come our way — we never know which ones will be once-in-a-lifetime chances. Opportunities that, when grasped, may just produce the equivalent of the "Butterfly Effect" in our lives.

For those who haven't heard of the Butterfly Effect, it is an aspect of chaos theory whereby tiny disturbances in one part of a chaotic system (like weather) can sometimes lead to major changes in the whole system. For example, it is theoretically possible that a butterfly flapping its wings in Brazil could create changes in air flow that cause a tornado in Texas.

THE MAGIC OF FIRSTS – PART II

Of course, in most cases the flapping of a single butterfly's wings makes no difference whatsoever, but on the rare occasion when the point of balance could go either way (like a spinning basketball on the tip of your finger), that tiny flutter may be just the thing that causes an amazing change.

That same principle applies to people. One opportunity seized, can, on occasion, change the world. Take for example, the story of Bill Gates and Microsoft. Until the early 1980s, IBM remained firm in their resolve not to get into the personal computer (PC) market. According to company executives, the market was just too small. However, with the success of companies like Apple, Atari and Commodore, they changed their minds. There was just one problem. Before they could manufacture their own PCs, IBM needed a new disk operating system (DOS) as their existing system was strictly for large mainframe systems. They decided to hire a small company with experience in this area to write the software for them.

As owner of that small company, Mr. Bill Gates met with IBM executives to make a deal (and this is where the butterfly effect comes in), but rather than build the DOS and sell it to IBM outright, Gates told them he wanted a royalty on every DOS sold. He also negotiated for a non-exclusive agreement, so when the PC market took off (as Gates predicted it would) and other companies began selling PC clones, Gates provided his operating system to them too. The rest, as they say, is history. That one decision led to Microsoft's domination in the software industry and made Gates the richest man in the world.

— The Runway of Life

WHEN WAS THE LAST
TIME YOU DID SOMETHING FOR
THE FIRST TIME?

BRING OUT YOUR GENIUS – WITH HUMOUR

C onsider the following problem: You are given a box of tacks, a candle and some matches and told to stick the candle to a cork board in such a way that when you burn the candle it doesn't drip wax onto the floor below. Could you do it? Turns out, your ability to complete the task successfully may depend on whether or not you're in a happy mood. That was the finding of psychologist Alice M. Isen and her colleagues in an experiment with students.

Before they were given the above problem to solve, two groups of students were shown either a comedy film of bloopers or a film on math (which was not funny at all, by the way). After watching the math film, 20 per cent of the students successfully solved the problem. However, 75 per cent of the students who watched the comedy film got it right. (By the way, the answer to the problem is to pour the tacks out of the box, tack the box to the board and then place the candle on the box and light it).

"Research suggests that positive memories are more extensive and more interconnected than negative ones, so being happy may cue you into a larger and richer cognitive context and that could significantly affect your creativity," explains Isen.

A good sense of humour is a trait we all admire, and for good reason. It's good for your health, your relationships, for relieving stress, it feels good and it even enhances your ability to solve problems, so make sure you keep it with you at all times. You never know when you're going to need it.

— Insight 2011

WHEN WE'RE FEELING
HAPPY, IT'S EASIER TO SOLVE
PROBLEMS AND BE CREATIVE.

CHEROKEE WISDOM

An old Cherokee tale tells of a grandfather teaching life principles to his grandson.

As they sat together beside the fire one evening, the wise old Cherokee said, "Son, on the inside of every person a battle is raging between two wolves."

"One wolf is evil. It's angry, jealous, unforgiving, proud and lazy. The other wolf is good. It's filled with love, kindness, humility and self-control. These two wolves are constantly fighting," the grandfather said.

The little boy thought about this for a few moments and then asked, "Grandfather, tell me, which wolf is going to win?"

The grandfather smiled and said knowingly, "Whichever one you feed."

Within each of us there is the potential for both productive and destructive behaviour. It's up to us to decide what we will focus on and what we will give attention to.

Which part of your personality are you feeding?

Are you negative or positive?

Are you developing good habits or bad habits?

How do we change our bad habits, the ones that bring negative consequences? It's quite simple, quit feeding them and choose to nourish positive, healthy habits.

As you go about your day,
think about which
wolf you are feeding and
remember, you always
have a choice.

HOW HUNGRY ARE YOU?

Ryan Walter played more than 1,000 games over 15 seasons in the NHL during his hockey career. He was captain of the Washington Capitals. He played nine seasons with the Montreal Canadiens and won a Stanley Cup. He finished his career in his hometown of Vancouver as an assistant captain of the Vancouver Canucks.

Born in Burnaby, B.C., Ryan is now a much sought-after motivational speaker and leadership coach. I had the pleasure of hearing him speak at my church and one of the key questions that he asked the members of the congregation was, "Are you hungry?"

According to Ryan, the difference between first place and second is not about talent and it's not about coaching; it's about being hungry enough to go out and do what it takes to get the job done, whether it's scoring goals, scoring new accounts or scoring a promotion.

The opposite of hungry isn't "not hungry." It's ambivalence, which really means, "I don't care." Take that attitude on a hockey team and it won't be long before you find yourself out of a job. Take that attitude in life and chances are you won't get very far either. Why? Because in the same way that hockey championships are won by the teams that are generally the most hungry, so too is the business world dominated by those companies that are willing to deliver above and beyond what their competition does. And the people who are most successful in life? They're the ones who want it so bad that they can actually taste it.

How hungry are you to achieve your dreams; your goals in life; the vision you have for your company, your career, your family, your community?

— *The Power to Soar Higher*

STAY HUNGRY AND SEE
WHAT HAPPENS!

LIFE ON YOUR OWN TERMS – PART I

I love a good rags-to-riches story, particularly one that includes British motor cars. John Cox's life was just that kind of story.

John told me that he came to Canada from London in 1956 with $50 in his pocket. Until then, his had been one of those lives that drift in and out of misadventure.

He left school as all Cockneys of his generation did at the age of 14, "to start work or steal or whatever one has to do to survive," he explained. "You learn a lot in the streets of London."

An adventurer, John served in the Norwegian Merchant Navy, the British National Service and even a stint with the military police where he was sent to Korea. It was about this time that he came to the realization that you can make choices about life. As he saw it, he could choose to continue to live by his wits and drift around or he could take control of his life.

John chose to come to Canada and fell in love with the country. Life here as a young man fresh from army service was one of delivering bread, working on an assembly line and yearning to race motor cars and get rich quick.

He set his sights on motor racing. He made his decision on a Friday and he had asked for the day off from the assembly line. The foreman said no.

"So I looked at all of the people there and I thought, do I want to spend the next 20 years of my life here just to get a pension? I said to the foreman, 'Who's the next guy to be laid off?' and he pointed to a guy across the room.

LIFE ON YOUR OWN TERMS – PART II

So I said: tell him he's got my job. And I left." John had the drive to succeed, but at that point, no car and no prospects.

That same day, he answered an ad in the newspaper looking for people to run an auto business. Foregoing the promised salary, commission, fringe benefits and demonstrator car, he was hired along with six others from amongst a field of hundreds of applicants.

Using the gift of the gab that he had picked up on the streets of London, John became a salesman and eventually came to own a company called Rolls-Royce on Bay Street in downtown Toronto. From the busiest corner in the city, he sold Rolls-Royces, Bentleys, Jaguars, Rovers and other fine cars. At one point (with his business partner), he also owned part of the company that made Aston Martins.

I asked John how he did it and he shared with me his four "driving" rules for success:

1. Believe in yourself — totally and completely.

2. Do what you know and understand.

3. Be committed — from the inside, way down deep where it counts.

4. Be willing to gamble on your own judgment.

John passed away in 2009 at the age of 77. He never did become a champion race driver, but he did find wealth and a satisfying career while living life on his own terms. A eulogy for John posted on Wheels.ca described him this way: "A Cockney barrow boy who was even invited to the wedding of Charles and Diana. You'd have to say he done good. The increasingly corporate car retailing world will never see his like again."

— How to Soar With the Eagles

WHAT DOES LIVING LIFE
ON YOUR OWN TERMS MEAN TO YOU?
ARE YOU DOING IT?

DIFFICULTY DEFINES CHARACTER

"There's something bad in everything good and
there's something good in everything bad."
— Michael Lewis (author of *Liar's Poker*)

How you deal with tough times really defines your character and tells the whole world who you truly are. Following is a list of some famous people who overcame great adversity to accomplish great things:

Sarah Bernhardt was the most famous actress in France in the 19th century, and even after her leg was amputated in 1915 following a serious knee injury, she continued her career undiscouraged.

Marlee Matlin lost her hearing at 18 months of age but went on to win an Oscar for her debut role in the film *Children of a Lesser God.*

Woodrow Wilson had a learning disability but still served as President of the United States from 1913 to 1921.

Albert Einstein is heralded as a scientific genius in spite of rumours that he suffered from a learning disability and did very poorly all through school.

Ludwig von Beethoven, the famous composer, had become deaf by the time he created his magnificent *Symphony No. 9.*

John Milton had turned completely blind by age 43 but went on to write his most famous epic poem, *Paradise Lost.*

Thomas Edison had a learning disability, but his inventions have significantly changed the world.

Canadian hero Terry Fox lost his leg to cancer and still went on to run a "Marathon of Hope" across Canada to raise millions for cancer research.

— *Make Your Life a Masterpiece*

"ADVERSITY IS LIKE A STRONG WIND. IT TEARS AWAY
FROM US ALL BUT THE THINGS THAT CANNOT
BE TORN, SO THAT WE CAN SEE OURSELVES AS WE
REALLY ARE. "— Arthur Golden

FOCUS ON WHAT IS IMPORTANT

There is an amusing story about the painter Picasso, who, by the way, was the first living artist to ever have his work exhibited at the Louvre Museum in Paris.

One day, Picasso was riding on the train and a gentleman sitting next to him suddenly turned and addressed him, asking in a pointed way, "Why don't you create paintings that look realistic — just like your subject?" To demonstrate what he meant, the man reached into his pocketbook and pulled out a photograph of his wife to show Picasso.

Picasso looked at the picture and then replied, "She's awfully small and flat."

As the son of an art teacher, Picasso discovered his passion for painting at a very early age. He exhibited his first paintings in Barcelona at the age of 12 and went on to create many masterpieces. Picasso continued to pursue his life's passion right up until his death in 1973 at the age of 91. During his lifetime, he is said to have produced approximately 20,000 paintings, sculptures and drawings. The sculptor Henry Moore once called Picasso one of the most "naturally gifted" artists since Raphael.

Picasso could have painted "realistic" paintings and the world would never have known the genius that lay within him. He chose instead to focus on expressing how he saw the world, what was important to him.

We all face critics in our lives, people who believe they know better than we do what we should be doing and how we should do it. But in the end, it's not those people we have to answer to, it is ourselves. Focus on what is important to you.

— *Make Your Life a Masterpiece*

DON'T BE DISTRACTED
BY CRITICS, FOCUS ON WHAT IS
IMPORTANT TO YOU.

LEAP – WITH FAITH

Michael Gates Gill, author of *How Starbucks Saved My Life*, is a great proponent of leaping with the faith that something good will happen. Nearing retirement, Gill lost everything that he thought was important in his life. A Yale-educated advertising executive making a six-figure salary, he was let go from his job, saw his marriage disintegrate and was diagnosed with a brain tumour (I can't imagine that many of us would ever have to face so much all at once).

As the son of famous *New Yorker* writer Brendan Gill, during Michael Gill's childhood years, the family's social circle had included the likes of Ernest Hemingway and Jacqueline Onassis. At the age of 63, desperate and without health insurance, Michael found redemption and a new sense of purpose where he least expected it: working as a barista at Starbucks. Gill's humble story, which was derived in large part from a journal he kept to help him make sense of what was happening to him as his life fell apart, became an instant best-seller with the movie rights getting picked up by Tom Hanks.

Having accepted the job at Starbucks on a leap of faith, with no expectation about where it might lead, Gill soon found himself feeling useful and happy for the first time in many years despite the fact that he was now the one serving instead of the one being served.

In an interview prior to his book tour, Gill was asked what message he has for others who find themselves in difficult circumstances. He said that he really has two messages, "Be ready to be happily surprised in life and don't be afraid to make a fool of yourself."

— *The Power of a Dream*

SOMETIMES WE FIND
WHAT WE NEED IN THE MOST
UNLIKELY PLACE.

LEADERSHIP SECRETS OF THE SALVATION ARMY

William Booth, founder of the Salvation Army, was once asked to telegraph his officers using just one word to describe what the Salvation Army is all about. After much thought, the one simple word that he came up with was, "OTHERS."

"It is not about us," he said. "It's about others."

The Salvation Army has been true to this one word for more than a century — helping the needy, the sick, the downtrodden and the disheartened. When William Booth died on August 20, 1912, at the age of 83, 40,000 people filled the auditorium to pay their respects. So how did this one man leave behind an organization so prepared for the future that it could continue growing strong for 100 years after his death? Robert Watson has written a book titled *Leadership Secrets of the Salvation Army*. It is based on five laws that govern every aspect of this institution. They are:

Clarity of Mission: Applying a laserlike focus to evaluate everything it does in terms of a mission to preach the gospel and meet human needs without discrimination.

Ability to Innovate: The Salvation Army's investment in people gets incredible returns because it encourages each person to engage all of their skills and resources; making it as much a venture capitalist organization as it is a charity.

Measurable Results: A unique way of setting, monitoring and celebrating the achievement of measurable goals ensures the Salvation Army delivers on the mission.

Dedication: It's how the Salvation Army accomplishes so much with just a small cadre of officers.

Putting Money to Maximum Use: Maintaining a lean organization means focusing on making the most of every resource and ensuring that all operations are self-sufficient.

— *Leadership Secrets of the Salvation Army, foreword*

WHAT ARE YOU DOING FOR FREE?

Whenever we are in Palm Springs, my wife and I like to visit a favourite restaurant, LG's Steakhouse, owned and operated by Leon and Gail Greenberg. As Leon is fond of saying, LG's is locally owned and nationally known. He's not kidding. The restaurant has been in Tom Horan's Top Ten Steakhouses Hall of Fame for more than six years. It has also received the Wine Spectator Award of Excellence and the Zagat Survey's rating of "Best Steakhouse in Town."

Located just minutes from Palm Springs in the town of Palm Desert, California, part of LG's charm comes from being housed in the oldest adobe building in town. After receiving a personal tour of the entire operation, I can say that they take their steak very seriously. So seriously, that they dry-age their prime beef on premises. If you're not a steak aficionado, dry-aging enhances and intensifies the distinctive flavour and tenderness associated with prime steaks. It is a time-consuming and costly method, but for LG it is one of the special touches that set their restaurant above the competition.

Another special touch is the fact that LG's is one of the few remaining restaurants that make a special Caesar salad right at your table. No prepared dressing here, starting from scratch, they prepare a perfect dressing right before your eyes. In addition, every customer they serve receives a printed copy of the Caesar salad recipe to take home, absolutely free. They have been doing this for 16 years and based on their continued success, I'd say it's a winning strategy.

— The Power to Soar Higher

WHAT ARE YOU DOING FOR 'FREE' TO ADD
TO YOUR SUCCESS? AND WHAT
SPECIAL TOUCHES COULD YOU BE ADDING TO SET
YOURSELF ABOVE THE COMPETITION?

MAKE HARD WORK A HABIT

We first make our habits and then our habits make us.

Ivan Seidenberg relates how hard work paid off early in his career: "My first boss — he was the building superintendent and I was a janitor — watched me sweep floors and wash walls for almost a year before he mentioned that I could get tuition for college if I got a job with the phone company. When I asked him why he'd waited so long to tell me, he said, 'I wanted to see if you were worth it.'"

Today, Ivan Seidenberg is the chairman and former CEO of the global communications company Verizon.

The message: Work hard, have high standards and stick to your values, because somebody is always paying attention.

Motivational author Og Mandino had this to say about hard work: "One of the greatest undiscovered joys of life comes from doing everything one attempts to the best of one's ability. There is a special sense of satisfaction, a pride in surveying such a work, a work which is rounded, full, exact, complete in its parts, which the superficial person who leaves his or her work in a slovenly, slipshod, half-finished condition can never know. It is this conscientious completeness which turns any work into art. The smallest task, well done, becomes a miracle of achievement."

— *Make Your Life a Masterpiece*

"IN THEORY, THERE IS NO
DIFFERENCE BETWEEN THEORY AND
PRACTICE. BUT IN PRACTICE,
THERE IS." — Jan van de Snepscheut

THE COMPARISON GAME – PART I

C omparison is a game you can never win. Comparison always leaves us wanting more, which in turn brings unhappiness. Thankfulness helps us to realize all that we have and learn to let go of comparison so we can focus on our own talent.

It's not always easy to keep from being envious of what other people have accomplished, however. Geraldine Laybourne, who was the founder and former chairman and CEO of Oxygen Media, recalls a company policy that dealt with exactly that challenge.

"When I was at Nickelodeon," she says, "We had 10 commandments that we followed. To me the most important one was, 'Thou shalt not covet thy competitor's success.' This is especially true in television, where so many people just keep their eye on what the other networks are doing. They'll try to find the next *Desperate Housewives*, but the look-alikes never amount to a whole lot. I've done that a couple of times and fallen flat on my face. So I try not to get distracted by what worked for others. I always have an eye on the competition, but it's not to do what they're doing. It's to see where the holes are. I've built businesses by looking at conventional wisdom and going exactly the opposite way."

In his book, *Good to Great*, author Jim Collins observed that the most successful companies are those who have leaders who are humble visionaries. They lead with passion but are happy to give plenty of credit to anyone and everyone else. If we want to be leaders, we need to let go of comparisons and recognize that the success of others in no way diminishes our own talents or worth.

Tomorrow, we'll look at three ways to help you get past comparisons.

THE COMPARISON GAME — PART II

"The meaning of life is to find your gift.
The purpose of life is to give it away."
— Joy J. Golliver

1. Develop your own strengths.
Our interests and experiences shape us all in different ways. That means that we are all experts in something. The key is finding what you are passionate about and then having the courage to develop it. Whether that means honing your skills to be the best salesperson you can be, investing in yourself by going back to university to study to be an urban planner, or using your love of technology to develop the latest computer software program, you absolutely have something of value to offer this world. Only you know what that is.

2. Network with those same people you feel intimidated by.
Seek out people who are infinitely more successful than you, those who are living your dream life and find out what steps they took to get where they are. Most people are happy to answer your questions and share some of the wisdom they have accumulated on the way to the top.

3. Surround yourself with optimistic people.
People who love their lives and make the most of every moment inspire others to do the same. If you want to develop your inner strength, surround yourself with people who are actively engaged in living. Join associations, volunteer in the community, reach out to people who share your interests and while you're busy doing that, watch how quickly your own self-confidence begins to soar. No comparisons needed.

— *Make Your Life a Masterpiece*

DON'T COMPARE YOUR LIFE
TO OTHERS, YOU HAVE NO IDEA WHAT
THEIR JOURNEY IS ABOUT.

PAYBACK

Often, in the question period following a speech, someone will ask me, "Why is it that you are so energetic?" I suspect, in part it comes from a belief that we are as happy as we make up our mind to be. Another very important part comes from the fact that as an only child of parents who were loving and encouraging, I always knew my mom and dad truly believed in me. Although they were not wealthy during my early years living in England, they worked hard and saved money to be able to send me to private school.

Later, my parents had the foresight to know that life for the Legge family would be better in Canada. They decided that my father would travel to Vancouver ahead of us to get settled, then send for mom and me.

Landing on the East Coast, my dad took a train all the way to the last stop in New Westminster, B.C., where he tried his hand at just about everything, picking blueberries, working as a short-order cook, whatever he needed to do to make money, but he couldn't find anything permanent. Lonely and discouraged, a year later he accepted a job in a smelter in Kitimat, B.C., to earn enough for a ticket back to England. However, just a few days before he was to start, he heard about a job as an inside sales rep for a cement plant in New Westminster. He got the job.

My parents sacrificed a lot for me and I always wanted them to be proud. I also wanted to be successful and have my life amount to something to show them just how much I appreciated all they have given me.

— *The Runway of Life*

HAVE YOU THANKED
YOUR PARENTS
FOR INVESTING IN YOU?

STAYING POWER

D o you think that Nelson Mandela knew when he first chose to raise his voice against apartheid in South Africa that he would spend more than 27 years of his life in a prison cell? Amazingly, when he was released from prison, Mandela was neither bitter nor discouraged. With his optimism, hope and a willingness to forgive his captors and forge a new start, Nelson Mandela set an example for all of his countrymen and the entire world. He went on to become the first post-apartheid president of South Africa, to begin the process of reconciliation and healing between blacks and whites and to realize his dream of a democratic South Africa. Who is to say what the world would look like today if Mandela had not had the tenacity to persevere?

Albert Einstein is quoted as saying, "It's not that I'm so smart, it's just that I stay with problems longer." Even if Einstein were being hopelessly modest in this statement, his line of reasoning is compelling. The world would never have benefited from his theories and equations if he had not pursued them far beyond the point where even the most dedicated theoretician would likely have given up (that's why there's only ever been one Einstein). Of his approach to problems, Einstein said, "I think and think for months and years. Ninety-nine times, the conclusion is false. The hundredth time I am right." Imagine the determination it must take to be wrong 99 per cent of the time and still keep your mind focused on getting to that one time when you finally get it right.

— *The Runway of Life*

"PERSISTENCE IS THE TWIN SISTER OF
EXCELLENCE. ONE IS A MATTER
OF QUALITY, THE OTHER, A MATTER
OF TIME." — Marabel Morgan

USE YOUR MARBLES

Nearly 20 years ago, I met a young man who had escaped, along with his family, from the tyranny of Idi Amin's regime in Uganda leaving behind all that he owned including a very prosperous supermarket business.

Arriving in Vancouver, Sadru knew that he would need to find a company to hire him, start at the bottom and work hard. He chose an import food brokerage company called National Importers Ltd. and started as the cleanup man in the warehouse. With a natural enthusiasm for the food business, within 10 years Sadru was managing director of the company and the company was thriving.

I learned a lot from Sadru, including this helpful lesson about delegating.

Whenever Sadru would hire a new staff member, along with the office, the desk and whatever else was needed, he also gave them a jar of marbles with each marble representing a particular responsibility or job function.

He would then tell the employee that from time to time, he would be giving them more marbles. Perhaps once a month or once every couple of months and they would be added to the jar. However, at no time must the marble jar overflow. Therefore, before the new job goes in the jar, the employee must choose another job (or marble) to be delegated out for the balance in the jar to be maintained. The jar was Sadru's way of reinforcing to his staff the importance of setting priorities and not taking on more than they could manage.

— How to Soar With the Eagles

USE YOUR MARBLES, FILL A JAR
OF YOUR OWN AND USE THEM TO HELP YOU
DETERMINE WHICH TASKS YOU SHOULD
BE DOING YOURSELF AND WHICH YOU CAN
DELEGATE TO OTHERS. JUST REMEMBER,
WHEN ONE MARBLE GOES IN, ONE
MUST COME OUT.

WHEN THINGS GO WRONG

"The man who does things, makes many mistakes,
but he never makes the biggest mistake of all —
doing nothing." — Benjamin Franklin

Here are some tips on dealing with mistakes:

Accept responsibility when something goes wrong.
You don't have to admit to the whole world that you have made a mistake, but you do have to admit it to yourself and anyone else who will be affected by it — and the sooner, the better. Also, never use your authority to mask a mistake. If you make one, admit it, explain it, apologize for it and above all else, learn from it. Allowing others to see how you accept responsibility and learn from your errors can go a long way towards healing any loss of faith.

Ask for help.
If you're determined to fly solo through every storm, eventually you're going to crash and burn. But it doesn't have to be that way; it's all up to you. Sometimes, a fresh perspective — especially from someone who doesn't have an emotional attachment to the problem — is just what you need to get things moving forward again. So don't be afraid to ask for input and use it to your advantage.

Don't overanalyze your errors.
Despite the fact that you made a mistake, there is no need to wallow in endless rounds of coulda, shoulda, woulda. Once you admit that you've made an error, look to the future. What have you learned? How will you keep from making the same mistake again? Where do you go from here?

— *Make Your Life a Masterpiece*

THERE ARE ONLY TWO REAL MISTAKES A PERSON CAN MAKE
ALONG THE ROAD TO SUCCESS, NOT GOING ALL THE
WAY AND NOT STARTING. YOU CAN SURVIVE EVEN THE BIGGEST
MISTAKE IF YOU ARE WILLING TO KEEP GOING.

BIG LESSONS CAN HAPPEN
IN THE SMALLEST PLACES – PART I

I hold a special place in my heart for the Williams Lake Cattlemen's Association. Not because of any particular love of cattle or because of any particular individuals within the association; rather, it is because they taught me an important life lesson.

During my speaking career, I've jetted in the best seats, performed in amazing international venues, checked into luxurious hotels and been served the finest food and wine. On one such occasion, I was scheduled to speak in Vienna, Austria, and my hosts had spared no expense, arranging to fly both myself and my wife first class and provide a suite in a posh hotel where our every whim was catered to. I'll tell you, it isn't difficult to become accustomed to that sort of lifestyle. And then I was invited to speak at the annual meeting of the cattlemen's association in the small town of Williams Lake, B.C.

I asked the booking agent if they would be flying me up in a jet.

"Certainly!" she responded.

Picking me up in a limo?

"Of course," she assured me.

Would I be speaking at the convention centre?

"Absolutely!"

With a state-of-the-art sound system?

"Most assuredly!"

Satisfied, I accepted the engagement.

As it turned out, the private jet was a Dash 8 on the milk run. When I arrived at the airport, there was no one waiting at the gate to meet me and as the small terminal quickly cleared and I walked outside, it was obvious that there was no limo either, just a dusty yellow mini bus idling at the curb.

"I'm expecting a limo," I told the driver who was waiting beside the bus.

"You must be Mr. Legge," he said smiling. "Hop in, this is your limousine."

BIG LESSONS CAN HAPPEN
IN THE SMALLEST PLACES – PART II

I took a seat and we bumped along into town, but instead of arriving at the convention centre, the bus pulled up in front of the local arena. Apparently this was to be my speaking venue. As for the state-of-the-art sound system, it was nothing more than a microphone used by the announcer at hockey games. To make matters worse, the whole place was stale, dank and dusty.

I was not a happy camper. After all, I was used to the best. It wasn't until I walked into the men's room and caught a glimpse of myself in the mirror that I realized the truth. As I stood there sulking and feeling sorry for myself, the face staring back at me was that of a spoiled, petulant brat.

"Who are you to demand limos and fancy venues?" I asked my reflection. "These people are as honest, genuine and welcoming as anyone and they've provided the best they have."

I snapped myself into shape, straightened my tie, combed my hair, added a big smile and went out there to give them my best.

Looking back, I don't think I've ever made a more inspired, genuine presentation. What I remember most is the standing ovation they gave me. I also remember the warmth they showed me with their smiles and handshakes. I flew home feeling exhilarated, having learned an important life lesson about letting my ego and expectations get in the way of doing my job. I also learned that while fancy jets and limousines are nice, they've got nothing on genuine hospitality.

— *The Power to Soar Higher*

DON'T LET YOUR EXPECTATIONS — OR YOUR
EGO — GET IN THE WAY OF TREATING
EVERYONE YOU MEET WITH THE RESPECT
THEY DESERVE AND DOING YOUR JOB TO THE
VERY BEST OF YOUR ABILITIES.

LESSONS FROM A NEAR-DEATH EXPERIENCE

As anyone who has been through a near-death experience will tell you, it's beautiful, it's frightening and it's very real.

The stories vary depending on the individual, but a common thread runs through them. There is invariably a feeling of departure from one's body, of travelling upwards, often through tunnels of light, into more light beyond. People say they are very conscious of what's going on. They can "look down" at a scene that often includes themselves, at grieving relatives and friends, at accident scenes, at whatever "killed" them. They remain ambivalent, there is no real sadness for those "left behind" and no apprehension about what may lie ahead. In fact, the prospect of some kind of journey is exciting.

But death doesn't happen. It's *near* death — and at some stage in this strange journey, the life force takes over once again and the individual suddenly snaps to the realization that they are not ready to go. And just like that, the heavenly chorus stops singing, the bright lights disappear and they're back in their body once again.

It's not an experience that's soon to be forgotten. In fact, it never really leaves those who have it. They are forever changed. Most interestingly, these people say the thought of dying no longer worries them, that when death comes for real, they will be ready. Even more importantly, having gone through a near-death experience, each seems to have a better understanding of what life is all about; how precious it is, how none of us can afford to waste a minute — and they start doing things they never did before, they get to the point much more quickly, get on with things and make better, faster choices.

— *You Can If You Believe You Can*

TODAY, LIVE LIKE YOU'RE
DYING. MAKE THE
MOST OF EVERY MOMENT.

NOVEMBER

SHOW THE WORLD YOUR ATTITUDE

W. Clement Stone once said, "I can't guarantee you will be successful with a positive attitude, but I can guarantee that you won't be without one."

Our attitude is one of the few things we have total control over in life. We have about as positive an attitude as we make up our minds to have. It all really comes down to choice and the first choice of the day. The choice to approach whatever the day may hold with a positive attitude is critical.

I'm sure I've mentioned this before, but psychiatrists say the first encounter of the day affects the next 13. Think about those people you meet and greet in the first 90 minutes of the day — your spouse, your children, the neighbours, the guy behind the counter at your favourite coffee shop, the person filling your tank at the gas station, the person on the other end of the line when you make your first call of the day. We affect and infect everybody with our attitude.

Think about what kind of people you want to encounter in the first 90 minutes of your day and then take a look in the mirror — are you one of them?

Think about that when you go to bed tonight and then first thing tomorrow morning when the opportunity clock goes off (that's what Zig Ziglar calls it), jump out of bed, strip off naked, stand in front of the mirror, look at yourself and say, "I am unstoppable" and then jump. Even the mental image of performing this should bring a smile to your face because some things will jiggle around that you haven't seen before — and that will definitely bring a smile to your face.

Now you're ready for the day.

— *The Runway of Life*

THE RULES OF ENGAGEMENT

K nowing the rules of etiquette for different situations is very helpful. Most behaviour that is perceived to be disrespectful, discourteous or abrasive is unintentional and can be avoided by practicing good manners and observing proper etiquette for the occasion. Basic knowledge and practice of etiquette is a valuable tool due to the fact that in many situations a second chance is just not possible or practical.

If you're not sure about a particular setting, do your homework (there are many books and websites on the subject) or ask someone who knows. As a public speaker, I have often learned the hard way by sticking my foot in my mouth. One such incident occurred at a Sovereign Order of Saint John of Jerusalem meeting in San Francisco where I was asked to do the toast to the president of the United States — at the time it was Bill Clinton.

It was a fabulous black-tie affair with medals and uniforms and all the formality you would expect. So I stood up to present the toast and it went something like this:

"Ladies and gentlemen, would you please be upstanding as we toast Bill Clinton, President of the United States."

Half of the people in the room were Republicans and the other half Democrats and I was taken aback when a good number of my fellows booed my toast. As I sat back down, feeling a bit puzzled, one of my American colleagues leaned over and said, "If you're wondering why you got boos, you always toast the office of the President of the United States, never the man. That way, you embrace everybody."

— *The Power of Tact*

IT IS ALWAYS IMPORTANT
TO KNOW WHERE YOU ARE
AND WHOM YOU'RE
TALKING TO BEFORE YOU
OPEN YOUR MOUTH.

IT'S NOT UNUSUAL

M any of you have heard of the entertainer Tom Jones (particularly if you are over 50). He had several hit songs in the '60s and '70s including "It's Not Unusual," "Delilah" and "What's New Pussycat." However, it is much less likely that you've heard of Tom Jones, the brick-layer or "hod carrier," as they're known in England and Wales (where Jones was born). They're called hod-carriers because they actually carry bricks on their back.

At one point after he'd made it as a star, Jones was scheduled to do a production number with some back-up singers at a TV station in London, England. The previous night he'd been partying and drinking heavily. So, he arrived at the station in his Rolls-Royce not at all in the mood to perform.

As he got out of his car he looked up and saw a labourer carrying bricks up a ladder. It so happened that the labourer knew Jones used to do the same job. He looked down at Jones and said, "Hey Tom, do ya wanna give me a hand?"

At that moment it dawned on Jones that hangover or no, he had no right to complain about having to perform and the privileged lifestyle it afforded him. He had a God-given talent and was being paid handsomely to do something he loved to do. People all over the world knew his name and bought his records, women swooned when they heard him sing and men wanted to be him. In an instant, he snapped to attention, realizing just how fortunate he was and headed into the studio to do the show.

— *The Runway of Life*

IT'S NOT UNUSUAL
TO TAKE WHAT WE HAVE
FOR GRANTED. SOMETIMES WE NEED
A REMINDER OF JUST HOW
GOOD WE'VE GOT IT.

FOUR IMPORTANT WORDS TO REMEMBER

An endless number of books come out each year touting the latest strategies for success, yet all too often it's the basics that really matter. Here's a little reminder about four words you should never forget to use.

The first two words are the first and last name of your client.

You may be saying to yourself, "Hey, I've got 600 clients, how am I supposed to remember everyone?"

It's a good point, but it's not as difficult as it sounds. What I suggest is that when you know you're going to be seeing a client, make sure you know that client's name and use it often during your exchange. People love being called by name.

"Good evening, Mr. Legge, your table is ready."

"Mr. Legge, nice to see you again!"

Who wouldn't want to be greeted like that?

Carry a cheat sheet if you must or use mnemonics. I play a little game with my wife for the times I forget the names of people I should know. If she notices I'm not using the name of a client or I have not introduced her, she moves right in and introduces herself, easily eliciting the name of the client (we'll call him Bill). Taking my cue, I quickly follow up with, "Oh Bill, I didn't realize that you and Kay hadn't met." Works like a charm.

The other two words, not surprisingly, are please and thank you (technically three words). I am amazed at how many professional men and women seem to have forgotten these simple, powerful words.

Whether you are talking to a store clerk, your assistant, the maître d', your boss, spouse or a child, please and thank you are a vital part of everyday common courtesy.

— *How to Soar With the Eagles*

INCLUDE COMMON
COURTESY IN EVERY INTERACTION
YOU HAVE TODAY.

CHECK YOUR COURTESY QUOTIENT – PART I

*"No one is too big to be courteous, but some
are too little."* — Unknown

I was browsing the Internet when I came across a blog site where a group of people had been discussing the topic of courtesy in modern times and one of them provided the following definition of courtesy, which I quite liked: "Courtesy is the ability to acknowledge in a friendly way the human dignity of those around you, whatever the circumstances."

Courtesy is so important to me and how my company does business, that the last thing I do before I hire a senior-level person is to take them out for lunch to observe their manners and how they treat restaurant staff throughout the meal. It gives me a good indication of how they will treat my customers and the staff who will work for them.

How every employee treats our customers is important to business. Late-night TV host Jay Leno once joked about this on a segment of his show when he told of a shopping experience. After making a purchase, he mentioned to the clerk that she forgot to say thank you. To which she curtly responded, "It's printed on your receipt."

Here are some questions to help you check your courtesy quotient:

Do you return phone calls and emails in a timely manner?

Do you regularly express gratitude to those around you, especially when someone has done something nice for you?

Are you available to others without making them feel like they're imposing?

Do you make sure never to keep people waiting more than a few minutes to meet you?

Have you trained your staff to respond with courtesy and politeness in all situations?

CHECK YOUR COURTESY QUOTIENT – PART II

Do you regularly ask others for input on issues that concern them and genuinely consider what they have offered?

Do you open the door for others or hold the door for those entering behind you?

Do you always say please and thank you at restaurants, when you shop or when someone has helped you in some way or extended a courtesy to you?

Do you shut off your cellphone or set it to vibrate (for emergency calls) when you are meeting with someone?

Do you allow the person with one item to go ahead of you at the check-out?

Do you conduct yourself in a polite manner when someone has made a mistake and you are contacting them to get it sorted out?

Do you allow other vehicles to move into the lane in front of you without honking your horn at them or becoming angry/aggressive?

Do you pay your bills on time, or let your creditors know if you cannot?

Do you make sure never to put down your competitors or speak ill of them?

Do you make every effort to curb your tongue when you feel like flying off the handle?

While all of these niceties may seem like small things — it really is the small gestures that we make towards others that leave a lasting impression. If you're not sure how you measure up, do a courtesy check on yourself.

"Outcomes rarely turn on grand gestures or the art of the deal, but on whether you've sent someone a thank you note." — *Bernie Brillstein*

— *Make Your Life a Masterpiece*

TREAT EVERYONE WITH COURTESY, EVEN THOSE
WHO ARE RUDE TO YOU — NOT BECAUSE THEY ARE NICE,
BUT BECAUSE YOU ARE.

THE MARRIAGE MYTH

S ome people think marriage should be easy. My wife and I have been married for over 40 years. If anyone were to ask us how we have managed to stay married and committed for this length of time, almost in unison, we would both say, "Hard work." Other married couples nod in agreement when we share this.

The idea of an effortless marriage is a myth. The truth is, marriage isn't for sissies, it's damn hard work and although the elements required for a good marriage are very simple, like many simple things, it can still be difficult to get it right. Creating a lasting marriage is a humbling experience that takes part skill, part luck and a whole lot of effort on the part of both partners.

Here are 12 strategies (offered by couples with experience) to help keep a marriage strong:

- Focus on your passion for life and for one another.
- Be friends. Have fun together, laugh and use humour in healthy ways.
- Forgive one another. Don't hang on to disappointments or past hurts. Be willing to let go and move forward with your lives.
- Comfort, encourage and affirm one another.
- Continue to be committed to each other and celebrate your commitment.
- Stand on your own feet as a couple, independent (financially or emotionally) of your parents.
- Respect one another's need for privacy and space.
- Parent your children together.
- Deal with crisis and adversity as a team.
- Always fight fair.
- Accept your differences and don't try to change your spouse.
- Keep romance alive in your marriage and continue to build intimacy.

THE WHALE

I read a front-page story in the *San Francisco Chronicle* about a female humpback whale that became entangled in a web of crab traps and lines. She was weighted down by hundreds of pounds of traps and struggled to stay afloat. She also had hundreds of yards of line rope wrapped all around her body, including her tail and a line tugging in her mouth.

A fisherman spotted her just east of the Farralone Islands and radioed an environmental group for help.

Within a few hours, the rescue team arrived and determined that the whale was in such dire straits that the only way to save her was to dive in and untangle her. It was a very dangerous proposition considering that one slap of her tail could kill a rescuer.

The team worked together for hours with curved knives and eventually freed the whale.

When she was free, the divers say she swam in what seemed like joyous circles. She then came back to each and every diver, one at a time, and nudged them gently as if to say, "Thank you for helping me."

Some of the team members said it was the most incredibly beautiful experience of their lives.

It's important to realize that there are some things we cannot do alone (no matter how big and strong we are) and we will need the help of others, just as there will be times when others need us to step up and help them.

— *The Power to Soar Higher*

MAY YOU BE SO FORTUNATE
AS TO BE SURROUNDED BY PEOPLE WHO
WILL HELP YOU GET UNTANGLED
FROM THE THINGS THAT ARE BINDING YOU
— AND MAY YOU ALWAYS KNOW
THE JOY OF GIVING AND
RECEIVING GRATITUDE.

THE WHY AND THE HOW — PART I

Over the years, I've done a lot of travelling and bought a lot of books. Mostly books filled with wisdom, biographies, business success stories and philosophy — the wisdom of others that I can consume and appreciate in the quiet miles of the sky.

Sometimes the books I want aren't readily available though. They have gone out of print, are only available in a particular country, or have simply disappeared.

Some time ago, my wife and I went on a bus tour through parts of England that I hadn't seen for years and on one sunny afternoon we ended up outside a bookstore called Blackwell's in Oxford.

"This store, ladies and gentlemen," said the driver, "has any book you want."

That's quite a boast. But knowing what I wanted and couldn't get elsewhere, I walked right into the store and asked the clerk, "Do you have Victor Frankl's book, *Man's Search for Meaning*?"

He clicked away on his computer and then led me directly to a bookshelf that contained six copies of the book. I bought all of them.

If you're not familiar, *Man's Search for Meaning* was published in Austria in 1946. Dr. Frankl spent three years as a prisoner in four different concentration camps and learned about every conceivable extreme of human suffering. After he was freed, he used his experiences to find ways of healing sickness of the mind and spirit. His belief is that man has amazing powers to go on living.

"He who has a why to live can bear with any how," said Frankl.

On one occasion, after he had been persistently beaten, as he froze and after he had watched friends and family die beside him, as he was forced to march to work and dig in icy ditches, Frankl wrote:

THE WHY AND THE HOW — PART II

Occasionally I looked at the sky, where the stars were fading and the pink light of the morning was beginning to spread behind a dark bank of clouds. But my mind clung to my wife's image, imagining it with an uncanny acuteness. I heard her answering me, saw her smile, her frank and encouraging look. Real or not, her look was then more luminous than the sun which was beginning to rise.

"A thought transfixed me: for the first time in my life I saw the truth as it is set into song by so many poets, proclaimed as the final wisdom by so many thinkers. The truth — that love is the ultimate and the highest goal to which man can aspire. Then I grasped the meaning of the greatest secret that human poetry and human thought and belief have to impart: The salvation of man is through love and in love . . ."

". . . In a last violent protest against the hopelessness of imminent death, I sensed my spirit piercing through the enveloping gloom. I felt it transcend that hopeless, meaningless world and from somewhere I heard a victorious 'Yes' in answer to my question of the existence of an ultimate purpose."

Ever since my visit to Blackwell's in Oxford, I have been inspired time and again by the hope that Frankl expressed.

Everything *can* be taken from us, but *not* the last human freedom — the freedom to choose our attitude in any given set of circumstances, to choose our own way.

— *How to Soar With the Eagles*

IF YOU ARE STRUGGLING
WITH SOMETHING IN YOUR LIFE,
FOCUS ON THE WHY
AND IT WILL BE MUCH EASIER
TO DISCOVER THE HOW.

WHO'S PACKING YOUR PARACHUTE?

Charles Plumb was a U.S. Navy jet pilot in Vietnam. After 75 combat missions, his plane was destroyed by a surface-to-air missile. Plumb ejected and parachuted into enemy hands where he spent six years in a communist prison in Vietnam. He survived the ordeal and today lectures on lessons learned from that experience.

One day, when Plumb and his wife were sitting in a restaurant, a man at another table came up and said, "You're Plumb! You flew jet fighters in Vietnam from the aircraft carrier Kitty Hawk. You were shot down!"

"How in the world did you know that?" asked a very surprised Plumb.

"I packed your parachute," the man replied.

Plumb gasped in surprise and gratitude.

The man pumped his hand and said, "I guess it worked!"

Plumb assured him, "It sure did. If your chute hadn't worked, I wouldn't be here today."

Plumb couldn't get to sleep that night, thinking about the man who had packed his parachute.

"I wonder how many times I might have seen him and not even said, 'Good morning, how are you?' or anything at all because I was a fighter pilot and he was just a sailor."

Plumb reflected on the many hours the sailor must have spent at a long wooden table in the bowels of the ship, carefully weaving the shrouds and folding the silks of each chute, holding in his hands each time, the fate of someone he didn't even know.

Now, when Plumb speaks to an audience, he always asks them, "Who's packing your parachute?"

— *The Power of a Dream*

EVERYONE HAS SOMEONE WHO PROVIDES WHAT THEY NEED TO MAKE IT THROUGH THE DAY. TAKE TIME TO RECOGNIZE THE CONTRIBUTION THAT OTHERS MAKE TO YOUR SUCCESS AND BE THANKFUL FOR THE PEOPLE WHO PACK YOUR PARACHUTES.

THE VALUE OF A SMILE

I suspect sometimes that it is not easy for a flight attendant to stand at the doorway of a 747 and extend a smiling greeting to 400 people who are about to embark on a flight to goodness knows where.

Unlike us passengers, who stumble down the aisle looking for our seat number, these people must be bright, shining, smiling ambassadors of the airline, making us feel welcome and helping to prepare us mentally for the journey ahead.

What value there is in a smile. Hands down, it is the most comforting of human gestures, providing a sense of calm and welcoming all at once.

I came across some words that tell it all. The author is unknown, but the words are wise. It's called *The Value of a Smile*.

> *A smile costs nothing, but gives much. It enriches those who receive, without making poorer those who give. It takes only a moment, but the memory of it sometimes lasts forever.*

> *None is so rich or mighty that he cannot get along without it and none is so poor that he cannot be made rich by it.*

> *A smile creates happiness in the home, fosters goodwill in business and is the countersign of friendship.*

> *It brings rest to the weary, cheer to the discouraged, sunshine to the sad and is nature's best antidote for trouble.*

> *Yet it cannot be bought, begged, borrowed or stolen, for it is something that is of no value to anyone until it is given away.*

> *Some people are too tired to give you a smile. Give them one of yours, as none needs a smile so much as he who has no more to give.*

— *You Can If You Believe You Can*

JOHN WOODEN'S WISDOM – PART I

In 2006, I wrote a book titled *Make Your Life a Masterpiece* to celebrate Canada Wide Media's 30th anniversary. It included many stories from our staff; they really are the masterpieces behind our success.

John Wooden, coach at the UCLA Recreational Sports Center, passed away on June 4, 2010, just a few months before his 100th birthday. During his career, he led UCLA to an unprecedented 10 national championships and had an 88-game winning streak.

Over the years, I've read many of John's books on leadership and it was one of his famous quotes, "Make each day your masterpiece," that was the motivation for me to write *Make Your Life a Masterpiece*. To illustrate the quote, John told a story about watching his players in practice one day and realizing they were not giving 100 per cent. So he pulled them aside and said:

"I know you're tired and perhaps didn't do well on an exam or maybe your girlfriend broke up with you. Whatever the reason, I see that you're only giving me about half today. I also know you're thinking that tomorrow you'll give 150 per cent; but you can't give 150 per cent, you can only give 100 per cent. What you leave on the table today, you leave for good."

I don't know how John's players felt, but I was inspired by his words . . . John believed it was necessary to live every day as though it were your last because one day you'll be right and you don't want to leave anything on the table. You can Google books written by John Wooden — most of them are still available and any of them would be a great addition to your library.

On the following page is a little more of Wooden's wisdom.

JOHN WOODEN'S WISDOM — PART II

Things turn out best for the people who make the best of the way things turn out.

Never mistake activity for achievement.

Be more concerned with your character than your reputation, because your character is what you really are, while your reputation is merely what others think you are.

Be prepared and be honest.

Be quick, but don't hurry.

You can't let praise or criticism get to you. It's a weakness to get caught up in either one.

You can't live a perfect day without doing something for someone who will never be able to repay you.

Winning takes talent; to repeat takes character.

If you don't have time to do it right, when will you have time to do it over?

Failure is not fatal, but failure to change might be.

Consider the rights of others before your own feelings, and the feelings of others before your own rights.

Do not let what you cannot do interfere with what you can do.

Don't measure yourself by what you have accomplished, but by what you should have accomplished with your ability.

Talent is God-given. Be humble. Fame is man-given. Be grateful. Conceit is self-given. Be careful.

Success comes from knowing that you did your best to become the best that you are capable of becoming.

Success is never final; failure is never fatal. It's courage that counts.

— Insight 2010

MAKE EVERY MOMENT COUNT

According to the human resources experts at Robert Half International, the average employee works only 50 per cent of the time they are at work. The other 50 per cent is largely wasted on idle chit-chat with co-workers, late arrivals, extended coffee breaks and lunches, early departures, private phone calls, Internet surfing, checking email and other personal business.

"Don't major in the minors," my dad always told me. "Do the tough things first and take control of both your career and your future."

It's good advice and I would also add the following, "Resolve to work all of the time that you are at work. If you are finding it difficult, try giving yourself a little reminder like 'back on track' each time that you realize you've gotten distracted from what you need to be doing."

Contrary to what some experts will tell you, there is no magic formula when it comes to getting the hard work done or reaching your goals. If you wait around for inspiration to get you going, you might be waiting for a long time. A much more practical approach, and the one that has worked for me, is to methodically work towards your goals. If you want to know how effective what you are doing is, break it down into every action and ask yourself this question, "Will what I am doing right now take me toward my goals or away from them?" If you're hanging around the water cooler talking about last night's crop of reality shows or trading gossip, I think you know the answer.

— *Make Your Life a Masterpiece*

WE DO NOT MANAGE TIME.
WE CAN ONLY MANAGE
OURSELVES. CHOOSE TO MAKE THE
MOST OF EVERY MINUTE.

NOBODY LAUGHED

As a motivational speaker, it's in my blood to focus on the positive, but that doesn't mean I never mess up. I do. I will never forget one such occasion that taught me a valuable lesson.

Early in my career, I did the rounds as a comedian in the U.K. and figured I'd go straight to the top. But in show business there are always dues to pay. So there I was in Wales, on a circuit of 20 working men's clubs, offering blokes who had been down in the mine all day a laugh to go with their beer.

I knew nothing of Wales, couldn't even pronounce the names of half the towns I visited, but that didn't matter. Humour has universal appeal and so on a rainy night in a small Welsh town, right after the singer and the magician, on comes Peter.

I went right into my jokes about kids, stories about how rotten they can be, how unruly and ungrateful they are, really funny stuff that had cracked 'em up in London.

Not a laugh. Twelve minutes later I gave up and walked off the stage, right into the arms of the furious club owner who promptly showed me the door.

Hurt, puzzled and upset, I headed to my hotel.

"Aberfan," I said, reading the signs along the high street. "Aberfan."

And then it clicked.

A month earlier, from high on a hill above the primary school, a tip (the monstrous pile of leftovers from a coal mine) had slipped and raced down the hillside. It slid like a grey blanket over the school and took the lives of 170 people, mostly children. Many of the working men in the pub that night were the fathers of those children.

I felt absolutely awful. And I learned a valuable lesson that night.

— *How to Soar With the Eagles*

IT'S ALWAYS IMPORTANT TO KNOW WHERE YOU ARE
AND WHO YOU'RE DEALING WITH.

SERVE THE COMMUNITY – PART I

While there are nearly as many reasons to serve the community as there are ways to serve it, by far the strongest and most enduring is love of the place you call home, whether it's a particular street, neighbourhood, city, or as was the case with James. F. MacDonald, inlet.

James "Mac" MacDonald first set eyes on the inlet in question, on B.C.'s South Coast, in 1919. He was a young man and from the first moment, he fell in love with Princess Louisa Inlet. Needing to earn a living, Mac spent the next six to seven years prospecting in the Southern U.S. After striking it rich in Nevada in 1927, Mac immediately returned to buy 45 acres of land surrounding Chatterbox Falls at the head of the inlet. There he built a log cabin and made it his home.

For years, Mac acted as host to visiting yachtsmen and sailors, telling everyone who visited that, "this beautiful, peaceful haven should never belong to one individual." Mac never wanted to see the inlet used for commercial purposes. In his opinion, he was simply a custodian of Nature and it was his duty to extend every courtesy to those who visited.

In 1953, Mac turned the title to Princess Louisa Inlet over to the boating public in trust and the Princess Louisa International Society (PLIS) was formed to preserve the inlet in its pristine state for future generations. In the trust, it was stipulated that Mac would always have a place near Chatterbox Falls to moor his houseboat and he continued to spend time there until 1972. For the last five or six years of his life, Mac was unable to return to the place he loved. He died in 1978.

Twelve years after the PLIS was formed, the property became Princess Louisa Provincial Marine Park under the care of the B.C. government.

SERVE THE COMMUNITY – PART II

To this day, the inlet remains as beautiful as ever, thanks to Mac's generous spirit. You see, Mac could have sold his property in 1953 (he was offered $400,000, a fortune at the time) and retired a very wealthy man.

Having spent some summers in Princess Louisa Inlet myself, I had the opportunity to meet Mac on a number of occasions, although I never imagined that I would one day be asked to conduct his memorial service.

The first few times I met Mac, I was a teenager attending a Young Life Christian camp on the inlet called Malibu. In those summers we knew him as Mac of the Princess. He would come to the camp to share stories about his life in the wilderness and the area's First Nations history.

I returned to Malibu in the late '70s as camp manager. So, it was a Saturday afternoon when we noticed all kinds of boats coming into the inlet. As I headed to the dock to check it out, a gentleman stepped off his boat and declared loudly, "I'm looking for a preacher."

It turned out, all of the people were there to scatter Mac's ashes and hold a memorial at Chatterbox Falls. Despite having no experience in such things, I was volunteered to speak at Mac's memorial the next day.

Sunday was a cool, rainy day. I performed my duties to the best of my ability, speaking to 300 people in the pouring rain about Mac's love of the inlet. In some way, I owe the discovery of my talent as a motivational speaker to Mac of the Princess.

— *Make Your Life a Masterpiece*

IF YOU TRULY WISH
TO LEAVE A LEGACY, SERVE
THE COMMUNITY.

LAW OF THE GARBAGE TRUCK

O ne day I hopped in a taxi and asked the driver to take me to the airport. We were driving in the right lane when a black car suddenly shot out of a parking space right in front of us. Thankfully, my taxi driver was paying close attention and slammed on his brakes. We skidded and missed the other car by mere inches.

Suddenly, the driver of the other car whipped his head around and started yelling, gesturing wildly and cursing at us. My taxi driver just smiled and waved at the guy. And I mean, he was really friendly.

So I asked him, "Why did you just do that? This guy almost crashed your car and sent us to the hospital."

The taxi driver then shared with me what I now call the law of the garbage truck. He explained that many people are like garbage trucks. They run around full of garbage, full of frustration, full of anger and full of disappointment. As their garbage piles up, they need a place to dump it and sometimes they'll dump it on you.

Don't take it personally. Just smile, wave, wish them well and move on. Don't take their garbage and spread it to other people at work, at home or on the streets.

The bottom line is that successful people do not let garbage trucks take over their day. Life's too short to wake up in the morning with regrets about the way we've treated others.

So, love the people who treat you right and have some compassion for the ones who don't (just imagine how much garbage they must be hauling around every day — it must stink!).

And remember, life is 10 per cent what you make it and 90 per cent how you take it.

— Insight 2011

HAVE A GARBAGE-FREE DAY.

BAMBOO WISDOM

The bamboo of China is one of the world's most fascinating bits of flora. It is used for scaffolding in the building of skyscrapers, as a conduit for irrigation, in the crafting of furniture, household goods, flooring and countless artifacts. Like fine porcelain and brush painting, it's one of the many beautiful and mysterious things we associate with this intriguing country.

But perhaps the biggest fascination about the bamboo of China is the nature of its growth. Before you ever see the first missile-shaped sprout of the bamboo, it lies underground as an undeveloped corm. Not just for a year must the bamboo be nurtured, nor two, or three, but four. It takes four years to bring a bamboo plant to visible life.

Then in the fifth year it explodes into visible being. Overnight, a dewy sap-soaked black sprout pushes from its earthen prison and in just one day it can grow a whole foot and sometimes more. The next day, with all of those years of nurturing behind it, it adds another foot, then another and another until it reaches a height of almost 100 feet in almost as many days.

I like the bamboo (the fact that it is so strong and yet flexible) and I like the way it comes into being. It reminds me of how life often is. If you want something that is truly spectacular, you have to be willing to work for it, you have to nurture it and you have to be patient because it doesn't always happen as quickly as you might like.

— *How to Soar With the Eagles*

TODAY, THINK ABOUT
WHAT YOU WOULD LIKE TO NURTURE
AND GROW IN YOUR LIFE.

FEAR VERSUS COURAGE

"Once when Marshal Ney was going to battle,
looking down at his knees which were smiting together,
he said, 'You may well shake; you would shake
worse yet if you knew where I am going to take you.'
Napoleon was so much impressed with the courage
and resources of Marshal Ney that he said, 'I have two
hundred millions in my coffers and I would give
them all for Ney.'" — Orison Swett Marden

Who builds the barriers that would keep us from being all that we can be? A stonemason named Fear, one who is highly skilled at building powerful barriers from nonexistent stones. Where does this craftsman live? In our minds. He's always there, but it's up to us whether he lives in the back of our minds or if he is permitted to come to the front because fear goes exactly where we tell him to go.

We move fear to the front by shifting our concentration away from our own courage and choosing instead to focus on that which frightens us. And then, as we give over our power, fear begins to grow stronger.

Fear is the sworn enemy of adventure and when we let it take over, we close ourselves off to opportunity. When fear defeats us, it does so because we have lost our mental focus. And unfortunately, the strength we pass along to fear is the very strength we need to overcome it.

Courage is the opposite of fear, it is also the antidote. Originating from the Latin word "cor," which means heart, courage is like a muscle. The more we exercise it, the stronger it becomes and the easier it is to push fear back where it belongs, in the shadows.

— *Who Dares Wins*

PUMP UP YOUR COURAGE
AND PUSH
FEAR OUT OF THE WAY.

APPRECIATE YOUR OWN VALUE

As a professional speaker, I know the importance of getting an audience's attention to drive a point home and nothing gets people's attention like offering them free money. Here's what one well-known speaker did to make a point that I think you'll appreciate.

As he started his seminar with a group of about 200 people, the speaker held up a $100 bill in his hand and asked, "Who would like this $100?"

Not surprisingly, hands shot up all around the room. Then he said, "I am going to give this money to one of you, but first let me do this." He crumpled the $100 bill up in his hand. He then asked, "Who still wants it?"

Still the hands went up in the air.

"Well," he said next, "What if I do this?" And he dropped the money and started to grind it into the floor with his shoe. When he picked it up; it was all crumpled and dirty. "Now who still wants it?"

Still the hands went into the air.

"Isn't that interesting," he asked the rapt audience, "No matter what I did to the money, you still wanted it because even though it was crunched up and dirty, you knew that that did not decrease its value. It is still worth $100."

Many times in our lives, we are dropped, crumpled and ground into the dirt by the decisions we make and the circumstances that come our way. As a result, sometimes we start to we feel as though we're worthless. But no matter what has happened or what will happen, remember that you will never lose your value.

— Insight 2011

NEVER LET YESTERDAY'S
DISAPPOINTMENTS GET IN THE WAY
OF TOMORROW'S DREAMS.

LOOK FOR THE "WOW" IN NOW

In 2008, I accepted nine speaking gigs in 12 days, all but one of them in Western Canada (with the final one in Seattle, Washington).

My second-to-last gig was in Taber, Alberta. I was picked up in Calgary at noon and driven the three hours to Taber for my presentation and then back to a hotel in Calgary. I arrived at the hotel at 12:30 a.m. completely exhausted yet knowing that I'd have to get up in the morning, fly to Vancouver, drive to Seattle and do my last presentation.

I tossed and turned all night, so when my wake-up call came in the morning, I was overtired and grumpy. Arriving at the airport, I checked in and then headed to Starbucks for a much-needed coffee.

On the plane, I found my seat then sat thinking how much I was dreading the flight. Just then, a blonde girl in pigtails stepped onto the plane. From the look of excitement on her face, it was clear she had never been on a jet. As she stood there looking down the long rows of seats, she turned to her mother and said, "Wow, mommy, this is amazing!"

At that moment, seeing her reaction to something I take for granted, it hit me, "Wow indeed!" I was flying business class and when I arrived in Vancouver I was going to get in my Jaguar and drive to Seattle where I would be paid to speak — something I absolutely love to do — and then I would return home and spend a relaxing weekend with the love of my life.

For the remainder of the flight, I thought about all of the "wow" things I enjoy in my life every day.

— *The Power to Soar Higher*

WHAT "WOWS" DO YOU TAKE
FOR GRANTED?

I WISH YOU ENOUGH — PART I

A s noted elsewhere in this book, a number of years ago I suffered a pretty serious stroke. For anyone who makes their living as a public speaker — something I have been doing for more than 40 years — a stroke can be a career-ending experience. This is because it can often seriously damage the centres in the brain that control the ability to speak and to comprehend language.

Thankfully, after many months of rehabilitation, I recovered fully. In fact, I would say that since my stroke, I am better than ever before; perhaps because I came out of the situation with a renewed appreciation for the fragility of life and the determination to make the most of every moment I have. The experience also provided me with a much greater understanding of just how important it is to truly appreciate all that we have, because it can be gone in an instant.

It reminds me of a story that Tashon Ziara, who helps me to write my books, sent to me a while back. It was the story of a fellow who was waiting for a flight at the airport who overheard a father and daughter in their last moments together as the daughter was preparing to get on a plane.

Standing near the security gate, they hugged and the father said, "I love you, my dear, and I wish you enough."

"Dad, your love is all I ever needed," the daughter replied. "I wish you enough too."

They kissed and the daughter left.

November 25

I WISH YOU ENOUGH – PART II

The father walked over to the window where the fellow traveller was watching the planes take off and land. He was clearly holding back tears as he watched his daughter depart. The father turned to the stranger and asked, "Did you ever say goodbye to someone knowing it would be forever?"

"Yes, I have," the stranger told him. "Forgive me for asking, but why was this a forever goodbye?"

"I'm old and she lives so far away," the father said. "I have challenges ahead and the reality is — the next trip back will be for my funeral."

"When you were saying goodbye, I heard you say, 'I wish you enough.' May I ask what that means?"

He began to smile. "That's something that has been handed down from other generations. My parents used to say it to everyone." He paused a moment and looked up as if trying to remember the exact words. Then he smiled and spoke:

I wish you enough sun to keep your attitude bright no matter how grey the day may appear.
I wish you enough rain to appreciate the sun even more.
I wish you enough happiness to keep your spirit alive and everlasting.
I wish you enough pain so that even the smallest of joys in life may appear bigger.
I wish you enough gain to satisfy your wanting.
I wish you enough loss to appreciate all that you possess.
I wish you enough hellos to get you through those times when you will have to say goodbye.

Clearly overcome with emotion, he then turned and walked away.

— *The Runway of Life*

TAKE TIME EVERY DAY TO APPRECIATE THE LIFE
YOU HAVE BEEN BLESSED WITH . . . AND REALIZE THAT NO
MATTER WHAT TODAY BRINGS, IT WILL BE ENOUGH.

BANISH A BAD MOOD

Are you having one of those days — or weeks — when every little thing seems to annoy you? Are you wondering if your little black cloud will ever disperse, letting you enjoy the sunshine once again? Instead of putting up with feeling down, try these five little steps to help identify and banish whatever's got you down.

1. Stop and *listen* to what's on your mind. Be your own best friend and give yourself an empathetic ear. What exactly is it that's bothering you? What are you feeling? Disappointment? Resentment? Jealousy? Frustration? Admitting to yourself what you are really feeling is a good first step.

2. Give yourself a few minutes to ruminate on whatever it is that's bothering you. If you're feeling jealous, resentful or disappointed, just own it. We all have feelings that we're not proud of or that aren't quite rational. Ignoring them doesn't make them go away; it just makes us feel worse.

3. Give yourself a pep talk. Here again, being your own best friend is the key. What would a good friend say to give you a morale boost? Okay, now say it to yourself! Your subconscious doesn't care where the encouragement comes from, only that it gets what it needs to feel better.

4. Refocus on your goals. Remind yourself what is important to you and that you aren't going to let anyone or anything distract, deter or derail you from your priorities. Let your passion recharge your batteries.

5. Remember to laugh at yourself. You can take what you do seriously, just don't take yourself too seriously. Remember, in the end no one gets out alive, so you may as well enjoy every moment you can.

— *If Only I'd Said That: Volume II*

CONTROL YOUR MOODS,
DON'T LET
THEM CONTROL YOU.

PLAY TO YOUR STRENGTHS

My wife Kay and I were on an assignment at Disney World in Florida and played a game of golf at one of the Disney courses. We were teamed up with a fellow named Jack Haley and his wife. They both looked a little old for us and we thought the game was going to be a cinch — no competition at all. How wrong we were!

Jack was two under par by the ninth hole — the turn, as they call it. He walked very slowly, almost purposefully, to the men's washroom. While he was there, Kay and I couldn't help but quiz his wife. "Tell us about Jack! Who is he? How does he play so well?" we asked.

She told us that Jack was a retired PGA pro and that they came to Orlando from time to time.

"Why does he walk so slowly?" I asked. She told me he had had an operation on his heart and it didn't take.

"He is on constant medication, but no more operations, they are too dangerous," she said. "You see, Peter, he is going to die."

"When?" I asked.

"It could happen any minute," she told me.

Just then, Jack returned to our foursome and we continued the back nine. I asked Jack about the pending end to his runway of life and how he handled it moment by moment.

Jack simply told me, "Play to your strengths."

Business coach Gary Lockwood concurs with this advice, "Conventional wisdom says we should work on improving our weaknesses. What a terrible waste of time, talent and opportunity. Imagine what would have happened if Chopin, Einstein or Pavarotti had followed that advice. Focus on your strengths and experience the immense satisfaction that comes with being superb at something."

— *The Runway of Life*

TUNE IN TO YOUR INTUITION

Everyone has intuition. Successful people learn to develop this muscle and follow their inner guidance. If you want to leverage your innate wisdom to create greater success, you must learn to tune in to your intuition.

Legendary hockey player Wayne Gretzky always had that sense on the ice and he explains it this way, "I skate to where I think the puck will be."

Well, that sounds easy, right? And Gretzky always had a way of making it look easy too. But for some of us, it can take a little practice to tune in to that little voice that whispers quietly to each of us. Here are a few tips:

Most often, intuition will appear as nothing more than a gentle nudge so you have to be paying attention. Quiet time and meditation can help to clear your mind of distractions as well as help you tune in to the subtle messages your intuition is sending you.

Worrying about the past or future bends your antennae. If you're too focused on what has happened or what will happen, you're likely to be distracted and miss what is happening right now. Keep your attention on the present.

Don't be afraid to ask your intuition for help. Pose the questions you are struggling with and you'll be surprised at the answers that come your way.

— *The Runway of Life*

"THE INTELLECT HAS LITTLE TO DO
ON THE ROAD TO DISCOVERY.
THERE COMES A LEAP IN CONSCIOUSNESS,
CALL IT INTUITION OR WHAT
YOU WILL, AND THE SOLUTION COMES TO YOU
AND YOU DON'T KNOW HOW OR WHY."
— Albert Einstein

WAIT FOR THE BRICK

A young, successful executive was driving home, going a bit too fast in his new Jaguar. Suddenly, a brick came flying out and smashed into the Jag's side panel. He slammed on the brakes and reversed the car. Seeing a kid standing on the road, the angry driver jumped out of the car, grabbed the kid and pushed him up against a parked car, shouting, "What was that all about? Just what the heck are you doing? That's a new car and that brick you threw is going to cost a lot of money. Why did you do it?"

"Please mister, I'm sorry, I didn't know what else to do," the young boy pleaded. "I threw the brick because no one else would stop."

With tears dripping down his face, he pointed to a spot just around a parked car. "It's my brother," he said. "He rolled off the curb and fell out of his wheelchair."

Sobbing, the boy asked the stunned executive, "Would you please help me get him back into his wheelchair? He's hurt and he's too heavy for me."

The driver tried to swallow the lump rising in his throat as he lifted the brother back into the wheelchair, then took out his fancy handkerchief and dabbed at the fresh scrapes and cuts on his arms and legs. A quick look told him everything was going to be okay.

"Thank you," the grateful child told the stranger.

Too shaken up for words, the man simply watched the little boy push his wheelchair-bound brother down the sidewalk. It was a long, slow walk back to the Jaguar. The damage was noticeable, but the driver decided to keep the dent as a reminder not to go through life so fast that someone would have to throw a brick to get his attention.

The same applies to each one of us, we can slow down and pay attention . . . or wait for the brick!

THE POWER OF OPTIMISM

Putting a stop to negative thinking and learning to view things from a positive perspective can have a profound effect on your health and your work life. The simple act of maintaining an optimistic outlook has been linked to lower rates of anxiety and depression, reduced risk of cardiovascular disease, stronger immune systems and a longer life expectancy. An optimistic outlook can also contribute to increased job satisfaction and improved outcomes at work.

The difference between a pessimist and an optimist lies in how they interpret events. Pessimists see positive events as temporary and limited and negative events as permanent and far-reaching, while optimists see things in reverse. Optimists also look for an external cause for events, while pessimists tend to blame themselves.

Optimism isn't denial. It's simply taking positive action to overcome setbacks rather than accepting defeat. Approaching challenges or failure as learning experiences teaches you strategies and coping methods that can boost your skills and keep you healthy, happy and productive.

Optimism can also be learned. Here are some tips to help you focus on the positive:

- Set goals and write them down. Everything looks brighter when you're working towards a goal.
- Never assume you can't do something. Challenge these beliefs.
- When you feel yourself crowding your mind with self-criticism and worry, stop and challenge yourself to find one positive thing to focus on.
- Tap into positive stories from your past, rather than constantly revisiting unhappy memories.
- Banish negative self-talk. Learn to recognize what triggers negative thinking so you can anticipate and redirect your thoughts in a positive direction.
- Practice reacting positively to new situations. In time, it will become second nature.

DECEMBER

JUST BE YOURSELF

Like many of us, Tsawwassen First Nation Chief Kim Baird sought out the advice of mentors as a young woman embarking on her career, but some of the advice she received didn't fit with her own values and that created a problem.

"Earlier in my career, I actually had a mentor tell me I was naive because of my approach, because I wasn't pounding the table with my fist," she says. "It really undermined my confidence for a period of time. I had to learn the hard way that I could be effective just being myself and since then I've been successful by following my own style of leadership. Ultimately the best advice is something I've heard from many places, which is to be yourself. Now they have a fancy word for it: authenticity. It just means that you can be effective without having to have a persona. I've found that, as a young woman, I have a very collaborative style, which is not seen as typical of Indian chiefs and negotiators."

As a chief, one of Baird's biggest dreams has been to sign and implement British Columbia's first urban land treaty (Tsawwassen is located within the Metro Vancouver region) and she is now living that dream. As chief since 1999 (she was recently re-elected for her sixth consecutive term in office), Baird represented her people throughout the negotiation process that ended in April 2009 with a treaty giving the Tsawwassen Nation full autonomy.

By staying true to herself and her own dream, Baird has accomplished something that many people believed impossible and she continues to pursue her dreams — based on her own values and doing it on her own terms.

— *The Power of a Dream*

BE YOURSELF AND
TRUST THAT THE WORLD
WILL VALUE WHAT YOU
HAVE TO OFFER.

WHERE DO YOU STAND?

"When your values are clear, decision-making is easy." — Roy Disney

In the 1990s, researchers Peter Kim and James Patterson wrote the book, *The Day America Told the Truth*, presenting some incredible statistics that reflected a widespread shift away from traditional moral values.

Of their response group, they asked: Do you lie regularly? Ninety-one per cent said yes.

Would you lie to achieve an important business objective? Twenty-nine per cent said yes.

Have you done anything in the last year that you are ashamed of? Twenty-five per cent said yes.

And then there were the money questions.

If you could pick up a quick $10 million, would you abandon your family? Twenty-five per cent said bye-bye to their family.

Would you abandon your faith? Another 25 per cent said yes.

Would you be a prostitute for a week? Twenty-three per cent said yes.

Give up your spouse? Sixteen per cent said yes.

Kill a stranger? Seven per cent said yes.

Finally, the same group of people was asked: Should we teach values and ethics in our schools? Eighty per cent of these men and women who would deceive, plunder and kill said: "Absolutely!"

I suppose that's somewhat of a relief, considering the sort of moral education and guidance the children of these people might be receiving at home.

A speaker friend of mine from Seattle tells about crossing the border between Washington State and British Columbia. When he got to the customs agent, he was asked:

Who are you? Where are you going? What do you have to declare?

These questions work well at the border because the answers can say so much. They also work for life.

— You Can If You Believe You Can

December 3

LET YOURSELF MAKE MISTAKES

Social psychologist Heidi Grant Halvorson has an interesting take on mistakes. According to her research, people who give themselves "permission to screw up," actually make fewer mistakes and master new skills faster. The reason for this is that they take a "get better" approach to goals rather than a "be good" approach.

Here's how it works.

When we have a be-good mindset, we put a lot of pressure on ourselves to perform well and this can create a lot of anxiety, particularly when it is a task that we haven't performed many times before. Nothing interferes with performance quite like anxiety and that makes us much more prone to mistakes and, ultimately, failure.

However, when we tackle a goal with a get-better approach, our focus turns away from our performance to learning and improving. As a result, we accept that it is okay to make some mistakes along the way, which allows us to stay motivated and focused on our goal despite any setbacks that may occur.

Halvorson, who is the author of *Succeed: How We Can Reach Our Goals*, offers three helpful steps for reframing goals:

1. Start by embracing the fact that when something is difficult and unfamiliar, it will take time to really get a handle on it. You might make some mistakes and that's okay.

2. Remember to ask for help when you run into trouble. Needing help doesn't mean you aren't capable — in fact, the opposite is true. Only the very foolish believe they can do everything on their own.

3. Don't compare yourself to others. Instead, compare your performance today to your performance yesterday; focusing on getting better is about progress, not perfection.

— Insight 2011

WHEN YOU GIVE YOURSELF PERMISSION
TO MAKE MISTAKES, THE FOCUS
SHIFTS FROM YOU TO YOUR GOAL.

WHY LIFE SHOULD BE MORE LIKE KINDERGARTEN

Innovative Internet giant Google is famous for its play areas. At Google, promising employees are allowed to use 20 per cent of their work hours on a project of their choice, building 'recess' back into the workplace culture. Known as 'free time' or '20 per cent time,' this play period has produced some of the company's most successful products, including AdSense and Google News. Just like in kindergarten, where play allows children to develop new skills in a safe environment, being able to play at work allows employees an opportunity to experiment with new ideas and out-of-the-box thinking without being judged on their performance.

Microsoft is another company that encourages playtime and promotes it as a benefit to new staff. There, employees are encouraged to spend at least some part of their time engaged in activities that have nothing to do with their job, such as performing in the company orchestra, participating in a theatrical production or playing a sport.

Although some people may view play as little more than a frivolous perk, in reality it is so much more than it appears to be on the surface. By distracting the conscious part of the brain with an amusing activity, we can unlock the unconscious brain and allow it to wander around unrestricted, essentially allowing it to do the awake version of what it does when we are asleep. This adult 'play time' offers a perfect way for the subconscious brain to attend to problems that we've been focused on without the awake brain butting in with its annoying rules and limitations. Play also allows us to see things in a new way and come up with innovative ideas.

GET IN TOUCH WITH YOUR
INNER KINDERGARTENER AND ADD MORE
PLAYTIME INTO YOUR LIFE.

FAILURE IS SNEAKY

In Volume III of my series *If Only I'd Said That*, Jim Rohn shares the formula for failure. As Rohn explains in the article, failure in life isn't the result of one cataclysmic event, but rather the effect of an accumulation of poor choices and bad decisions over a long period of time.

For example, those who regularly eat foods that are highly processed and full of sugar, sodium and saturated fats are contributing to future health problems, but the joy of the moment greatly overshadows any consequences so they continue to overindulge. It's the same for people who continue to smoke, take drugs or drink to excess year after year. The consequences aren't immediate; therefore, they are lulled into a false belief that it doesn't matter.

But as Rohn tells us, "Failure's most dangerous attribute is its subtlety." In the short term, all those little indiscretions and poor choices don't seem to make a difference, so we let them slide and continue to drift from one day to the next making wrong choices until the day we finally wake up and realize we have a much bigger problem on our hands.

That's the formula for failure and it can be applied to almost everything we do, whether it is failing to communicate with our spouse, failing to spend time with and guide our children as they grow or failing to do our job to the best of our ability. The best way to inoculate ourselves from failure is to realize that the little choices we make every day — how we spend our free time, who we associate with, and how we feed our mind, body and soul — all of these choices matter: a lot.

— *The Power to Soar Higher*

FAILURE IS THE INEVITABLE
RESULT OF POOR
THINKING AND POOR CHOICES.

HOPE

Hope + substance = a life worth living.

Samuel Johnson once said, "It is necessary to hope." He went on to say, "Hope itself is happiness and its frustrations, however frequent, are less dreadful than its extinction."

We hope . . . for the future, as yet unknown.
We hope . . . for a successful career.
We hope . . . for happiness, fulfillment and a meaningful life.
We hope . . . to devote our talents for the good and to use them to their fullest.

When we apply substance to our hopes — take action and put some meat on the bones — they turn into dreams and only then are we in a position to bring them to life. My dream for this book is that it will encourage and inspire you to figure out what your dreams are and to get moving on them, for the time left on our runway of life grows ever shorter. And the last thing we want, I believe, is to be at the end of our life asking the questions, "Why didn't I act on that dream? Why didn't I walk through the doors that opened for me? Why didn't I seize the opportunities that presented themselves?" Because as we close our eyes and take our last breath, it will be too late.

So, get moving today. You have within you enormous resources, untapped talents and abilities, intelligence and opportunities that have been denied to many. Seize today — carpe diem!

— *The Power of a Dream*

WHEN WE ADD SUBSTANCE
TO OUR HOPES, WE
BRING LIFE TO OUR DREAMS.

IN HIS BROTHER'S HANDS

Back in the 15th century, the Dürers, a family of 18, lived in a house outside the city of Nuremberg, Germany. The father worked three jobs just to keep food on the table.

Two of his sons, Albrecht and Albert, were artistically inclined and wanted to attend the academy in Nuremberg — however, with so many mouths to feed, there could be no expectation of financial help for both to realize their dreams.

One Sunday morning, they decided to solve their dilemma with the toss of a coin. The winner would go to the academy; the other would work in the mines to help pay and, four years later when the winner graduated, the roles would be reversed. They agreed and tossed the coin. Albrecht was to go to Nuremberg. Albert became a miner.

Albrecht Dürer was an immediate sensation. His engravings and watercolours were spectacular. He began to get commissions and win adulation throughout Europe. Four years later, Albrecht returned home to celebrate his accomplishments with his family and more importantly, to toast the four-year sacrifice by his brother that had made it possible.

"Albert," he said, holding his glass high, "now it is your turn to study and my turn to take care of you." All eyes turned towards Albert, who sat with his face in his hands and tears in his eyes.

"It's too late, brother," he said. "In four years, the bones in my hands have been broken by work and arthritis has crippled my fingers."

Albert Dürer never entered the academy in Nuremberg. But the hands that were so much a part of the sacrifice he made were immortalized by his brother in his famous painting, *Praying Hands*.

— *You Can If You Believe You Can*

TODAY, HOW CAN YOU
SHOW THANKS FOR THE HELP
YOU HAVE RECEIVED?

THIS TOO SHALL PASS

In the Bible, it states 323 times, "This too shall pass." Nowhere does it say, "Get used to it, this situation is here to stay." Buddhists also have a word to describe the state of impermanence that applies to all things. They call it anicca. If we learn to understand and accept that all moments must pass, we can better appreciate the good times and cope with the not so good. By accepting change as a natural part of life, we are better able to live in the present moment and embrace the beauty of the time while allowing the difficulties to strengthen us.

If we stop to think about it, everything in the world is continually changing — and not even one of us is the same person we were 20 years ago. All of the cells in our body, our appearance, our personality, our feelings and emotions, even our problems have changed. Good or bad, with time, everything changes and with change come challenges.

The most difficult challenge for many people is knowing when to let go of things that are no longer serving us. The second is being able to embrace the changes that come our way. Our attitude towards change can determine the happiness we experience in life, and most things that seem insurmountable can be managed if we simply choose to face up to the situation.

Knowing that our difficulties are not permanent gives us hope and knowing the good times are also fleeting, helps us to savour them. Remembering that even the most beautiful times will be gone reminds us to live fully in the moment, enjoying every second of happiness that comes our way because . . . this too shall pass.

—The Power to Soar Higher

HOW CAN YOU EMBRACE
CHANGE TODAY?

YOU'RE STILL ALIVE — THAT'S FANTASTIC!

I was speaking at the Mirage Hotel in Las Vegas for Jaguar Canada and had to take an early flight from Las Vegas to San Francisco. Upon leaving the hotel at 5:30 a.m. dressed in a smart business suit, I bounded up to the checkout counter, which was manned by a young fellow in his twenties, to pay my bill.

Other than a couple of diehards playing blackjack and a few people on the slot machines, no one else was around. As I approached the counter, the young man, who was just finishing his shift, asked rather grumpily, "How are you this morning?"

"Just fantastic, thank you," I replied.

To this he said, again in a rather somber voice, "And what makes you so fantastic this morning?"

I thought quickly and responded, "You know young man, 3,200 60-year-old men didn't wake up this morning. They're dead."

He looked at me with a startled expression on his face and then suddenly he brightened a little and said, "I'm starting to feel better already."

Now I have no idea if that statistic is true or not; I just made it up on the spot because I had a big day ahead of me and I didn't want any negativity from him to slip into my spirit. I paid my bill, bounced out of the hotel feeling great and hopefully affected the next 13 people with my positive attitude — the bellman, the cab driver, the ticket agent, the security guard, the coffee shop attendant, the airline check-in clerk, the air hostess, my seatmate and ultimately my next audience in San Francisco.

— *The Runway of Life*

WHEN YOU REALIZE JUST HOW LUCKY
YOU ARE THAT YOU WOKE
UP AT ALL THIS MORNING, YOU CAN'T
HELP BUT FEEL FANTASTIC.

DON'T ALLOW IT TO DRAG YOU DOWN

In his book, *The Art of Happiness*, the Dalai Lama relays a story based on one of the interviews he did with Dr. Howard Cutler, who co-authored the book.

During the interview, the pair were talking about guilt and regret and Dr. Cutler asked the Dalai Lama if there was anything he had done in his life that he felt bad about.

"Oh yes, many things," replied the Dalai Lama. "For example, an elderly monk came to me and asked me about doing these yogic practices which required a lot of physical ability, sort of designed for 18-year-olds and I advised him against it because I said I thought he was too old. And he seemed to take that well and he left, and then I heard that he had committed suicide. Because of his belief system, he thought that if he committed suicide, he would get a younger body and he could do the exercises."

As a result, the Dalai Lama was left with the regret that no matter what his intention had been, he was responsible for this man's death, for his suicide.

"Oh my goodness, how did you ever get rid of that feeling?" Dr. Cutler asked.

And the Dalai Lama paused for quite a long time and really thought about that and then he said:

"I didn't. It's still there. I just don't allow it to drag me down and pull me back. I realized that being dragged down or held back by it would be to no one's benefit . . . not mine or anybody else's, so I go forward and do the best I can."

— *Insight 2011*

LIFE LESSONS ARE ONLY
VALUABLE IF WE USE WHAT WE HAVE LEARNED
AND KEEP MOVING FORWARD.

AND THEN SOME

Retired business executive Carl Holmes was asked the secret of his success. Here's what he said:

AND THEN SOME . . . these three little words are the secret to success.

They are the difference between average people and the top people in any field. The top people always do what is expected, and then some . . .

They are thoughtful of others, they are considerate and kind, and then some . . .

They meet their obligations and responsibilities fairly and squarely, and then some . . .

They are good friends and helpful neighbours, and then some . . .

They can be counted on in an emergency, and then some . . .

I am thankful for people like this, for they make the world more livable. Their spirit of service is summed up in three little words . . .

AND THEN SOME.

In every study of successful people — athletes, executives, entrepreneurs, self-made millionaires — the most obvious habit they all have in common is they work much longer and harder than their co-workers or competitors.

If you do more than you are paid to do, sooner or later, you will be paid for more than you do. Unfortunately, this is not a widely accepted truth. Many people take the opposite approach, saying, "When they pay me what I'm worth, I'll give them what they pay for." The problem with this line of reasoning is that if you aren't willing to give something in order to get something, you never give anyone the opportunity to value your contribution.

In many ways, ours is a society based on instant gratification and entitlement, we want what we want, when we want it, whether we have earned it or not!

— *Make Your Life a Masterpiece*

HAPPINESS DOES NOT COME FROM DOING EASY WORK, BUT FROM THE AFTERGLOW OF SATISFACTION THAT COMES AFTER THE ACHIEVEMENT OF A DIFFICULT TASK THAT DEMANDED OUR BEST.

December 12

WHAT ARE YOU BUILDING?

A tourist walked up to a couple of London bricklayers who were working on a wall with considerable care.

"My good man," he said to the first, "what are you doing?"

"Building a wall," he said. "I'm a bricklayer."

"And you?" he asked the second man.

"Me?" he answered. "I'm buildin' a cathedral to the glory of God. Strong it will be and true. An' its bricks and mortar will last for a hundred generations."

"That's pretty stupid, mate," said the first bricklayer. "You're supposed to be building a garage."

You've got to admire that second bricklayer. Despite the fact that he might have been a bit off track, he did his job with obvious purpose and he knew beyond a doubt that whatever he was doing, it was bigger than mere bricks and mortar. No matter what we do for a living, we should all feel that way about the contribution we are making to the world.

From the dreams of designers, the money of financiers, the plans of architects, it always comes down to, or to put it another way, it's really up to the steelworkers, the bricklayers, the electricians, plumbers and painters — the army of men and women who really make buildings, bridges and cathedrals. They know what they're doing and they do it well.

As with bricklayer number two, our purpose must be about more than just doing a job. It's what pride is all about. In our day-to-day lives, we do so many things that don't seem to add up to much — and sometimes our efforts don't. But sometimes they do.

— *How to Soar With the Eagles*

THINK ABOUT THIS AS YOU GO
ABOUT YOUR DAY:
WE CAN LAY BRICKS OR
WE CAN BUILD CATHEDRALS.

SIMPLY GIVE

The great Law of Cause and Effect dictates that you and I live in an orderly world in which everything happens for a reason. Sometimes it may not seem that way, but I believe that it is. There are no accidents.

For example, it's no accident that so many of the most successful people in the world, such as Bill Gates and Oprah Winfrey, have discovered a great sense of fulfillment from giving back to the communities that helped make them successful.

An infatuated follower once told Mother Teresa that he intended to follow her around the world to learn her philanthropic secrets first-hand. He bought a plane ticket and was about to embark with her on a trip to South America, another leg in her worldwide, lifelong mission of service. Mother Teresa was flattered, but said simply: "Sell your ticket. Give the money to the poor."

It was a simple, yet profound lesson.

We can line up to shake hands with kings, queens, prime ministers and movie stars and probably learn nothing. Those same kings, queens, prime ministers and movie stars would line up to meet Mother Teresa. Mother Teresa simply says "give," then goes her quiet way and we stand in open-mouthed wonder to ponder her wisdom.

As Mother Teresa and other spiritual visionaries such as the Dalai Lama have been telling us all along, making the world a better place isn't complicated. All we need to do is find someone who could use our gifts and talents (a charity, advocacy group or even an individual) and offer them up, no strings attached.

— You Can If You Believe You Can

You don't need to be Bill Gates or
Oprah Winfrey to make a difference in the world.
Share what you have today.

CHOOSE TO BE A LIFELONG OPTIMIST

"I can't change the direction of the wind,
but I can adjust my sails to always
reach my destination." — Jimmy Dean

One of the most powerful and uplifting mental habits that we can — and should — master in our lives, is that of being an optimist. If you believe, as I do, that you become what you think about most of the time, it only makes sense to keep your thoughts focused on the positive ways in which you can move your life forward and achieve your goals. Optimism motivates and stimulates us to perform at higher levels. Best of all, it is also contagious. Therefore, if you haven't yet got it, make a point of hanging around with optimistic people and you will soon catch it.

Former U.S. Secretary of State Colin Powell talks about the power of optimism and the effect that a leader's attitude can have on those around them.

"The ripple effect of a leader's enthusiasm and optimism is awesome. So is the impact of cynicism and pessimism. Leaders who whine and blame engender those same behaviours among their colleagues. I am not talking about stoically accepting organizational stupidity and performance incompetence with a 'What, me worry?' smile. I am talking about a gung-ho attitude that says, 'We can change things here, we can achieve awesome goals, we can be the best.' Spare me the grim litany of the 'realist,' give me the unrealistic aspirations of the optimist any day."

— *Make Your Life a Masterpiece*

FEW THINGS IN THE WORLD ARE MORE
POWERFUL THAN A POSITIVE PUSH. A SMILE, A WORD
OF ENCOURAGEMENT AND HOPE — THESE CAN
MAKE ALL THE DIFFERENCE WHEN THINGS ARE TOUGH.
CHOOSE TO BE A LIFELONG OPTIMIST.

December 15

HELPFUL INSTRUCTIONS FOR LIFE

Not all of the instructions we receive make sense, sometimes for the simple reason that somewhere along the way, the message got mixed up. As a speaker, I have travelled quite a lot and I like to read instruction labels, sometimes sharing the best ones with my audiences, like these:

> On a hair dryer in a hotel room in Atlanta were the words, "Do not use while sleeping."

> On a bar of soap in Toronto, "Directions: Use like regular soap."

> On a tiramisu dessert package, "Do not turn upside down." Of course, the message was printed on the bottom of the package.

> Operating instructions for a clothes iron, "Do not iron clothes on body."

When I'm speaking I like to make sure I offer at least a couple of pieces of practical advice. Here are a few for you to think about today:

> If there is something you must do but find it a struggle, do it every day and make it a habit.

> If you're tired at work, rotate tasks every 30 minutes to stay productive.

> If you need better sleep at night, block out all sources of light and sleep in total darkness (light makes your brain want to stay alert).

> When you wake up in the morning, complete the following sentence, "My purpose today is to . . ."

> No matter how you feel, get up, dress up and show up because no matter what happens, it will be better than doing nothing at all.

> What other people think of you is none of your business; focus on living according to your own values.

— Who Dares Wins

THANKS FOR THE MEMORIES

We all need to laugh and no one could make people laugh like Bob Hope. For those of you too young to remember, ask your grandparents — what a wonderful man he was.

TV Week magazine once hired Bob Hope to be the guest entertainer at a big awards banquet some years ago at the Hotel Vancouver. We were also helping raise money for a Mel Zajac charity project. Bob was sensational. I hope his insights will put a smile on your face and in your heart.

Bob Hope on turning 70 . . .
"You still chase women, but only downhill."
On turning 80 . . .
"That's the time of your life when even your birthday suit needs pressing."
On turning 90 . . .
"You know you're getting old when the candles cost more than the cake."
On turning 100 . . .
"I don't feel old. In fact, I don't feel anything until noon. Then it's time for my nap."
On never winning an Oscar . . .
"Welcome to the Academy Awards or, as it's called at my home, Passover."
On presidents . . .
"I have performed for 12 presidents and entertained only six."
On receiving the congressional gold medal . . .
"I feel very humble, but I think I have the strength of character to fight it."
On his family's early poverty . . .
"Four of us slept in the one bed. When it got cold, Mother threw on another brother."
On his six brothers . . .
"That's how I learned to dance. Waiting for the bathroom."
On his early failures . . .
"I wouldn't have had anything to eat if it wasn't for the stuff the audience threw at me."

THE STARFISH

One morning just before sunrise, an old man walked along the beach and every few steps, he stopped to pick up a starfish and toss it back into the sea.

A young jogger watched him for a while and eventually asked, "What in the world are you doing?"

"I'm picking up stranded starfish and returning them to the sea," said the old man. "The sun is coming up and the tide is going out. If I don't, they will die."

The young man laughed. "That's ridiculous," he said. "There are 30 miles of beach and a million starfish ahead of you. How can you possibly expect to make a difference?"

The old man took a couple more steps and stooped to pick up yet another sand-covered starfish. With all the strength he could muster, he sent it in an arc toward the rising sun and the coolness of the sea.

Then he turned to the young man, smiled and said, "It made a difference for *that* one, didn't it?"

Have you ever wondered why some people accomplish amazing things in their life and others just seem to drift around aimlessly?

There is something very special in each and every one of us. We have all been gifted with the ability to make a difference. And when we become aware of that gift and choose to use it, we have the power to shape the future. We must each find our own starfish. And if we throw our stars wisely and well, the world will be a just a little bit better as a result.

— *The Runway of Life*

NO MATTER WHAT ANYONE ELSE MIGHT
THINK, YOU HAVE THE ABILITY
TO MAKE A DIFFERENCE. GO AND
FIND YOUR STARFISH.

WORTH THE STRUGGLE – PART I

In the summer of 2001, I made a commitment to my youngest daughter Amanda that I would be a speaker at a teachers' conference she was helping to organize for 300 to 400 of her colleagues in September. I was looking forward to the event, seeing it as a great opportunity to show her how proud I am of her work as a teacher. Then, just a few weeks before I was scheduled to speak, I suffered a serious stroke.

While I was recovering, Amanda came to me and said, "Don't worry, Dad, you don't have to speak at the conference."

"There is no way I'm going to miss that conference," I told her determinedly. "I don't know how, but I will be there."

Not being able to drive myself, on the day of the conference I arranged for a car to pick me up and drive me to the school. Amanda met me at the curb and helped me inside where she showed me to a private waiting room. I appreciated the few minutes of time alone to gather my courage, given the fact that the stroke had distorted my facial features and I was feeling more than a little self-conscious.

When it was time for me to speak, Amanda came to escort me to the stage. One side of my body was nearly lifeless and she literally had to hold me up and help me onto the stage where I clung to the podium for 40 minutes as I spoke. Following my remarks, I was touched to receive a standing ovation from the teachers and Amanda helped me back to my seat. During the coffee break, she helped me back to the waiting car and I went home and straight to bed.

WORTH THE STRUGGLE – PART II

S ometimes, after I have spoken to a group, people will come up to me and comment that I make what I do on the stage look so easy. I can tell you for a fact that day certainly wasn't easy for me, but it was important and the reward that I got at the end was worth any amount of struggle on my part. The very next week, I received the following card:

Dear Dad,

I am so proud and honoured that you were a part of our school conference. With daring and courage you came to our conference knowing you were not 100 per cent, but also knowing that you were not going to let me down.

I hope you know that had you not been able to speak, I would have been as proud of you as I am today. I am honoured that you gathered all your strength and talent for me.

You have often told me the story of how you chartered a jet to get home for my graduation ceremony, doing whatever it took to keep your word. I think because I was younger I couldn't truly appreciate the lengths you were willing to go to make our family and me a priority.

Today, as an adult, I have experienced first-hand what courage it took for you to speak at our conference and I know what this means.

I thank you — not only for speaking, but more importantly, for making me feel like the most important person in the world to you, as you so often do, and once again for modelling courage, commitment and dedication.

I love you,
Amanda

— Make Your Life a Masterpiece

"SURMOUNTED DIFFICULTIES NOT
ONLY TEACH, BUT HEARTEN US IN OUR FUTURE
STRUGGLES." — James Sharp

WORRY WILL GET YOU NOWHERE

I enjoy regular lunches with my friend and mentor, Joe Segal. He always has a few pearls of wisdom to share. During one such lunch, he told me that working hard is exhilarating, but worrying hard is literally a killer. According to Joe, who has more than 85 years of life experience, as much as 92 per cent of the things we worry about never happen, so what's the point of worrying about them.

Here are more reasons why we shouldn't worry:

Worry robs you of your power to be proactive. When you worry it's like being stuck on a merry-go-round. You're so preoccupied with feeling sick that you aren't able to see other options available to solve whatever problem you face.

Worry distorts reality. When you worry, all of your focus is on what's not working, rather than what is, making it difficult to keep problems in perspective.

Worrying is bad for your health. When you worry, damaging physical changes take place in your body. Some of the symptoms include: increased blood pressure, excess stomach acid, muscle tension and headaches.

What to do if you are a worrier:

Just because you've always been a worrier doesn't mean you can't change. The first thing to do is recognize that worry is a habit and like other unhealthy habits, you can choose to break it.

It's also helpful to stop trying to be in control of everything in your life. Things rarely go as planned; being able to roll with the punches is a useful life skill.

Face your fears. The things we worry about are rarely as bad as we imagine and when we face them head on, we take away the power they hold over us.

As Dale Carnegie so wisely advised in his 1944 book, it's time to stop worrying and start living.

IF IT'S GOING TO BE, IT'S UP TO ME

I have always believed that we are totally responsible for our lives; including our moods, behaviours, attitudes, good and bad habits, manners, personalities, work ethic, the way we dress — literally everything.

If you believe all of this, then we are also responsible for the success that we seek and the happiness that goes along with a career and a life of significance and meaning. General Dwight D. Eisenhower often used these three powerful words: "enlightened self-interest." No one will be more interested in you — than you. And that's very natural and appropriate.

The world doesn't give me a living —
"If it's going to be, it's up to me."

Society won't give me a moral and ethical character —
"If it's going to be, it's up to me."

The university will not give me an education —
"If it's going to be, it's up to me."

Psychology cannot give me well-being —
"If it's going to be, it's up to me."

Religious institutions will not save my soul —
"If it's going to be, it's up to me."

The minister won't give me a lifetime of happiness and harmony in my marriage —
"If it's going to be, it's up to me."

The medical establishment can't give me good health —
"If it's going to be, it's up to me."

The economy will not deliver financial security to my purse —
"If it's going to be, it's up to me."

A new sunrise doesn't promise to give me a great day —
"If it's going to be, it's up to me."

— *Who Dares Wins*

DON'T BE AFRAID
TO LAUGH AT YOUR MISTAKES

The ability to see humour in a problem can make the lesson it has to teach us much more palatable. Former NBA centre and coach Johnny Kerr tells a story about the time when he was coaching the Chicago Bulls. At the time, Kerr was struggling with the challenges of coaching an expansion team and in the midst of a major losing streak. He tried to pump up the team by giving them a pre-game pep talk before they headed out onto the floor in Boston.

"We had lost seven in a row and I decided to give a psychological pep talk before a game with the Celtics," Kerr explains.

During the talk, Kerr told Bob Boozer to pretend he was the best scorer in basketball, he told Jerry Sloan to pretend he could stop anyone in the game, then he told Guy Rodgers to pretend he was the top point guard in the league, and finally, he told six-foot-eight Erwin Mueller to pretend he was a shot-blocking, rebounding machine.

"We played the Celtics at the Garden and lost by 17 points," Kerr recalls. "So I was pacing around the locker room afterward, trying to figure out what to say to the team when Mueller walked up, put his arm around me and said, 'Don't worry about it, Coach, just pretend we won.'"

— *Make Your Life a Masterpiece*

"To ERR IS HUMAN, BUT WHEN
THE ERASER WEARS OUT
AHEAD OF THE PENCIL,
YOU'RE OVERDOING IT." — Josh Jenkins

DO IT ANYWAY

The following poem was taken from a sign on the wall of Shishu Bhavan, the children's home in Calcutta supported by Mother Teresa:

People are unreasonable, illogical and self-centered.
LOVE THEM ANYWAY

If you do good, people will accuse you of selfish, ulterior motives.
DO GOOD ANYWAY

If you are successful, you will win false friends and true enemies.
SUCCEED ANYWAY

The good you do will be forgotten tomorrow.
DO IT ANYWAY

Honesty and frankness make you vulnerable.
BE HONEST AND FRANK ANYWAY

What you spend years building may be destroyed overnight.
BUILD ANYWAY

People really need help but may attack you if you help them.
HELP PEOPLE ANYWAY

Give the world the best you have and you'll get kicked in the teeth.
GIVE THE WORLD THE BEST YOU'VE GOT ANYWAY

Mother Teresa dedicated her life to helping others without any expectations about what she would receive in return. It's not a bad philosophy for the rest of us as we pursue our many dreams. Take these eight principles and apply them to your life, your career, your family and your community and you will discover that this wisdom will move you from success to significance.

— *The Power of a Dream*

"YOU MUST BE THE CHANGE
YOU WISH TO SEE IN THE WORLD."
— Mahatma Gandhi

COUNT YOUR BLESSINGS

Whenever I speak to an audience about how much abundance we have in our lives, I always say that we can all come up with at least 15 things to be grateful for. When you are verbally grateful for the blessings in your life it changes everything . . . most importantly, it changes your attitude. Consider this:

If you woke up this morning with more health than illness, you are more blessed than the millions who will not survive this week.

If you have never experienced the danger of battle, the loneliness of imprisonment, the agony of torture or the pangs of starvation, you are more fortunate than 500 million people in the world.

If you can attend a religious meeting without fear of harassment, arrest, torture or death, you are more blessed than three billion people in the world.

If you have enough food to eat, clothes on your back, a roof overhead and a place to sleep, you are richer than 75 per cent of this world.

If you have money in the bank, in your wallet and spare change in a dish someplace, you are among the top eight per cent of the world's wealthy.

If you hold up your head with a smile on your face and are truly thankful, you are blessed because the majority can, but most choose not to.

If you can hold someone's hand, hug them or even pat them on the shoulder, you are blessed because you can offer a healing touch.

Count your blessings every day.

—*The Power to Soar Higher*

WHEN YOU SAY OUT LOUD
EVERYTHING YOU'RE GRATEFUL FOR,
THE THINGS THAT AREN'T
EXACTLY PERFECT IN YOUR LIFE
SEEM TO PALE IN COMPARISON.
TRY IT TODAY.

THE SECRET TO HAPPINESS

The secret to happiness and well-being is no mystery. All it takes is the ability to do the following:

Forgive.
Apologize.
Admit errors.
Take responsibility.
Keep your temper.
Act on good advice.
Make the best of things.
Maintain high standards.
Avoid repeating mistakes.
Learn from your experiences.
Think first and act accordingly.
Help others whenever you can.
Look for the bright side of the situation.
Smile.

— *The Power to Soar Higher*

TRY SLIPPING AS MANY OF THESE
"SECRETS" INTO YOUR DAY
AS POSSIBLE. YOU'LL SOON REALIZE
THAT YOU HAVE A MORE
POSITIVE OUTLOOK ON LIFE.

JUST BREATHE

Holding on to anything, according to Deepak Chopra, whether it is events of the past or a preconceived idea of what the future should be, is like holding on to your breath. Ultimately, you will suffocate. Letting go of things and learning to live in the present moment can be extremely difficult (I know it is for me), but mindfulness practice, as it is often called, can be as simple as breathing. Seriously, one of the most simple ways to experience living in the moment can be done as you go about your daily activities and it involves focusing on your breathing.

Focusing on the sound and rhythm of your breath (especially when you're upset) can have a calming effect and help you stay grounded in the present moment.

Here's a simple exercise to try. It involves breathing from your belly, not your chest.

First, sit or stand in a relaxed position. Now, slowly inhale through your nose until you feel that you can't take in any more air. As you prepare to slowly exhale, firm up your belly and tighten your abdominal muscles to push the air up and out of your lungs. Repeat this process several times. That's it!

Here are a few more helpful tips:

1. As you breathe, let your abdomen expand outward rather than raising your shoulders. This is a more relaxed and natural way to breathe. It also helps your lungs fill more fully with fresh air and push out more old air.

2. Try a few breaths any time you want to release tension or for several minutes as a form of meditation.

3. If you like, you can make your throat a little tighter as you exhale so the air comes out like an exaggerated sigh. This type of breathing is used in yoga and can bring additional relaxation.

TAKE SOME TIME TO RELAX
AND BREATHE EVERY DAY.

THE MOST IMPORTANT THING
THAT MONEY CAN'T BUY

L ucy Hyslop is a freelance writer, editor and communicator with a
wealth of British and North American journalistic and social media
experience. Earlier this year, she had lunch with my mentor Joseph Segal to
talk about life, business, philanthropy and what it's like to still have game at
the age of 86. She shared some of her insights from that conversation in an
article for *BCBusiness* magazine.

"I don't play golf" is Joe's favourite explanation for why he still enjoys the
entrepreneurial game so much. And there's no doubt that when it comes to
the art of deal-making, Joe's still got more enthusiasm than most men 50
years younger than he is. Still, they have something that Joe covets more
than anything else in the world: time.

A prolific mentor, Joe shared a story with Lucy about a 30-year-old
young man facing bankruptcy who came to him seeking advice.

"I quickly told him that I would give him everything — the money, the
houses, everything — if he could just make me 30 again," said Joe. "He may
be broke, but he has more than I have: time is his asset. I'd rather be his age
on welfare than to face the inevitable fact that I'm running out of time. I'm
not done living yet."

— Insight 2011

TIME IS FREE, BUT IT'S PRICELESS.
YOU CAN'T OWN IT, BUT YOU CAN USE IT.
YOU CAN'T KEEP IT, BUT YOU CAN
SPEND IT. ONCE YOU'VE WASTED
IT, YOU CAN NEVER GET IT BACK.

December 28

BUILD STRENGTH THROUGH ADVERSITY

*"I realized that they had already taken everything
from me except my mind and my heart. Those they could
not take without my permission. I decided not to give them away
. . . And neither should you."* — Nelson Mandela

Adversity reveals our true character. This was noted by the 14th-century mystic Thomas Kempis, who said, "Adversities do not make a man frail, they show what sort of man he is."

Oliver Wendell Holmes noted, "If I had a formula for bypassing trouble, I would not pass it around. Trouble creates a capacity to handle it. I don't embrace trouble; that's as bad as treating it as an enemy. But I do say meet it as a friend, for you'll see a lot of it and had better be on speaking terms with it."

It has often been said that experience is the toughest teacher because she gives the test first and then the lesson. Those who face personal trials either rise to the occasion or fall down in despair. A crisis strips away all pretense, revealing true character, and it is up to each one of us to choose whether we will be beaten down by the problems in our life or "use the difficulty" and build strength of character.

— Make Your Life a Masterpiece

WE ONLY GROW WHEN
WE FACE THE CHALLENGES
OF LIFE HEAD ON, NOT BY
RUNNING AWAY.

WRITE YOUR OWN OBITUARY

S tephen Covey, author of the bestselling *Seven Habits of Highly Effective People*, sometimes tells his seminar audiences to "find a quiet place and go and write your own obituary" — a rather somber task. Covey is not trying to be morbid; rather, he explains that it is a useful way of deciding what we wish to accomplish and what really matters to us in life.

In this life it is a fact that where we put our time and effort is where we will gain the greatest rewards. With this in mind, we need to take a look at our goals and dreams from the other end. Are they going to get us where we want to go?

Writing our own obituary is an excellent way to test our priorities. It's also a reminder that we need to live our life with the end in mind.

Lord Baden-Powell, the founder of the Boy Scouts movement, is said to have lived out the precept that every minute was "60 seconds" worth of distance run. Within a century of its founding, there were Boy Scouts troops in 110 nations and the organization is still going strong today. What a legacy!

Sir Winston Churchill once said, "What is the use of living if it be not to strive for noble causes and to make this muddled world a better place to live after we are gone."

It is up to us to live up to the legacy that was left for us and to leave a legacy that is worthy of future generations.

— *The Runway of Life*

WHAT IS IT YOU WOULD LIKE
TO BE SAID ABOUT
YOU WHEN YOU ARE GONE?

ONLY A MATTER OF TIME – PART I

Have you been waiting for the right time to reach for your dreams? Have you been waiting for the right circumstances? Perhaps you've been waiting for the right opportunity to go after your dreams?

My, you are patient, aren't you?

You could be waiting forever, you know. Time is an illusion. Circumstances are what you make them. Opportunity is a whisper that waits for your invitation; it doesn't burst in and shout its arrival. Now is the right time. Circumstances change when you take action. Opportunity is yours for the making. So what are you really waiting for?

Value every minute, every day — time waits for no one. It's time to power up your dreams.

Lance Bowerbank of Westcoast Moulding & Millwork Limited sent me this updated version of a story that you may have seen before. It's worth keeping in mind as you consider when and how you are going to implement the important dreams in your life.

Imagine that you have won the following prize in a contest: each morning your bank will deposit $86,400 in your private bank account for your own personal use. However, this prize has rules, just as any game undoubtedly has certain rules.

The first set of rules:

1. Everything that you don't spend during each day will be taken away from you.

2. You may not simply transfer money into some other account. You may only spend it. Each morning upon awakening, the bank opens your account with another $86,400 for that day.

The second set of rules:

1. The bank can end the game without warning; at any time it can say, "It's over, you're done!"

2. The bank can close the account in an instant and you will not receive a new one.

ONLY A MATTER OF TIME – PART II

W hat would you personally do? Most likely, you would buy anything and everything you wanted, right? Not only for yourself, but for all the people in your life. Maybe even for people you don't know, because you couldn't possibly spend it all on yourself and the people in your life, right? You would try to spend every single cent and use it all up every day, right?

Actually, this game is a reality, but not with money!

Each of us is in possession of such a magical bank. We just don't always realize that is what it is.

The magical bank is time.

Each morning we awaken and receive 86,400 seconds as a gift of life and when the day is done, any remaining time is gone, there is no carry-over balance and no credit. What we haven't lived up to that day is lost forever. Yesterday is forever gone.

Each morning the account is refilled, but the magical bank can dissolve our account at any time . . . *without warning.*

So, what will *you* do with your 86,400 seconds today? Think about that and always remember this: enjoy every second of your life, because time races by so much quicker than we think. Take good care of yourself and savour the life you have. Live each day to the fullest, be kind to one another and be forgiving. Harbour a positive attitude and always be the first to smile, because hey, you won the lottery!

— *The Power of a Dream*

HERE'S WISHING YOU
A WONDERFUL, BEAUTIFUL 86,400
SECONDS, EACH AND EVERY DAY.
NOW GO AND LIVE YOUR DREAMS!

About the Author

PETER LEGGE, O.B.C. • LL.D. (Hon) • D.Tech. • CSP • CPAE • HoF

Peter Legge is an inspiration to anyone who meets him. He lives his life's dream as an internationally acclaimed professional speaker and bestselling author, and as Chairman and CEO of the largest, independently owned magazine publishing company in Western Canada — Canada Wide Media Limited. Peter is a community leader who tirelessly devotes his time to many worthwhile organizations and he is a past Chair of the Vancouver Board of Trade.

His presentations are based on his everyday experiences as a community leader, husband, father and CEO. Peter has published 14 previous books including *The Runway of Life*, *Make Your Life a Masterpiece*, *The Power of Tact*, *The Power to Soar Higher* and, most recently, *The Power of a Dream*. His books have motivated thousands of people towards positive change.

Toastmasters International has voted Peter "Golden Gavel Award Winner" and "Top Speaker in North America" and both the National Speakers Association and the Canadian Association of Professional Speakers have inducted him into the Speakers Hall of Fame.

Peter is also a member of the prestigious Speakers Roundtable, an invitation-only society comprising 20 of North America's top professional speakers. He has received honorary doctorate degrees from both Simon Fraser University and Royal Roads University, and most recently received an honorary doctorate of technology from the British Columbia Institute of Technology.

In 2005, Peter was presented with the Nido Qubein Philanthropist of the Year Award in Atlanta, Georgia. The following year, he was awarded the Ambassador of Free Enterprise by Sales and Marketing Executives International in Texas, and later in 2006, the Peter Legge Philanthropist of the Year Award was introduced by the Canadian Association of Professional Speakers. Peter was the first recipient of this award.

In June 2008, the province's highest honour, The Order of British Columbia, was presented to Peter for his lifelong commitment to serving the community.

To contact Peter, write to:

Peter Legge Management Company Ltd.
4180 Lougheed Hwy, 4th Floor
Burnaby, BC V5C 6A7 Canada
Telephone: 604-299-7311
Email: plegge@canadawide.com
Website: www.peterlegge.com

To order Peter's books, CDs and other products, please contact Heidi Christie at the address above, or email hchristie@canadawide.com